Frederic Gardiner

The Old- and New Testaments in their Mutual Relations

Frederic Gardiner

The Old- and New Testaments in their Mutual Relations

ISBN/EAN: 9783742811394

Manufactured in Europe, USA, Canada, Australia, Japa

Cover: Foto ©Lupo / pixelio.de

Manufactured and distributed by brebook publishing software (www.brebook.com)

Frederic Gardiner

The Old- and New Testaments in their Mutual Relations

THE
OLD AND NEW TESTAMENTS

IN

THEIR MUTUAL RELATIONS

BY

FREDERIC GARDINER, D.D.

PROFESSOR IN THE BERKELEY DIVINITY SCHOOL.
AUTHOR OF "HARMONY OF THE GOSPELS IN GREEK," ETC.

NEW YORK
JAMES POTT & CO., PUBLISHERS
14 AND 16 ASTOR PLACE
1885

COPYRIGHT, 1885,
BY JAMES POTT & CO.

Press of J. J. Little & Co.,
Nos. 10 to 20 Astor Place, New York.

PREFACE.

THE following pages give the substance of a course of lectures in the Berkeley Divinity School. In preparing them for the press two changes have been made: as far as possible everything technical has been omitted, and especially the use of Hebrew and Greek words, that the matter may be more easily intelligible to a larger circle; and the division of the lectures into portions occupying nearly equal times has been neglected for the more convenient arrangement of the subjects. With these modifications the lectures remain substantially as they were delivered, and are printed in accordance with the wish of those who heard them.

There have been many works, both elaborate and popular, upon the same general subject; but none of them cover exactly the same ground, or supply the want these lectures were designed to fill.

F. G.

MIDDLETOWN, CONN., *June*, 1884.

CONTENTS.

                                                                                      PAGE

LECTURE I. THE ESSENTIAL UNITY OF THE OLD AND NEW TESTAMENTS.. 1

    Both come from God and are written by men. Differences arising plainly from time and circumstances. Christ taught that the New Covenant was the culmination of the Old. His disciples did the same. The Epistle to the Hebrews. Other epistles, addressed to Gentiles. Common object of both. Nevertheless there are great differences. Anthropomorphism. Progress in revelation. The laws of marriage; of revenge; of slavery. The federal and individual relations of man. The wars of Israel. Sacrifice. Faith. Summary.

LECTURE II. THE PROGRESSIVE CHARACTER OF REVELATION........ 28

    On à priori ground it must have been progressive. The records of revelation which have been preserved the only basis of discussion. The ordinarily accepted order of revelation accepted as a "working hypothesis," because best in accordance with the phenomena. The smallness of revelation at the birth of Abraham. The Mosaic legislation and subsequent prophetic teaching; their harmony, yet the latter an advance. The theories which reverse this order, and the objections to them. The progress of revelation in the New Testament. Summary.

LECTURE III. THE OLD TESTAMENT PREPARATORY FOR THE NEW... 62

    The Old Testament prepared for the New, and was given for this purpose. The evidence from the calling of Israel;

from its history; from the consciousness of the people from prophecy; from the teaching of the New Testament. The conduct of the heroes of the Old Testament; Abraham; Jacob; the Judges; David.

LECTURE IV. THE RELATION OF THE PRECEPTS OF THE LAW TO THE GOSPEL.................................. 90

The precepts arranged in classes; national precepts were preparatory for the Gospel by separating the people from contaminations of the heathen; educational precepts, by teaching them in concrete form until they should be able to receive principles; typical, by symbolically foreshadowing truths they were yet unable to understand in their full and clear expression. Particular precepts concerning the sacrifices and the priesthood.

LECTURE V. SACRIFICE................................ 111

The Patriarchal sacrifices, burnt offerings and peace offerings. The sacrifices of the Law. The Passover. Four general classes, with some subdivisions and special sacrifices. The burnt offering, with its ritual and significance. The peace offerings. The sin and trespass offerings. The day of Atonement. The sacrifices had a certain absolute ceremonial value, but were intrinsically insufficient for the forgiveness of sin. Treatment of the sacrifices by the Prophets. Their relation to the Gospel. The consciousness of sin, the holiness of God, and His unity; the necessity of the shedding of blood; the personal act of the worshipper; the character of the offerer; the intervention of an authorized mediator; the equality of men before God; the insufficiency of the sacrifices in themselves and the consequent prophecy contained in them.

LECTURE VI. THE PRIESTHOOD....................... 138

Priesthood and sacrifice correlative terms. At first the head of the family, then of the tribe, and finally the monarch, the priest, and this made necessary the appointment of an order of priests. In Israel the priests always sharply separated from the monarchs. At first no monarchs. The priests appointed by God as mediators for their people. The various

CONTENTS. vii

duties. Types of Christ, in several points. They could be only typical. Christ the only true priest. The word never applied in the New Testament to Christian Ministers. The relation between the two Dispensations in the priesthood.

LECTURE VII. THE KINGDOM OF GOD.................. 149
Ordinarily the constitution of society has passed from the tribal to the monarchical. In Israel this process was arrested that the nation might be under the immediate government of God. Afterwards a monarchy was conceded to the sinfulness of the people, but only on condition that it should continue a theocracy. When Solomon attempted to pervert it into an earthly empire, the nation was broken up. The idea of a kingdom under an invisible King was always made prominent. Combined with this was the primeval promise with its various renewals, and the teachings of the prophets. A kingdom of righteousness was foretold. The people were thus prepared for the announcement of "the kingdom of God" in the New Testament. There it appears as a development and present realization of the teachings of the Old Testament. The part of the prophets in connection with this kingdom. In both Testaments this kingdom is based upon the idea of a Covenant. The worship of this kingdom of old and under the Gospel.

LECTURE VIII. PROPHECY........................... 170
Definition of the term. Proofs of the existence of prophecy. The methods in which prophecies were given: (1) By distinct utterances; (2) By means of institutions in their nature temporary; (3) By prophetic types; (4) By educational precepts; (5) By history foreshadowing the future; (6) By typical characters. The way in which the prophecies are regarded in the New Testament. Quotations "by way of accommodation" set aside and each of the above classes considered. The Old Testament as a whole considered as prophetic in the New.

LECTURE IX. TYPOLOGY. I. HISTORY AND GENERAL PRINCIPLES...................................... 195
Distinction between type and allegory. Treatment in the

early Eastern and Western Church. Reaction at the Reformation. The Cocceian school. Opposition to this. School of Marsh. Examination of Marsh's principle. Definition of type: in the New Testament; in theological literature. Canons for the determination of true types. Discussion of these. There may be several types of one antitype, and several antitypes of one type.

LECTURE X. TYPOLOGY. II. SPECIAL CLASSES OF TYPES. 220

1. Ritual or legal types; examples, the sin offering; the priesthood. 2. Historical types. Reasons for expecting them. Proofs of their existence. Illustrations. Apparent defects in these types. Their importance. Indications of their typical character in the Old Testament. Combination of historical and prophetical types. 3. Prophetical types, of three forms: (*a*) types in the past or present are foretold as to appear again in the future; (*b*) a type not expressly, but in its essential principle is embodied in prophecy; (*c*) the type itself is future and is foretold.

LECTURE XI. TYPOLOGY III. PRINCIPLES AND DIRECTIONS FOR THE INTERPRETATION OF PARTICULAR TYPES... 247

Only principles can be laid down to be applied with judgment. 1. Nothing sinful in the Old Testament can be a type of the good things of the Gospel. 2. The meaning of types is to be determined partly by the light thrown back by the Gospel; shown (*a*) by the nature of types, (*b*) from the analogy of prophecy, (*c*) from the history of Israel, (*a*) from the use of the word "mystery" in the New Testament, (*e*) from the analogy of God's works. 3. A type must be *preparatory*. 4. A type has only one main idea. Explanation and modification of this rule. 5. Regard must be had to the essential difference between type and antitype. Summary.

LECTURE XII. THE ALLEGED "DOUBLE SENSE" OF SCRIPTURE... 262

Definition. Grounds for asserting the existence of a "Double sense." Examination of these. Objections to the existence of such a sense. Quotations by "accommodation."

CONTENTS.

LECTURE XIII. THE NEW TESTAMENT TESTIMONY TO
THE AUTHORSHIP OF THE OLD TESTAMENT BOOKS......... 274

Different views on the subject. Examination of the facts. Elimination of irrelevant matter. Examination of Jude 14, 15; of several quotations; Ps. cx. 1, xvi. 7–10. Enumeration of Books quoted by name. Examination of Acts, iii. 24; of Matt. ii. 17, 18; of Mark, i. 2, 3. Result thus far. Passages in which quotations are made by name. Conclusions.

LECTURE XIV. THE NEW TESTAMENT USE OF THE OLD.. 310

General features of anonymous quotations. The way in which the Old Testament was regarded by New Testament writers. Quotations (1) for purposes of argument, with illustrations; (2) expressing general truth belonging to all ages; (3) as illustrations; (4) use of sacred and familiar words simply to express the thought of the writer. Other uses of the Old Testament in the New.

LECTURE XV. CONCLUSION............................ 332

The relations examined indicate One Being as the Author of all Revelation. They show the eternal verity of the Old Testament, and the finalty of the New. Bearing of "the progress of Revelation" upon its order. Character of this progress. The Divine love in adapting Revelation to the needs and capacities of man.

INDEX OF SCRIPTURE TEXTS................ 343

THE OLD AND NEW TESTAMENTS

IN THEIR

MUTUAL RELATIONS.

LECTURE I.

THEIR ESSENTIAL UNITY.

THE two parts of the sacred volume which pass under the general name of the Bible are commonly known as the Old and New Testaments. They are more accurately called the Old and New Covenants. The former derives its name especially from the Covenant made in the Sinaitic legislation, but includes the record of the earlier revelations and of the lives of the patriarchs, as well as the subsequent history of the chosen people and the prophetic teachings given them; the latter contains all that has been authentically preserved of the life and teachings of our Lord and of His immediate followers. Whatever differences of opinion may exist in connection with this book, it is yet recognized by all who profess the name of Christ as in some sense coming from God, and as having been actually written down by men.

It has, therefore, both a Divine and human side, and both of these aspects must be recognized in any intelligent treatment of its contents.

The two parts of this Book are widely separated from one another by the languages in which they were originally written, by the times in which they were published, by the condition and development of the people to whom they were first given, and by the general character of the revelations they proclaim. Each of the single books, indeed, composing these parts, is also, in several of these respects, distinguished from every other; but there is a still broader line of distinction between the two collections. In as far as these differences can be at once recognized as arising from the circumstances of the times and the condition of the people, they call for no remark. Every intelligent person can see that such differences were both necessary in themselves, and were required for the accomplishment of the purposes of Revelation. But there are other differences which, although they are fully explained to the thoughtful mind by the consideration of these facts, yet to a more superficial observation have often seemed to involve a certain antagonism between the two Dispensations. This apparent opposition is increased by the continued rejection of the New Covenant, even to the present day, by the mass of the people to whom the Old was given; by the misunderstanding of some passages of the New Testament which speak directly of the Old; and by the contrasted teaching of the two on a variety of subjects, such as revenge, polygamy and slavery, and, above all, by their general teaching in regard to the means whereby man may obtain acceptance with God.

But before these points are examined, it must be shown that, notwithstanding these or any other marks of unlikeness, there is really an essential unity underlying both Testaments so strong and clear as to prove them to be parts of one great work. I do not know how this enquiry can be entered upon more satisfactorily than by observing how the Old Testament was regarded by those whose office it was to promulgate the New.

First among these utterances must stand the angelic declarations which ushered the Gospel into the world, and the teachings of the Author of the New Covenant. The very birth of His forerunner was heralded as God's beginning "to perform the mercies promised to our fathers" and "the oath which He swore to our father Abraham."* His own birth was announced as that of one who should sit "upon the throne of His father David," and should "reign over the house of Jacob forever."† He conformed His life to the requirements of the law and everywhere represented Himself as the Messiah foretold of old, and as "not come to destroy the law or the prophets, but to fulfil," ‡ adding with solemn asseveration, "One jot or one tittle shall in nowise pass from the law till all be fulfilled." § He summarized the law in its two great commandments as embodying His own teaching of the duty of man.‖ He rested His own new treat-

---

* Luke, i. 72, 73. † *Ib.* 32, 33. ‡ Matt. v. 17.
§ *Ib.* 18; Luke, xvi. 17. ‖ Matt. xxii. 37-40 ; Mark, xii. 29-31.

ment of the law of marriage upon the record of its original institution in the narrative of Genesis.* He justified His dealing with the Sabbath by examples taken from the sacred history of old.† He read passages from the Prophets in the Synagogue and declared that they were fulfilled in Himself. ‡ He argued with and convicted His enemies from the Scriptures, § which He says "cannot be broken." ‖ He reproved His disciples for being "slow of heart to believe all that the Prophets have spoken of" Him, and "beginning at Moses and all the Prophets, He expounded unto them in all the Scriptures the things concerning Himself." ¶ But not to multiply proofs of so obvious a fact, it may be said broadly that He rested His whole life and teaching upon the Old Covenant, declaring Himself to be the Redeemer to whom that Covenant had looked forward from the first, the culmination of all its hopes and promises, and always represented His teaching as the more perfect setting forth of the will of the same God who had spoken by the Prophets of old. For all this there is and can be but one explanation: it is inconceivable that the Author of the New Covenant could have taken this position unless He believed in the essential unity of the two Dispensations, and looked upon Himself as the point where they met and coalesced.

The teaching of His immediate followers is always

---

* Matt. xix. 4-6 ; Mark, x. 6-9.
† Matt. xii. 3-5; Mark, ii. 25, 26 ; Luke, vi. 3, 4.
‡ Luke, iv. 16-21.   § *E. g.* Matt. xxii. 15-46, etc.
‖ John, x. 35 ; cf. Matt. v. 19.   ¶ Luke, xxiv. 26, 27.

the same. Throughout the Book of Acts they are seen everywhere planting themselves upon the old Scriptures, whether in their private assemblies claiming the promises and prophecies given to their fathers,* or in their addresses to the unconverted, "reasoning with them out of the Scriptures .... that Christ must needs have suffered .... and that this Jesus is Christ." † So also their converts "mightily convinced the Jews .... showing by the Scriptures that Jesus was Christ." ‡ Particular instances are too familiar to need mention. Passing on, therefore, to the Epistles, one of the longer of them, the Epistle to the Hebrews, is wholly taken up with a masterly argument showing from the declarations of the Old Testament itself the superiority of Christ and of His Dispensation. It is addressed to men of Israelitish descent who clung with tenacity to the sacred oracles delivered to their fathers, and it recognizes in almost every line that these and the teachings of the Gospel are parts of one vast Revelation, coming from the same Source, given for the same object, and both perfectly true and authoritative, but that the older was in its form temporary and made provision for its own completion in the new. The key-note of the whole epistle is given in its opening sentence, "God, who at sundry times and in divers manners spake in times past unto the fathers by the Prophets, hath in these last days spoken unto us by His Son." §

---

* Acts, i. 16, 20 ; iv. 25, 26, etc.
† Acts, xvii. 2, 3; cf. ii. 30–36 ; iii. 18 ; ix. 22 ; xxvi. 6, 22, 23, etc.
‡ Acts, xviii. 28. § Heb. i. 1.

This epistle was written under peculiar circumstances, and addressed to a people trained under the old Dispensation. It has been argued, by those who would do away with its evidence of the unity of the two Dispensations, that the epistle does not represent the relations really existing between them, but is a case of special pleading. A careful examination of the epistle must dispel such a view. The difficulty in the mind of the Jew was that the Mosaic legislation should in any wise be superseded. He looked for its enlargement and completion, but was shocked at the idea of its sustaining to the Gospel such a subordinate position as is here insisted upon. But however this may be, the argument of the epistle stands upon its own merits; and whatever may have been its object, it does conclusively prove the unity of the two Dispensations.

Several of the other epistles were written to churches chiefly of Gentile origin. In most of them there were probably also converts of Jewish descent; but the Gentile element so preponderated that they are addressed collectively as Gentiles. Thus the Ephesians are bidden to "remember that ye being in times past Gentiles in the flesh;"* the Corinthians are told "ye know that ye were Gentiles;"† and the whole Epistle to the Galatians characterizes them as converts from heathenism, now in danger of being subverted by Judaizing teachers. Other epistles might also be enumerated, but these will suffice. One cannot fail in reading these epistles to be struck with the fact that wherever Christianity was received

---
* Eph. ii. 11. † 1 Cor. xii. 2.

among the Gentiles the Old Testament was likewise received, as a matter of course. The Apostle addresses his Gentile converts as familiar with its contents; he argues from its laws, its histories and its prophecies, as from things acknowledged to be sacred and authoritative by his readers. In the few epistles named above there are considerably more than a hundred quotations from, or allusions to the Old Testament. Many of these are distinct citations, used argumentatively. Neither this universal reception, nor this use of the Old Testament as of absolute authority in Christian argument could have been possible, except on the ground of the unity of the two revelations. In the Epistle to the Galatians St. Paul is very definite in speaking of the relations between them. He says that God "preached before the Gospel unto Abraham;"* that the law "was added because of transgressions, till the seed should come to whom the promise was made;" † and that "the law was our schoolmaster to bring us unto Christ." ‡ The first promulgators of Christianity, therefore, the men who had been immediately instructed by the Author of Christianity Himself, looked upon the law and taught their hearers to look upon it as a preparatory system, designed to lead men to the Gospel, and therefore in full harmony with its purpose and design.

Such unity is a necessary result of the common object of the two Dispensations. In both man is regarded as a fallen being, capable of restoration to

---
* Gal. iii. 8.   † *Ib.* 19.   ‡ *Ib.* 24.

his lost communion with God; and each revelation was divinely given to show him how he might attain this desired end. This will be again spoken of more fully. But meantime, when these revelations are examined, each by itself, it were folly to refuse to recognize that great differences are apparent. Particular precepts of the old are distinctly set aside in the new and others, of far greater moral purity and strictness, are substituted. "Ye have heard that it hath been said by them of old .... but I say unto you" * becomes the key-note of much of our Lord's teaching. Of more weight even than this is the fact emphasized and insisted upon, especially by St. Paul, that the general tone of the law as understood in his day was, "The man that doeth these things shall live by them," † putting man's salvation on the ground of perfect obedience to the divine requirements; while the teaching of the Gospel is distinctly that such obedience is impossible to fallen man, and that his only hope of salvation is through faith in Him whose obedience alone was perfect, and who by His death upon the cross has made atonement for human sin.

To appreciate the reasons for these differences and their consistency with the essential unity already described, it is necessary to take a general view of the history of the people of God and of their moral condition at various stages in their life. Such an examination may well begin by considering the anthropomorphic representations of the Deity in the Old Testament, which have been the occasion for so much cavil and criticism.

---

* Matt. v. 21, 27, 33, etc.   † Rom. x. 5; Gal. iii. 12.

It is to be noted at the outset that this whole question of the use of anthropomorphic language and descriptions is only one of degree. Human conceptions of that which is above us can only be formed from the conceptions of things around us, with a gradual elimination of all that is unworthy. Even now there is no philosophical language the roots of which may not be traced to sensible things, and there are no abstract terms which have not grown up from an original reference to sensible images. Perhaps in all language there is no higher description of the Infinite Being, no more fitting statement of his absolute supremacy and incomprehensibility than that in the epistle of the great Apostle to the Gentiles :— " Who is the blessed and only Potentate, the King of kings, and Lord of lords, Who only hath immortality, dwelling in the light which no man can approach unto; Whom no man hath seen or can see." * Yet all the words here used to express the most elevated idea which the human mind can form are taken from human relations and sensible actions. When the human race started on its career, it had not yet devised secondary and abstract meanings for its terms, because it had not yet developed ideas calling for the use of such abstractions. It could only be addressed, as children and the uneducated must be now, by concrete language and sensible images; and if God, in His lovingkindness, would reveal Himself to man at all, it could only be in terms adapted to his comprehension. Any other language must have failed of its purpose. Think of

---
* 1 Tim. vi. 15, 16.

the absurdity of talking to Adam or even to
Abraham in modern philosophic terms of "the Unknowable," of "a Power not ourselves which makes
for righteousness," of "a Power beyond nature
forever inscrutable to the human intellect," and the
like. To the simple minds in the early childhood of
our race, the idea of a Superior Being could only
be given as something higher than the highest thing
they knew; He must be spoken of substantially as
a man and yet above man. Yet that no false impression might be conveyed by such unavoidable
use of language, the Scriptures are careful to place
here and there statements, perhaps not fully understood at the time, but yet making it clear that the
Divine Being in His own nature was something infinitely more and higher than it was possible to express. Far back in the original Sinaitic legislation,
Moses is told at the very moment when he is vouchsafed a manifestation of the Divine Presence, " Thou
canst not see my face: for there shall no man see
me and live." * The earliest of the prophets, using
almost the words of the Divinely inspired Seer of
Aram, † declares that "the strength of Israel" "is
not a man that He should repent." ‡ The book of
Job,—whatever be its actual date—certainly the
most ancient Scripture in which anything of a philosophic tone is to be found, has many explicit
passages: "Canst thou by searching find out
God? Canst thou find out the Almighty unto
perfection? It is as high as heaven—what canst
thou do? Deeper than hell—what canst thou

---

* Ex. xxxiii. 20.   † Num. xxiii. 19.   ‡ 1 Sam. xv. 29

know?"* Such teaching is scattered here and there throughout all the sacred books, and must have shown man that the language in which he was obliged to speak of God and in which (in condescension to his weakness) God also spoke to him, was inadequate, and that he had—as we very fully understand that we have now—no words in which he could speak truly and sufficiently of the Infinite Being. In his own nature and essence the finite can never know Him except in so far as He is revealed to us through the Mediator, the God-man, partaker of both natures, and thus the one who brings together the incommensurable terms of the finite and Infinite.

But not only is this true of the bare mention of the being and attributes of the Supreme; the same thing must hold good also of the account given of His acts. When the Bible speaks of "the Lord God walking in the garden in the cool of the day" and calling to Adam "where art thou?"† the critic of our age sniffs at the narrative as fit only for children. Precisely; and further, only such narrative was adapted to the spiritual children who were the progenitors of our race. Probably few people of ordinary intelligence, unless determined to find fault, really have any great difficulty with such simple narratives, when they remember that only by means of this simplicity and anthropomorphic imagery could any idea be conveyed to the minds of men in those early ages. But the case is different when expressions are reached which seem to involve really untrue statements, when, *e.g.* it is said that "God repented," that His "wrath

---

* Job, xi. 7, 8. † Gen.iii. 8, 9.

burned like fire," that He loved one and hated another. It is apt to be forgotten how difficult it is to express the ideas intended to be conveyed by these terms without resort both to long paraphrases and to abstract expressions quite unintelligible to simple minds. Even in matters of physical science, when the utmost accuracy of language is expected, who objects to the statement that heat acts differently on different substances, expanding the iron and contracting the clay, or, as in the famous illustration of St. Augustine, burning up the chaff and purifying the gold?* We know that the so-called natural laws are uniform in their operation (although this conception of them has been reached only by long study and reflection), and we are now taught that heat is only "a mode of motion." Its different effects are simply the result of differences in the objects acted upon. Nevertheless, we are often compelled in popular language to describe differences of effects in terms which seem to imply difference in the action of the force itself. The light leads to very varied results as it falls upon the surface of the thermopile, upon the sensitive plate in the camera, upon the polarising crystal, or upon the refracting prism. The energy is the same in all these cases; but we speak popularly as if the light itself acted differently when such diverse results follow from its uniform action upon different objects. In spiritual things we are still less emancipated from a corresponding necessity. We cannot more conveniently speak of God's relation to His faithful servants than by describing Him as

---

* In Psal. xxi. 5; De Civ. Dei. I. c. 8.

their Father. We know that this is a figurative term; but we have no more satisfactory way of conveying the idea intended. We recognize fully that any change in the manifestation of the Divine action upon man depends upon a change in the persons acted upon; but we cannot better describe this than by saying that He changes whom we know to be unchangeable. In this last case the difficulty lies not merely in the language, but in the thought conveyed by it. It is hard for other than thoughtful minds to understand how precisely the same grace which softens and blesses one heart, hardens and consequently curses another. When occasionally this is plainly stated in Scripture, as when the Apostles speak of their preaching as "the savor of death unto death" "in them that perish" equally as "the savor of life unto life" "in them that are saved,"* much explanation is required by many minds before such passages can be understood. The same thing is true when God is said to have hardened Pharaoh's heart, † or to have sent a lying spirit into Ahab's prophets. ‡

Revelation having been given for men of all ages and all lands, must be adapted, on the whole, to the understanding of all. There must be statements which shall enable the cultured and thoughtful to explain what may seem strange in those adapted especially to more simple minds; but the great bulk of its teachings must be suited to the needs of the mass of mankind. It would be as hard to banish from it terms describing the Divine acts by their

---

* 2 Cor. ii. 15, 16. † Ex. viii. 13; ix. 12; x. 20.
‡ 1 Kings, xxii. 19–23.

sensible phenomena as it would be to banish from ordinary life the expressions "the sun rises" and "the sun sets." Even the most cultured and philosophic at the present day, as already said, cannot avoid using something of anthropomorphic language in speaking of the Deity and His acts, and it is plain that the same thing must have been tenfold more necessary to men in the dim twilight of knowledge. Our race, before it had been developed by reflection and science, needed to be taught spiritual truths in the same forms which we now use for our children; only those forms, being the clothing of Divine truth, remain still, not merely the delight of childhood, but the perpetual instructor of those who are able, by their spiritual maturity, to see beneath the forms the substance they were intended to convey.

Yet there is a manifest progress in this respect in the Scriptures—a progress so marked as to be numbered among the characteristic differences between the Old and New Testaments. Our heavenly Father has always revealed Himself quite up to, and even somewhat beyond man's capacity at the time; not so much beyond as to be unintelligible and prevent any good effect, but yet enough to raise man continually to a higher level as fast as his capacity would allow. It is to be expected, therefore, that as man has been improved and elevated by the earlier revelations, the later will become increasingly spiritual in their character, and the grosser forms of anthropomorphism will be more and more left behind. Yet the earlier forms were not only once necessary in the childhood of our race; but they are still required both for the actual child and for all that vast mass of mankind who remain permanently in a childlike stage of intellectual development.

This particular point has been dwelt upon at considerable length because it furnishes the key to the other differences between the Old and New Testaments which may now be spoken of more briefly. For it is quite as true of the substance as of the form of revelation, that in order to be of any use and value to man it must be adapted to his capacity. The sermon on the Mount would have been spoken quite in vain to the horde of slaves escaping from Egypt, or to the marshalled hosts of Joshua's army; and the glowing exhortations of St. Paul's epistles could not have moved the hearts of those who knew nothing of Gethsemane and Calvary. "If the fact be that God is what in the imperfection of our language we are fain to describe as merciful and loving, it follows that in any revelation He will not reveal Himself perfectly, but only partially, as man is able to bear it; and this must be, in a certain sense, untruly or erroneously (for whatever is imperfect is from one point of view erroneous). Revelation must, therefore, be marked in different ages by different degrees of this imperfection or so-called erroneousness of teaching. Men must be trained through inferior conceptions—such conceptions as it was possible to awaken in them without violating the laws of their nature—to enable them to rise to higher; they must be appealed to through motives and feelings they can understand, before they can be led up to those which at first they could not understand."* They must be taught simple and fundamental truth before they can be trusted with that which is less obvious and which rests upon the former as its foundation.

If, now, particular instances of the divergence of teaching between the two dispensations be considered, they will all be found to come under this general principle or under one or two others immediately connected with and dependent upon it. The difficulty from the recognition of easy divorce and of polygamy is not wholly removed by our Lord's argument from the history of creation, that monogamy was originally the Divine purpose, and that polygamy was only temporarily suffered for the hardness of men's hearts.† We may understand that a law of higher morality was originally proposed, and that when men evidently were unequal to its requirements God should simply not have enforced the law, should have forborne to punish men for its violation—that, as St. Paul says of His dealing with heathen polytheism and idolatry, "The times of ignorance, therefore, God overlooked;" ‡ but the difficulty here is that polygamy was not merely suffered, but expressly sanctioned by law; it was not only allowed, but it was recognized in positive enactments. Here two things are to be noted which have a much wider application than to this particular case. In the first place, in any system of legislation many things not really approved, but

---

* See an article, "Errors of the Scriptures," in the *Bibliotheca Sacra* for July, 1879, p. 510.
† Matt. xix. 8. ‡ Acts, xvii. 30 (Revision).

simply tolerated, must necessarily be recognized in the provisions of the laws. Thus if polygamy was to be tolerated, it must be guarded against abuses common among the surrounding heathen, and in order to this its existence must be recognized in the law. Yet this does not show that it was in accordance with the Divine will in any other sense than that it was suffered for the time being. Secondly, the distinction between toleration and command is not always quite so clear as it may seem at first sight. In regard to all those matters which are steps in education and in progress towards a higher state it may often be necessary to make positive enactments for the time being, although these are in themselves temporary and destined to be superseded or reversed in the future. It is the universal experience in a new country that laws are required in an unformed condition of society which must pass away as that society becomes more settled. The vast mass of the best system of jurisprudence in an old and cultured nation would be altogether out of place among pioneers in the wilderness; and correspondingly, the simple and summary rules so absolutely necessary in the one case would be tyrannical in the extreme and work the utmost injustice in the other. So it was also in the case of what may be called the spiritual pioneers of mankind. It was necessary that positive laws should be given to them which they were destined, by means of the very education they thus attained, to outgrow, and which, at a period of higher spiritual advancement, were to be superseded or even reversed. In the case of polygamy there is no occasion for such reversal; those laws which recognize it were simply made to prevent its worst abuses in view of the necessity of its temporary toleration.

The laws of revenge partly come under this head. In part, it is true, they have precisely the same character as those of polygamy. They were steps in a progress, restraining the people from the unlimited license of revenge and leading them through the principle of exact justice to the Gospel requirements of "love your enemies," "do good to them that hate you;" the law itself meantime embodying the precept "thou shalt love thy neighbor as thyself,"* that such as were able to receive it might understand the will of God and be prepared for the higher and fuller revelation. But the *lex talionis* of the Pentateuch unquestionably went beyond this. It was not merely permissive, but obligatory: "Thine eye shall not pity; but life shall go for life, eye for eye, tooth for tooth, hand for hand, foot for foot." † In the sermon on the Mount this very passage is quoted under the formula, "Ye have heard that it hath been said," and it is added, "but I say unto you, that ye resist not evil: but whosoever shall smite thee on thy right cheek, turn to him the other also." ‡ How are these contradictory precepts to be considered as the harmonious requirements of the same Being? In virtue of the principle just explained; because the condition of the people was such that they must first be trained under a lower, in order to become fitted for a higher standard.

---

* Lev. xix. 18. † Deut. xix. 21. ‡ Matt. v. 38, 39.

They must be taught the principles of justice to prepare them to receive those of love. The same order of Divine action which is thus required in spiritual things is familiar in regard to the Divine works in the natural world. "The monsters of the carboniferous era must precede the development of life in the tertiary, and that in turn must prepare the way for the age of man; yet to Him who ordered the earth from the beginning those carboniferous monsters were good in their day (although their existence now would be incompatible with the life of to-day), and on looking back we see no unfitness in their formation under the guiding hand of Him who was leading our earth to a higher state. So in the spiritual development of our race, as far as we can judge, it was necessary that God should govern man according to his capacities, and give him laws suited to his condition. Only thus could he be advanced to a higher standard; only by impressing on a lawless people, given to unbridled license of revenge, a sense of exact justice and of the rights of others could they be prepared for a higher teaching." *

Slavery comes under the same head as polygamy. It was suffered for the time "for the hardness of their hearts," but it was hedged about and restrained in a variety of ways, transforming the institution into one essentially different from that of the contemporary nations, and giving principles which would finally result in its abolition. Yet even Christianity

---

*See Art. in Bibl. Sacra *ubi sup.* p. 523. See also Mozley, *Ruling Ideas in Early Ages*, and Newman Smythe, *Old Faiths in New Light*.

could not proceed at once to its entire abrogation, and only after eighteen centuries of the gradual leavening influence of Christian principles has it been abolished even among civilized and Christian nations.

The punishment of the innocent family for the sins of its guilty head, and the extermination of whole nations, and that too in bloody wars, by the hands of the chosen people, strike strangely upon the Christian's ear, and sometimes lead him to doubt if the dispensation in which they were peremptorily commanded could have come from the Author of the Gospel of peace and love. The study of these facts opens another of those broad principles of the Divine dealings with man, and the last that will here need to be considered. Men always have stood, and they still stand, in a two-fold relation to God, individual and federal ; as single persons responsible for their own works and treated accordingly, and as members of a body acting together and dealt with collectively. This is seen everywhere in God's natural government of the world. Children inherit not merely the social position and the fortunes, but the physical and mental peculiarities of their parents ; families prosper or are ruined according to the conduct of their head ; whole nations are affected by the action of their rulers. Whether or not we can explain why the world should have been so constituted, it is plain that we must expect, if both come from the same Author, the same general features in revelation as in the constitution of nature. The existence of this two-fold relation in our own day may be illustrated by the Christian Church; whatever grace or blessing comes by its instrumentality is in consequence of the federal relation in which each believer stands to his Master, over and above his individual relation. Certainly the latter is the all-important and determinative relation; for "every man shall be judged according as his work shall be." Yet while man remains by his constitution a social being, the social relation can never be ignored, nor has it ever been in the Divine dealings with man. A great change, however, has gradually come about as the ages have rolled on. To the student of the history of revelation its progress is marked in nothing more strongly than in the constantly growing importance of the individual in comparison with the federal relation. In early times the latter was far more prominent. So strong was it in the time of Moses that the prophet could declare, God " hath not beheld iniquity in Jacob, neither hath he seen perverseness in Israel,"* at the very time when He was punishing tens of thousands of them for their gross and outrageous sins. In early days men—whether Israelites or heathen—looked upon the nation chiefly as an organic whole and upon the family as a possession of its head. When, therefore, such nations as the Amalekites or the Canaanites arrayed themselves against the Church of God they must be dealt with as a whole, in order that the Divine judgment should be intelligible or have any value in the minds of either friends or foes. Occasionally there occurred, it is true, such a striking instance of faith

---

* Num. xxiii. 21.

that Rahab could be spared in the destruction of the doomed city, but even so her whole family must be spared with her. Generally, however, men made little distinction between the individual and the body to which he belonged. The same thing is true also of the treatment of families; the Israelites could not have understood that God was seriously displeased with Dathan and Abiram, or afterwards with Achan, had not their whole families been involved in the sentence upon their heads. If the Divine judgments were to be of any effect in showing God's government of the world, they must be sweeping and comprehensive. This is still to some degree unavoidable; but it was far more so in the olden time, when the value of human life was so little understood. The only way in which the Divine detestation of the sins of the Canaanites could be conveyed to their minds was by the command that the whole people, like Sodom and Gomorrah, should be utterly swept away. The result showed the necessity of this command; for when the people failed in its execution, they also failed to understand the heinousness of Canaanitish sin. Their ideas could only slowly and gradually be raised above those of the rest of the world. Yet it is never to be forgotten that all those judgments in which the innocent were involved with the guilty, were temporal and not eternal in their character, they were like the earthquake which now destroys the city, or the catastrophe into which :the ship's company is plunged by the unskilfulness or error of the captain. The wife of Korah, who went down alive into the pit,* may yet have been received into Paradise; and many of the Ninevites, who heard "the preaching of Jonah," although their city was spared,† may have received the final doom of the impenitent.

It is hardly necessary to ask why the chosen people should have been made the instruments of these judgments, or why, in some instances, appeal should have been made to lower motives to nerve them for their task. The lesson of God's anger against Canaanitish sin could in no other way have been so impressed upon the Israelites as by making them the actual executioners of His wrath. Even thus their tendency to heathen abominations was so strong as to have been but imperfectly held in check by this most vivid personal impression. In regard to the appeal sometimes made to such reasons as hereditary hostility to the people of God, former injurious treatment and the like, as in the case of the Amalekites,‡ it may suffice to say that man is of a mixed nature, and in mercy to our weakness God has always appealed, in seeking to lead us to the right, not only to the motives of love and duty and gratitude, but also to self-interest. Such appeals are a help, are even essential to us now, in the full sunlight of the Gospel; how much more to those in their spiritual infancy in the dim twilight of the law.

There are no other particular instances of alleged opposition between the details of the Old and the

---

* Num. xvi. 32, 33. † Jonah, iii.
‡ 1 Sam. xv. 2, etc.; Deut. xxv. 17-19.

New Covenants which will not, upon reflection, be seen to fall under the principles which have now been discussed. It only remains that a word should be said upon the general scheme of salvation as set forth in them respectively.

It is abundantly clear that man, having once become alienated from God, and being an inheritor of a sinful nature, could never restore himself by his own exertions to that state of perfect holiness in which alone communion with an all-holy God is possible. However his history may be looked upon as on the whole an upward progress, yet the energy by which that progress has been made has always been from without and from above, and this energy it has been the office of all revelation to place within his reach. In other words, the old and the new revelation must necessarily have had the same common purpose of raising man from sin to a life of holiness, and thereby of communion with God. Before any step could be taken on this road, the sin already committed must be done away. Hence, after his fall, man resorted to sacrifice as a means of approach to God. How far he appreciated the imperfection of this means we do not know; but it is plain to every thoughtful man that it was intrinsically insufficient. There is an inherent want of correlation between human sins and the life of the lower animals; and hence, as the author of the Epistle to the Hebrews has taught, "it is not possible that the blood of bulls and of goats should take away sins."* Sacrifice, therefore, could only have ex-

---

* Heb. x. 4.

pressed on man's part his repentance and desire to be forgiven, and in so far as it was understood to be a Divine institution, some symbolic form of atonement. When sacrifices came to be systematically ordered under the Mosaic law, their typical character was abundantly shown in many ways. The heathen idea of the sacrifice as an adequate compensation to God for the offence, as a *quid pro quo*, was absolutely excluded. It was plain that there must be some other ground of acceptance with God, and this ground was expressly declared to Abraham in words which the New Testament has again and again referred to as containing the cardinal principle of the Gospel: Abraham " believed God and it was counted unto him for righteousness."* The true principle of salvation, perfect trust in God, was the same under both dispensations and binds them together in a perpetual unity. Nor can this unity be broken because, long centuries after the promise to Abraham, it became necessary for a time to control the wickedness and perversity of the people by a law of definite and detailed precepts lest they should relapse into utter ungodliness and heathenism. St. Paul justly argues, "The covenant that was confirmed before of God in Christ, the law, which was four hundred and thirty years after, cannot disannul," and the law " was added because of transgressions till the Seed should come to whom the promise was made." † When this was accomplished, the law had served its purpose, and, like

---

* Gen. xv. 6, cf. Rom. iv. 3; Gal. iii. 6 ; James, ii. 23.
† Gal. iii. 17-19.

everything else which has fulfilled its end, could only be a hinderance and obstruction if it continued to be maintained. The Apostle does not hesitate to call it then a "handwriting of ordinances that was against us, which was contrary to us," and which Christ "took out of the way, nailing it to His cross;"* but until then it was important, and the precepts of the law, as will appear further on, were thoroughly educational in their character, so that in its least as well as in its greatest points it "was our schoolmaster to bring us to Christ."† Its aim was to teach the necessity of holiness, and therefore of the forgiveness of sin, and that the ground of these things must be trust in God and submission to His will.

There are innumerable points which cannot now be touched upon, showing the thorough unity of the two covenants. Some of these, such as the prophecies of the Old Testament, and the quotations made from it in the New, will be discussed in the following lectures. For the present these points must suffice: The Author of the New Covenant presents Himself to mankind as the Redeemer promised under the Old, and declares that its purpose from the beginning was fulfilled in His work and teachings. His disciples, one and all, took the same position, and from the Scriptures of the Old Testament they mightily convinced the Jews that Jesus was the Christ. These Scriptures were carried everywhere among the Gentile converts as sacred and authoritative. The same fundamental prin-

---

* Col. ii. 14, 15. † Gal. iii. 24.

ciples characterize both covenants, and the differences between them all result from the application of these principles to different people at different times and under different conditions. And, finally, both have one common purpose: the restoration of fallen man to communion with an all-holy God, and that, too, by the very same means, of trust in Him and acceptance of His appointed way of salvation.

LECTURE II.

THE PROGRESSIVE CHARACTER OF REVELATION.

IN the last lecture it was assumed that Revelation had been progressive, and several explanations were based upon this fact. The fact itself needs to be more fully emphasized and illustrated; for without its constant recognition there can be no sufficient understanding of the Divine word. This lecture will be the expansion of the text, "God who .... spake in times past unto the fathers by the prophets, hath in these last days spoken unto us by His Son."*

There is a certain difficulty in the treatment of this subject. If revelation has been progressive and adapted to man's increasing capacity to receive it, then it may plausibly be argued that this correlation marks the sacred books as the mere outgrowth of man's advancing knowledge rather than as the Divine condescension to human needs. In other words, it shows them to be of human rather than of Divine origin. This position has been vigorously asserted in recent years, and has obtained no inconsiderable share of the public attention. It has a certain plausibility at first view, but on more careful examination it will be found inconsistent with the facts,

---
* Heb. i. 1.

as will be seen presently. Let us first look at the actual progressive character of revelation, since this lies at the basis of all just estimate of the relations and proportions of its different parts.

In the first place, it is plain on *à priori* grounds that any revelation, like every other form of education, in order to useful effect, must be given gradually. This may best be done by a series of revelations given in portions, and these must necessarily be progressive. Otherwise, if the later made no advance upon the earlier, there would be no reason why it should be given; if all that was meant to be taught of the Divine will was announced in the first, there would be nothing for the second to tell. Again: if the earlier revelations had any effect, if they did not utterly fail of their purpose, man must have been advanced by them in spiritual knowledge and thus fitted for further revelation. Historically, it is plain that this was actually the case, and that with each successive revelation man did attain to a higher knowledge of divine things, to better ideas of his own duty and purer conceptions of the Deity. Still this does not imply the necessity of a continuous flow of successively fuller revelations; if each revelation were somewhat above man's capacity at the period when it was given, time must be allowed for him to grow up to it before another could be required. Four centuries intervened between Malachi and Christ. Eighteen centuries have not yet sufficed to bring men up to the full standard of the Christian revelation, although the growth through successive ages has been real and marked. So, also, a higher revelation having been given in outline which the mass of the people were as yet unprepared to receive, it may be followed by one inferior in that the higher outlines of the earlier are overlaid by teachings better adapted to the capacities of the people, in order to lead them up gradually to that which has already been announced. Such St. Paul shows to have been the relation of the Mosaic legislation to the Abrahamic promise. The people had proved themselves unable to receive that which had been given. They must now be trained up from the level on which they stood. Nevertheless, on the whole, revelation is recognized by all as having been progressive.

Any examination of the character of the Divine revelations to man must be limited to those of which the record has been preserved. There may have been others given, especially in the earliest times, and the Mosaic record, itself a compilation of earlier documents, implies them. The Babylonian tablets, far outdating the age of Abraham,* seem to have preserved the trace of some primeval revelations overlaid by masses of myth and fable, the accretions of ages of human transmission. But it is reasonable to suppose that the most important have been preserved in the records which remain to us, and therefore that the knowledge divinely given at any time did not essentially surpass that which may be obtained from the existing Scriptures relating to that time.

---

* See Smith's *Chaldean Genesis;* and the volumes of *Records of the Past.*

The order of the several parts of the Bible, especially the older revelation, is by no means universally agreed upon. Of late years earnest discussion has arisen in regard to the date of considerable parts of both Testaments. This may be considered as now practically settled for the New Testament, at least in its main points, in favor of what is known as the traditional view; but in regard to the Old, we are still in the midst of the controversy. Details of the disputed points, such as the date of many of the Psalms, or of the latter part of Isaiah, or of the book of Daniel, important as they are in other connections, do not matter for our present purpose; but in treating of the progress of revelation, we must have before our minds some idea of the general order in which its main parts have been given. We must assume that the Levitical legislation either preceded or followed the prophetical teaching. Unfortunately, this forms now one of the chief points of critical discussion, and it is impossible here to consider the facts on which the question must ultimately be decided. It is necessary, therefore, to adopt as "a working hypothesis" that view which will best explain the phenomena before us. The newer criticism rests largely on what is supposed to be the orderly evolution of the several parts of the sacred word; but if it be once admitted that there is progress in revelation, that progress must surely be, in accordance with all the analogies of God's works, from the lower to the higher. Such a progress, as will presently appear, involves the acceptance of the traditional view. It will therefore be here assumed that broadly, and as regards their relation to one another, the several parts of revelation are connected chronologically as has generally been supposed until the times of the most recent criticism. While this is assumed here only as a working hypothesis, it is believed that it will be sustained by the most thorough and searching examination of the facts.

The mention of the birth of Abraham occurs in the eleventh chapter of Genesis. If any one will open his Bible at this point, and imagine for a moment that he has no other revelation than is contained in the previous record, he will see at once how very small a proportion of the whole bulk of the sacred volume precedes this event. In the vast period of earlier time, of which we have no certain chronology, the revelations recorded are few and of the utmost simplicity; but man is represented as in a shocking state of ungodliness, and with a strong tendency to evil. Such divine communications as were given were chiefly practical, relating to immediate and easily understood duties; yet there is a certain progress even in these, from the single childlike command laid on our first parents to the "covenant" established with Noah having the bow in the clouds as its token. With Abraham a new era was ushered in; a special family was singled out and prepared for the reception of a fuller revelation. The primeval promise had been given long ages before, but without details or explanation; now its fulfilment was limited to the patriarch's family: "in thy seed shall all the families of the earth be blessed." Abraham himself was vouchsafed many divine visions; God's dealings with mankind in various ways were made known to him; the course of the Divine training for his posterity during centuries to come was declared; and, above all, he was taught the great principle of faith as the means of acceptance with God, which, obscured in after ages, was finally brought into full light by the Gospel; and the fundamental fact of all true religion, the unity of God, altogether lost from sight, or only here and there maintained by the more intelligent minds among the nations of the earth, was most strongly impressed upon him and his descendants. It is particularly to be noted that up to this time, the revelation of God presented Him to human thought as the one universal God of all the earth, technically expressed, as *Elohim;* the revelation of Him in a peculiar relation to Israel, as *Jahve*, was not until later. He was not, however, even then revealed as a merely national Deity, but as the universal God in a special relation to His chosen people. Much clearer views of the character of God and of His dealings with man come out gradually in the lives of Abraham's immediate descendants. Still, if you were asked to cut off your Bibles at the close of Genesis and see how much of Divine knowledge you could obtain from that single book, you would, until you had thought upon it, be surprised to see how small and meagre and elementary was your information. If even this be compared with the legends of other nations covering the same period—with such a book, *e. g.*, as "the Chaldean

Genesis," its vast superiority is manifest. The Chaldeans were a far more civilized and powerful nation than the Israelites at the time of the Exodus. Yet either they had sunk from the level of primeval knowledge and purity, or else—what for our purpose is practically the same thing—the Hebrews had been elevated by revelation. The same thing is true of the Egyptians, the most powerful and the most advanced of all the nations of the period. Their priesthood still preserved the idea of the unity of God as an esoteric doctrine, and they held firmly to a future life whose awards depended upon the conduct of men here below; but the mass of the people were allowed to sink into the grossest polytheism and idolatry, and neither priests nor people appear to have had the slightest conception of the value of faith as the means of acceptance with God.

Passing from the narratives of Genesis to the next book of the Bible, we find that Israel has become a nation and a fresh chapter in the plan of redemption is unrolled. In the long struggle of Pharaoh against God, and the terrible judgments by which his pride was humbled, in the divine interpositions for the deliverance of the chosen people, and the miraculous support of their vast hosts in the wilderness, they were taught by personal experience that "man doth not live by bread alone but by every word that proceedeth out of the mouth of God." * But when at last they had encamped at the foot of Sinai and were to receive instructions in the will of God which should make them "a kingdom of

---

* Deut. viii. 3; Matt. iv. 4.

priests, and an holy nation,"* they proved unfit for their high vocation. They begged that they might no longer hear the voice of God directly, but that Moses should announce His will to them;† they turned aside again to their idolatries, and worshipped the golden calf.‡ "Because of transgressions" it became necessary that "a law should be added,§ by which their gross and carnal propensities might be held in check until they were further trained and prepared. Even this law was very imperfectly observed in the centuries that followed, until by long and severe discipline, by rejection of masses of the people, and by stern judgments on the remnant, they were at last brought to a better mind. Nevertheless, a real progress was made; and this law, in itself in some respects a backward step, was still at the time and in view of the condition and needs of the people, a vast and real advance. By it a church was established, with its sacraments, its typical sacrifices and worship, its hierarchy, and its government of the life of man by definite outward law. The duty of a loving obedience to God from the heart and of scrupulous regard to the rights of a neighbor is everywhere insisted upon, and the subordination of the passions and immediate selfish interests to a higher will is most emphatically taught. Above all, the unity and sole supremacy of God and the abomination of rendering homage to any other, is set forth with a distinctness that he may read who runs.

---

* Ex. xix. 6. † *Ib.* xx. 19, 20.
‡ *Ib.* xxxii. § Gal. iii. 19.

It is to be remembered in connection with these facts that Abraham was an exceptional man, whose spiritual character and discernment were far above those of either his contemporaries or of most of his descendants; while Israel at Sinai was a mass of average people. Higher truth could be understood by him than by them. Yet among them also were such better men as Moses and Joshua, and in the midst of the lower teaching for the mass, higher teaching was given for the spiritual nurture of such as could receive it.

It were too long to follow out thus in detail the successive revelations. They were given little by little, with great intervals between, as during the troubled and disorderly period of the Judges; or at other times in the fuller outbursts of inspired song and prophetic teaching, as when David had restored the independence of the nation and established the worship of God in a more regular and systematic way; or the great development of prophecy at other and later epochs, as at the time of the approaching captivity of the Northern kingdom in the days of Isaiah and his contemporaries, Hosea, Amos, and Micah; or again just before and during the Babylonian captivity, when Jeremiah, Ezekiel, and Daniel prophesied. One has only to read the various books in their ordinarily accepted chronological order to be struck with the steady progress of revelation, with the ever increasing knowledge of God and of man's duty brought out in the successive books, each fresh revelation pre-supposing all that had gone before, and therefore adding its own teaching without repeating what was already known. There are two points to which attention may be especially called: the teaching of the spiritual meaning of the law; and the definite preparation by prophecy for the still higher revelation yet to be made. On each of these a few words will suffice.

In regard to the former: the closing exhortations of Moses expressly and repeatedly set forth the loving obedience of the heart as the essential point in the fulfilling of the law. Yet these exhortations were little regarded by the people, who signally failed even in the observance of the outward commands. Further instruction was needed, and accordingly the constant teaching of the prophets, as well as the sacred songs of the Psalms, insist on spiritual service as alone acceptable, and describe in vivid terms the worthlessness of mere outward worship apart from that of the heart. All this had indeed been taught before; but the progress of revelation was marked by bringing this teaching into prominence and awakening the consciousness of the people to the true meaning and value of the revelation already given. As Christ "brought life and immortality to light,"[*] though they were known before; and as it could be said before our Lord's ascension, "the Holy Ghost was not yet,"[†] although holy men all along had been filled with His influence,[‡] and all the prophets had spoken under His inspiration:[§] so it was that the Psalms and the Prophets were practically a new revelation of the spirituality of the

---

[*] 2 Tim. i. 10.   [†] John, vii. 39.   [‡] Luke, i. 41, 67.
[§] 2 Tim. iii. 16; 1 Pet. i. 11; 2 Pet. i. 21.

law, although the same truth had existed, little noticed, in the law itself. On this account it has sometimes seemed, to superficial critics, that there is an opposition between the law and these subsequent writings; but it is plain on any just consideration of the people and their needs that this is not the case. The spiritual element had been all along in the law, only more dimly expressed, and obscured by the necessity of restraining and guiding a rude and lawless people by a multitude of definite outward precepts. The Israelites, with that perverse tendency which has always existed in the human heart, were bent on overlooking the spiritual element and relying on the mere outward performance of the letter of the law. It was one of the chief offices of subsequent revelation to show clearly, and by admonitions repeated from age to age, that the restoration of sinful man to communion with God was too great and real a change to be accomplished by any outward acts alone. There was no other opposition than that which must always exist between more partial and more perfect truth.

But all this would have been incomplete and insufficient without the other teaching. The later revelations, by giving higher ideas of God and of man's duty, showed the people the imperfection of the system under which they were living, and that what they really needed and the better spirits among them longed for, "the law could not do, in that it was weak through the flesh."* It was, therefore, necessary that the Psalms and the Prophets should

---

* Rom. viii. 3.

point forward to the Redeemer to come with a clearness and fulness not yet expressed either in the patriarchal revelations or in the Sinaitic legislation. He had been foretold in Paradise, He had been promised to Abraham, He had been prophesied of by Moses; but here, as before, it was the office of later revelation to make this promise more prominent and more full. All through the ages of Israel's history inspired men were raised up for this purpose, and their work was so thoroughly done that the Messiah's coming became the constant thought and the life-spring of every devout believer. By this means the greatest advance of all was made and the best preparation effected for the new and higher dispensation. Brought by the law to a sense of sin, having only means intrinsically insufficient for its forgiveness, they were thus taught to look forward to the "fountain opened .... for sin."* There is, therefore, in these successive revelations an order and logical development in accordance with the needs and the capacities of men. Let us review this order: First, after man's fall comes the fundamental but somewhat indefinite promise of the Redeemer; then a gradual schooling in the nature of God and of man's relations to Him, culminating in the announcement of the great principle of faith and the choice of a peculiar people to be the depositaries of the knowledge of God and examples of faithful obedience to His will. Proving unequal to this high vocation, the law was given them to be their "schoolmaster to bring them to Christ." Meantime, instruction in the spiritual

---

* Zech. xiii. 1.

meaning and character of the law was constantly given, and the hope that in the fulness of time it should find its consummation in a better and more perfect revelation was in every way nourished and strengthened and made more definite. Especially was advance made in revelation by the prophecy— which the sequel showed to be still far above the people's comprehension—that the Redeemer must reach His exaltation through the path of humiliation.

The theory of the so-called "advanced criticism," that the Levitical law was not prior, but subsequent to the teachings of the Prophets, would throw this order into confusion. According to the view here followed, there was first the example given in Abraham of trust in God as the fundamental principle of religion, and, when the people proved unequal to the reception of this principle, the law was "added because of transgressions," but while it was still in force and the people still under its pupilage, prophets were sent age after age to bring the people up by their spiritual teaching to that higher standard for which they had been unworthy. According to the view of the critics, we should have the strange phenomenon of the higher instruction given first and with all the emphasis and prolonged reiteration of the prophetic teaching, finally culminating in the relatively inferior teaching of the law. We should have the growing hope of the universal spiritual kingdom of the Messiah leading to the narrower national development of the strictly Jewish system. In the midst of progress there would be an enormous and long-continued retrogression. It is true that, if the prophetic teaching be compared with the prevalent ideas and practice of the mass of the people, such a retrogression may be made out; but no such comparison can fairly be made. Teaching must be compared with teaching and practice with practice, and in both there was a great advance. In the gross and sinful condition of the people the effect of the prophetic teaching was to rouse them gradually to a sense of their neglect of the letter of the earlier revelation, and they were thus brought to a better observance of this, although they continued to neglect its spirit as taught by the Prophets. Our Lord often reproved the people for this very failure to rise to the higher level set before them, and for their perverse clinging to the mere letter of the commandments.

The system of this school of critics is thus equally at fault whether the Scriptures be looked upon as the supernaturally revealed will of God, or as an evolution of human thought. These two views, opposite as they are in their fundamental conceptions, yet have before them the same phenomena of progress. For if the Almighty has condescended to adapt His revelations to human needs and capacities, they must have a growing development like that which would have resulted from ever-improving human ideas and conceptions during ages of successive enlightenment; but after this enlightenment had once reached the standard of the prophets it is inconceivable that the most advanced spirits of the nation, which the writers of the Pentateuch must have been, could have fallen back to the ceremonial part of the law. It is not hard to choose between the two views of the origin of the law on other grounds; but for the present, it is to be noted that the law can only be considered subsequent to the prophets on the supposition of an enormous backward step. This difficulty is partially met by the critics through the assumption that the greatest and most fundamental doctrine of all, the unity of God, was not clearly revealed to the earlier Israelites, but was only gradually brought to light and enforced by the prophets. To maintain this proposition they find it necessary to discredit the usually accepted historical data, and to represent what are stated in Scripture to be Divine rebukes of the people's sins, as the struggles of a more enlightened and advancing party against the general darkness and prevailing polytheism. Their argument is, that since the idea of the unity and spirituality of God had not yet been reached by the mass of the nation, that idea could not have rested upon any authoritative basis recognized by them.

One answer to all this might be, that such monotheistic conceptions were unknown at the time to all other nations of the earth, and that there was nothing in the character of the people of Israel to put them in advance of their contemporaries. A certain sort of monotheism (called "henotheism" by modern scholars to distinguish it), had long been received in India; but it was really the opposite extreme—Pantheism. In Egypt, too, there was a belief in the unity of God; but it was an esoteric doctrine of the priests, carefully hidden from the people, and it is by no means clear whether even this was really monotheism or only pantheism. The speculations of human philosophy, unguided by revelation, have always shown a pantheistic tendency; but the Israelites were too little given to philosophy to be much affected by this, and certainly their Scriptures show no trace of such a tendency. If the ideas of the unity and holiness of God were of merely human development, the critics would have strong reason for placing the date of their publication in Israel as late as possible; but no date consistent with admitted historical facts would be late enough to sustain their argument. These ideas are found among the Israelites far earlier than anywhere else, and there is no reason why this should have been so. About the time of the last of the Hebrew prophets, and, on any hypothesis, long after the unity of God had been proclaimed among them, Plato wrought out the idea as a result of the most profound thought; but, even then, he made small approach to the Divine perfection and purity as revealed in Israel. The mass of the Israelites themselves, down to the period of the captivity, showed a most obdurate attachment to polytheism and all its degrading superstitions.

But the views in question must be met on higher grounds. The main point is to determine whether the ideas of the unity and holiness of God with the consequent duties of man, contained in the Scriptures, were from a supernatural source, or a development of human thought. In the latter case, the position of the newer criticism, as has been seen, would have a cogent argument in its favor, although opposed to the best historical data in our possession, and not in accordance with the view of the Old Testament taken in the New; but if the former be true, there is no reason why these doctrines should not have been revealed at as early an era as could have been beneficial to man.

This is not the place for any extended discussion of the truth of revelation or of the inspiration of the Scriptures, but only for a few suggestions bearing upon the point at issue. No stress can here be laid upon the view of the older revelations taken by our Lord and His Apostles. Unquestionably these were regarded by them as of supreme and divine authority, and were quoted by them as conclusive of all argument; but it is a first principle with the "newer criticism" that in any scientific examination the Old Testament should be considered by itself and quite apart from the view taken of it in the New. It is not obvious why the bud can be better understood without reference to the flower, or the embryo without the light thrown upon its structure by the adult. Nevertheless, it may be well to see the conclusions to which we are led by the evidence of the Old Testament alone. Its writers certainly claim to speak by express command of God, and often preface their utterances by "Thus saith the Lord;" but to the critics this is inconclusive. We are told that this is merely an accustomed formula of the writers to express their belief that the best outcome of their own thoughts was really divine truth; that

they only meant to say that God spoke by them as
He speaks by every man who attains to worthy conceptions of Him and of His character and dealings.
The apparent force of these expressions is therefore
set aside.

Prophecy has been often appealed to, and was
appealed to in a very marked way by some of the
Old Testament writers themselves as a positive
proof that their utterances were directed from on
high. This will be considered in the Lecture on
Prophecy.* The distinct foretelling of future events
which could not be foreseen by human sagacity, and
which were accomplished as foretold, is admitted on
all sides as a conclusive proof of divine communication. But here, as everywhere else, the critics have
seized beforehand on every possible source of proof,
and declared it untrustworthy. Either the usually
accepted date of the prophecy is challenged and it is
made into a *vaticinium post eventum*, or, when this
cannot be done, it is interpreted as not meaning
what it has always been understood to mean. But
notwithstanding these and other objections, there
remain some prophecies the date of which is beyond
all gainsaying, and the interpretation of which is unquestionable. Instances will be given in the Lecture on Prophecy. Meantime this source of proof
must also be passed by.

Independently of any such specific evidence, there
are two broad and general considerations having an
important bearing on the question. One of these,
already alluded to, is the superiority of the Jewish

---

* Lecture VII.

system to any and all other religions which can be compared with it in antiquity. Take, as a single illustration, a point which directly or indirectly involves all man's relations to his fellow-man—the equality of all men before God. This was taught in the institutions of the law in every variety of form. There was precisely the same redemption money for every soul, the same sin-offering (except in some cases of official responsibility) for every transgressor, the same defilements, and the same means of purification; withal there was an equal division of the land, the fee of which was regarded as vested in God Himself, all inheritances were the same, and every one, priests and Levites not excepted, stood on precisely the same footing before the penal law. Slavery, greatly modified, was still suffered; but the slave stood on the same footing as his master before God. In no other nation on the face of the earth was anything like this equality of man recognized for a long course of centuries; in fact it has never been, to any practical purpose, except under the influence of Christianity. Again: if the Bible story of the creation and of the early history of mankind be compared with those of other nations, the vast superiority of the Hebrew record is acknowledged even by those most unwilling to recognize its divine Source. The best of them, as already noticed in regard to "the Chaldean Genesis," are pervaded with polytheism and with a mass of superstitious legend in strange contrast to the simplicity and purity of the Mosaic writings. The question of relative antiquity need not here be raised; the point is simply their comparative purity, truth, and excellence. Other illustrations, such as the duty of love to neighbors, of kindness to the poor and to slaves, and the like, will occur to every mind. The higher ideas of God, His omnipotence and omnipresence, His freedom from human passions and impurities, were known only to the Hebrew, except in so far as the shadow of them was recognized in the vagueness of pantheistic systems. This superiority of the Jewish system is a phenomenon to be accounted for. Human evolution is an insufficient cause in view of the character of the people as shown in their history, and of the immense interval of time by which their higher ideas were separated from those of other nations. There is but one other rational explanation: that these ideas were communicated to them from without; and, there being no other external source for them, this must have been from above.

The other consideration referred to as showing a superhuman origin of the Hebrew religion is, that this religion, universally recognized as so much above all others of its time, confessed its own insufficiency and looked definitely forward for its completion to the future. Something of this kind is, indeed, to be found everywhere. There certainly was such a thing as a Desire of all nations, and the Magi of the East looked for the birth of "the King of the Jews." God left not Himself without witness, and the echoes of the primeval promise are more or less dimly heard among all nations. It was generally felt that the world had gone awry, and that it must in some way be restored, and this hope was naturally connected with the expectation of a personal Restorer. There was also some perception that to this end wickedness must cease and a reign of righteousness be spread over the earth. These were precious rays from the Source of truth glimmering in the darkness, and, without doubt, helped much to prepare the minds of men for the reception of the Gospel; but in themselves they were either vague hopes or philosophical speculations concerning the ultimate outcome of all sublunary things. They had little living power over the hearts and lives of those by whom they were held, and the notion of righteousness, as connected with these expectations, was very confused and imperfect. With Israel the hope of the future had a very different character. It was constantly renewed and quickened and made definite by the successive prophetic utterances. With a far clearer revelation of God's righteousness, there was more of a sense of sin and of the need of repentance and of forgiveness. The sad attitude of heathenism is voiced by Plato, when, discoursing of the universal sinfulness of man and of the inefficiency of all remedies, he says that he stands in sore need of a deliverer, but knows not where to find him. Israel was taught to look for the Messianic kingdom with a personal Redeemer from all sin, and Teacher of all truth. This contrast between the religion of the Hebrews and that of all other nations is too plain and too generally recognized to need proof. With the Jews it was a practical belief, a daily thought of the knowledge and the bliss which the expected Messiah should bring to the earth; "Blessed is he that shall eat bread in the kingdom of God,"* was their common thought, and "I know that Messias cometh.... when He is come, He will tell us all things,"† was the belief which had passed over from them to their neighbors who held, in part, to the same Scriptures. The whole reason of their national existence was to prepare the way for the Messianic kingdom. Then all doubts were to be solved, all sin removed. But why should it have been so? Why this difference between Jewish and all other human thought? Was there any reason why the evolution of religious ideas among this people should have been in such contrast with the universal laws of evolution among all other nations? Again: there seems but one possible solution of the enigma; in the case of other nations there may have been, there undoubtedly were, some dim recollections of the early promise, and some uncertain expectations of the future; but to the Israelites the truth came with the clearness and fulness of special revelation.

The phenomena, then, sustain the claim which the Scriptures everywhere make for themselves, that they are a revelation from God. It remains, however, that this revelation was progressive, because only in that way was it possible that man could receive it. Nowhere is it possible for him to attain, or even to comprehend, perfect truth at a bound. He is obliged to gain first one elementary fact or principle, and then by means of this to advance to

---

* Luke, xiv. 15.   † John, iv. 25.

another which must often seriously modify his conception of the first. In the study of language, he must master the rule before he can learn the exception. The Ptolemaic system in astronomy was the necessary means of systematizing observations until they should lead to the Copernican; the Copernican must begin by the assumption of circular orbits and uniform motions of the planets until these could lead to the discovery of elliptical orbits and the doctrine of the radius vector. Still our present knowledge is imperfect. The law of gravity and the observed facts of astronomy are not in perfect accord. Each new discovery, as of the asteroids and of Neptune, brings about a closer harmony; but we cannot expect to see in nature a perfect realization of the law until we can look out upon its completeness from the footstool of the throne of the Omniscient.* The same thing is true of chemistry and of all other natural sciences, and indeed of all human knowledge. As already said, the elements, the most essential points, must be thoroughly fixed in the mind before it can receive their modifications. Were the process reversed and the fuller truth set at once before the untrained thought, the result could only be disastrous, and positive misconceptions take the place of simple imperfect apprehension. The child now, as well as the race in its childhood, must learn of the unity of God, before it can be profitably, or even safely, taught the doctrine of the Trinity. Any other course will be sure to lead to the error of Tritheism.

---

* See Cooke's *Chemical Physics*, at the close of § 166.

This, then, being the law of all human knowledge, it was plainly necessary that if revelation was to be useful to man, it should be conformed to the same method, and the fact that our heavenly Father has thus adapted the communication of His truth to our necessities, so far from implying that this communication is not from Him, does but show it to be in harmony with all His other works. It is the great merit of the so-called "theory of evolution" that it has brought all intelligent thought to a recognition of this fact. This cannot in the least do away with the necessity of recognizing Him as the Author of nature, but it does show that the manifestations of His work are in orderly and systematic succession. In history, in the science of language, in the development of character, whether in the individual or in the race, the same truth holds. Everywhere the same Unchangeable Being is consistent with Himself, and manifests Himself in similar ways. Theology owes a large debt of gratitude to the negative critics in bringing more fully to light the same characteristics in the progress of revelation. Only here, as in natural science, care must be taken not to mistake the method for the Source, and to imagine that because God adapted His teaching to man's needs and capacities, therefore man could have learned all that he needed himself.

But it is time to return to the examination of the actual fact of the progress of revelation. Of the immense advance made in passing from the Old Testament to the New there is no need to speak, for it is plain to every reader. A period of centuries had passed since the voice of the last of the prophets was hushed, giving the Church ample time for reflection. She had been led through strange vicissitudes of history adapted to impress strongly upon the people a sense of the overruling hand of God and of their utter dependence upon Him. When the voice of John, therefore, was heard in the wilderness, it came upon a people largely prepared for his message and ready to flock in crowds to his baptism of repentance in the immediate expectation of Him Who was to follow. It now becomes necessary to trace the same progress of revelation in the New Testament.* Here it is to be expected that the rapidity of the progress would be greatly accelerated, just as all human progress is ordinarily, in geometric ratio. First steps must always be slow, but when once made, become the means of more rapid advance. In tracing this progress it will be necessary to follow the order of the teaching contained in the various books rather than that of the publication of the books themselves. Some of the Epistles were written before any of the Gospels; but the subject-matter of the Gospels had long been taught orally, and therefore really came first.

Before entering on the subject itself it may be well to guard against a misapprehension. The whole New Testament teaching was comprised within the limits of much less than a century; eighteen centu-

---

* See on this subject *The Progress of Doctrine in the New Testament*, being the Bampton Lectures for 1866, by Rev. T. D. Bernard. An American edition was printed from the second London, in Boston, 1872.

ries have since passed away and there has been great progress in the appreciation and the practical application of the truth taught at first. Is this latter advance to be included in "the progress of revelation?" Certainly not. Revelation is from above. In the course of its communication to man there have ever been long pauses, that the truth already given might be sufficiently understood and assimilated by man to fit him for further disclosures. Such a pause, though not indeed absolute, followed for many centuries after the giving of the law; and total silence, again for centuries, preceded the Christian revelation. That revelation declared itself a finality and left nothing more to be communicated to man until by this he should be prepared for that higher state of existence in which he "shall see face to face" and "know even as he is known."* But meantime the revelation itself was so much higher and better than what had gone before that a very long period must be required for man to rise to its requirements. We can trace in history, in the improved recognition of the rights of man, in missionary enterprise, in benevolent activity of every kind, and above all, in an increased sense of responsibility and in higher ideas of duty to God, a most marked gain in the acceptance and the understanding of Christian truth; but this has nothing to do with the progress of revelation itself. That ceased for the time with the last line of the inspired Apostolic writing, and "the faith once delivered to the saints" became then complete, until the end of the present

---

* 1 Cor. xiii. 12.

dispensation shall bring forth a fresh flood of light in that life when we shall no longer "see through a glass darkly." Our present concern, therefore, must be with the New Testament itself, and not with the growing appreciation of this through the ages.

The New Testament begins with the Gospels. As already said, these were not the first books written, but they contain the record of what was said and done by the Author of our religion while still in the flesh. Even within these how great is the progress from the first announcement of the forerunner of the promised Messiah to the cross on Calvary, the resurrection and the ascension. Yet the Gospels as a whole, while they present the life and work of Christ, and record His pregnant teachings as the foundation of all that was afterwards to be more fully explained, must be considered, in reference to what follows, as elementary, and must close with the declaration of the Master, "I have yet many things to say unto you, but ye cannot bear them now. Howbeit when He, the Spirit of Truth, is come, He will guide you into all truth."* If the works and discourses of our Lord be followed in the Gospels in chronological sequence, a marked and visible progress is manifest from the Sermon on the Mount to the last discourse with the disciples. Perhaps no more obvious proof of this can be given than the way in which He was regarded by the people. In the early part of His ministry crowds pressed around Him, eager to see His works and hear His words. He "made and baptized more dis-

---

* John, xvi. 12, 13.

ciples than John."* At the close, notwithstanding the many who believed on Him, and the Hosannas of His triumphal entry into Jerusalem, He was "despised and rejected" by the great majority of the nation, and when He stood before Pilate, multitudes were found ready to cry "Crucify Him, crucify Him." This change was the result of the character of His teaching. At first He dealt gently with the ignorance of the people. He unfolded to them, indeed, the highest morality and deeper views than they had ever conceived of the nature of God and of the spirituality of His requirements; but when He began to show plainly that His "kingdom was not of this world," when He taught that the path to glory must lie through humiliation and suffering, that He himself must "be lifted up from the earth," and that His disciples must needs take up the cross and deny themselves if they would follow Him,—then, indeed, there was a progress in the revelation He was making, but a progress as yet above the capacity of the people, and they turned against Him. There are two points in our Lord's teaching which are of especial importance, and which may serve for examples of all. Every one will recognize at once the increasing clearness and fulness with which they are brought out during the course of His ministry on earth. The first of these points is the putting Himself forward as the centre and object of our faith, and belief in Him as the turning point between death and life. There is comparatively little of this in His early teaching of the mul-

---
* John, iv. 1, 2.

titudes. Yet it was no new point in His doctrine, as some have tried to think. It comes out in His private interview with Nicodemus, an intelligent and well-disposed ruler of Israel,* and it appears in His conversation, outside of the people of Israel, with the woman of Samaria;† but it does not enter as a marked feature into His public teaching of the people until His discourse on the bread of life, at Capernaum, at the time of the last Passover before His suffering,‡ and it only appears in its fulness after the institution of the Lord's supper in the few hours preceding His arrest and death.§ The other point is the foretelling His own death and resurrection. This again was intimated from time to time in private. It was suggested to Nicodemus; ‖ it was occasionally spoken of to His immediate disciples; but only after His transfiguration, during the last year of His ministry, did it become a frequent and express subject of His teaching. These two are among the most important points of all, and in regard to them there is a marked progress in the teaching. Even to His immediate disciples in His last discourse with them He said "these things I said not unto you at the beginning, because I was with you."¶ All these references have been cited from the Gospel of St. John. This Gospel relates, of course, to the same period as that covered by the Synoptic Gospels; but it was written later, and in the record it gives there is a progress so marked in the bringing out of the deeper signification and the

---

* John, iii. 13-18. † *Ib.* iv. 10, 14, 26 ‡ *Ib.* vi.
§ *Ib.* xiv.-xvi. ‖ *Ib.* iii. 14. ¶ *Ib.* xvi. 4.

spiritual force of our Lord's words as to have attracted the attention of its readers in all ages.

When one passes from the Gospels to the Acts of the Apostles he passes from the record of our Lord's human life upon earth to that of the teaching of His Apostles under the guidance of His Holy Spirit. Great events, of fundamental importance for the salvation of man, occurred on the confines of the two periods. Our Lord had given up His life upon the cross for the salvation of men, He had triumphed over death in the resurrection, and He had ascended to the glory which He had with the Father before the world was. In the last forty days He made definite provision for the establishment of His Church as an universal and visible organization in the Apostolic commission, " Go ye into all the world, and preach the Gospel to every creature. He that believeth and is baptized shall be saved."* The Apostles did not at first understand the significance of these things. They were not fully enlightened by His talking with them during the forty days before His ascension "of the things pertaining to the kingdom of God," and even to the last moment they could ask, in the full spirit of the Jewish expectation of temporal dominion, "Lord, wilt Thou at this time restore again the kingdom to Israel?"† But after the descent of the Holy Ghost on the day of Pentecost, a flood of light burst upon them, and thenceforward they began to preach "Christ and Him crucified." Jesus, put to death for our sins and risen again for our justification, became the

---
* Mark, xvi. 15, 16.   † Acts, i. 6.

burden of their teaching. The record of the Acts is a record of constant progress in the organization of the Church ; in the proclamation of faith in Christ as the means of salvation ; in the extension of Christianity outward from its centre and cradle in Jerusalem, first to other Jewish communities, and then to the Gentiles; in the discussion and decision of the question as to the continued obligation of the Gentile converts to observe the Mosaic law ; and in the establishment of the new faith as a universal religion in all the great centres of the world's activity.

Then come the Epistles, written to a considerable extent during the period covered by the history of the Acts, but also extending beyond. These found their occasion, in most cases, in special circumstances and in the needs of particular churches ; but they contain, nevertheless, the mature and deliberate setting forth, in some instances systematically, of Christian truth, both in its theoretical and its practical aspects. They contain nothing, it is true, which may not be found in germ in our Lord's own teaching in the Gospels, and in His life and death for the salvation of man ; and they necessarily lack the power which can belong only to the direct words of the Source of all truth. No new revelation is made in them; but the germ already given and not understood is here unfolded and developed under the Holy Spirit's guidance, as without that guidance it never could have been developed by man alone. It is not that they constitute a higher revelation in themselves; but they are a

Divine explanation of the Gospels, and thus lead us farther and deeper into their meaning than we could otherwise have gone. They make known to us that mind of God which was in the Gospels, but which we could only have imperfectly discovered without their aid. Thus, as the unfolding and explanation of that Divine teaching on which they were founded, they become the crowning treasure of Christian literature.

In the Epistles, too, there is a more frequent and express looking forward to the final goal of all progress since the world began, when the Church militant shall be swallowed up in the Church triumphant. The figurative language of the Apocalypse contains indeed the fullest description of the "heavenly Jerusalem" and of "the pure river of water of life;" but we hear also in the Epistle to the Hebrews of our coming "unto Mount Sion, and unto the city of the living God, the heavenly Jerusalem, and to an innumerable company of angels, to the general assembly and church of the first-born which are written in heaven, and to God the Judge of all, and to the spirits of just men made perfect, and to Jesus the Mediator of the New Covenant."* Both in the Epistles and in the Book of Revelation we learn of the time when "the Lord Himself shall descend from heaven with a shout, with the voice of the archangel, and with the trump of God, and the dead in Christ shall rise," when "we shall be caught up together with

---

* Heb. xii. 22-24.

them in the clouds,"* and the faithful of all ages shall be gathered before the throne to pour out their endless thanksgivings to the Lamb. Thus is unfolded something of the meaning of our Lord's reiterated teaching of the eternal life—beginning here below, but consummated above—which so warmed the heart of St. Paul, (as of every true believer), that he thought it "far better" to depart and be with Christ.

Thus looking over the whole course of revelation, from the material and typical Paradise in the Garden of Eden to the true Paradise above watered by "the river of life," there is seen throughout in the highest and truest sense an evolution of heavenly truth. I have tried to show that this could not have been a mere human evolution, but must have been from above, God ever limiting His revelation to the needs and the capacities of those to whom it was given. In this His action has been in most complete harmony with all His other works. PROGRESS is the most characteristic feature of the universe, and the great advance of modern science, in other words of the knowledge of God's works, has been in the recognition of this progress from the chaos of which Moses tells us to the wonderful cosmos spread out all around us. In a true and thoughtful recognition of that progress in revelation is to be found the solution of most of the difficulties which trouble the superficial reader of the Old Testament, and the warrant for our own highest hopes of the future.

---

* 1 Thess. iv. 16, 17.

The life of the race is mirrored in the life of the individual, and we can only progress in the knowledge of God and the grace of His Son and the enlightenment of His Spirit as we receive and assimilate in our own inner and outer life the knowledge and grace already given.

LECTURE III.

THE OLD TESTAMENT PREPARATORY FOR THE NEW.

THE essential unity of the two Dispensations having been pointed out in the first lecture, and the progressive character of all revelation in the second, it remains to show in the present that the Old Testament was given for the purpose of preparing for the New, and to say something of what seems to us the strange conduct of some of its heroes. The purpose of the many detailed precepts of the law must be reserved for the following lecture.

That, in fact, the Old Dispensation did prepare the way for the New is a matter of history; it is also true that it was given and continued for this very purpose. The Gospel was the *raison d'être*, the ground and cause of Israel's existence. This fact is left out of sight by the theory that Israel's religion was simply one among the many religions of the world, better perhaps than any other, but developed in the same way and having essentially the same purposes; for if the Old Dispensation did not exist for itself, but was designed as a preparation for the New, it is plain that such a theory cannot be maintained. Whatever may be said of the argument from design in nature, in revelation the design is expressed beforehand and cannot be gainsaid. That there was such design was the claim of our Lord, when speaking of the sacred books of the Jews in general, He said, "they are they which testify of Me."* The same thought was in the mind of St. Peter when he wrote, "Of which salvation the prophets have searched and enquired diligently, who prophesied of the grace that should come unto you."† Such in general is the understanding of all the writers of the New Testament, who continually and unhesitatingly speak both of the Old Dispensation itself and of its sacred records as a designed preparation for the New. This is most fully brought out in the Epistle to the Hebrews, because that epistle is occupied with the argument on this very point; but no reader of the New Testament can fail to see that it is the underlying thought of all its writers in their references to the older Scriptures. For the purposes of the present discussion, it is by no means necessary to assume the truth and reliability of the Scriptures. The point is simply that the Old Dispensation was for the sake of the New, and this is a question not depending upon the trustworthiness of either of them. It may be noted in passing that if this is once admitted, the Divine authorship of both can hardly be denied; but this is a consequence, and not a condition precedent. For the present the attention may be confined to the representations given in the Scriptures themselves.

The primary fact in the history of Israel is the migration of Abraham. If this had been an ordinary tribal movement, as some critics assume, it would

---

* John, v. 39. † 1 Pet. i. 10.

have little significance for our purpose; but the Scripture narrative does not so represent it. This expressly declares it to have taken place at the command of God Himself.* This command cannot be interpreted as a mere conviction of the patriarch's own mind, devoutly referred to the Being whom he worshipped; for it is grounded on the primeval promise, and is a limitation of its fulfilment to his posterity: "In thee shall all the families of the earth be blessed." † Throughout the whole story of Abraham's life it is clear that the Scriptures represent Abraham as called to leave his country and kindred in view of some great and universal blessing to come through him. A choice was made among his posterity, all his other sons were set aside, and the child of promise, Sarah's son Isaac, was selected with the same object. This was again repeated in the next generation, Esau was rejected and Jacob chosen as the heir of the promise. Then, when his descendants had multiplied to a nation and were made the chosen people of God, it was still on the ground that their God was the God of Abraham, Isaac, and Jacob, and would fulfil to them the promise made to their fathers. They were delivered from bondage and led to the foot of Sinai and the Mosaic legislation given them. The great features of this legislation were the sacrificial system and the priesthood. These I hope to show hereafter distinctly

---

* Gen. xii. 1; xv. 7.
† Gen. xii. 3. The gloss which would make this read, "by thee shall all the families of the earth bless themselves," seems hardly worthy of consideration, and is inconsistent with the whole narrative.

looked forward to the New Dispensation, and were only given in view of it. Minor features showing the same thing will be taken up in the next lecture. When the lawgiver was about to be taken away, he gave his parting charge to the people. They had feared to come themselves into direct communion with the Almighty and had begged that Moses might stand as a mediator between them. What were they now to do when he was gone? He tells them they shall not be left alone: " The Lord thy God will raise up unto thee a prophet from the midst of thee, of thy brethren, like unto me; unto him shall ye hearken." * The context, and the needs of the people to whom this promise was given, alike show that it had in view the whole long line of men who from time to time should be commissioned to make known the Divine will to the people; but it meant, and it was understood to mean, something more than this. There was to be a culmination of this line in a special Prophet, and for Him the people always looked as THE Prophet to come. This expectation was so strong as to have passed over even to their Samaritan neighbors.† The first preachers of Christianity shared in this interpretation of their people and believed the prophecy to be fulfilled in Christ.‡ Thus the very giver of the law of the Old Dispensation turned the thoughts of the people forward to a future Mediator. And thus was impressed upon their minds, that, however they might glory in their existing law, it was preparatory to something higher and better.

---

* Deut. xviii. 15.   † John, iv. 25.   ‡ Acts, vii. 37.

Beyond this point we have three sources of evidence: history, the consciousness of the people, and prophecy. The first of these can appeal only to those who recognize a distinctly Providential guidance of the course of Israel's history, such as is continually claimed in Scripture; but to such the evidence is clear. During the long troubled period of the Judges, the struggle was mainly for present national life, and little reference to the future is to be expected. Still even here, the prosperity and adversity of the people was visibly determined by their faithfulness or unfaithfulness to Him who had chosen them to be the depositary of the Messianic promises. They were rewarded or punished, not merely in view of the morality or immorality of their conduct, which was a consequence; but in view of their fealty to the God of Israel, or their defection from Him. He was the God of Israel by virtue of His promises of the coming Redeemer made to their fathers. The same fact is the fundamental and controlling fact of all their subsequent history. When the reign of David is reached and for the first time so much of order and national consolidation is obtained that the Divine teaching can expressly concern itself with the future, the monarch, forbidden—because he had " been a man of war and had shed blood "*—to carry out his cherished purpose of building a temple, is consoled first by the promise that this shall be done by his son, and then that to his posterity shall be given a " kingdom that shall be established forever,"† its absolute perpetuity being

---

* 1 Chron. xxviii. 3. † 2 Sam. vii. 12-16.

emphasized by a threefold repetition of the word *forever*. From this time forth "the kingdom of God" or "of heaven" and the everlasting throne of David became the constant theme of sacred song, and of the vision of prophecy. The people's minds were filled with the thought of the glorious future before them; they were accustomed to look upon the Dispensation under which they lived as preparatory for that which was to follow, and their habitual thought is expressed in the exclamation, "Blessed is he that shall eat bread in the kingdom of God."*

To return to the history: while the nation was kept to its purpose of a theocracy, a kingdom of God, leading towards a fuller development of an everlasting and direct Divine reign, it was prospered. As soon as it was perverted, under Solomon, to a magnificent earthly kingdom, its dismemberment was threatened, and under his son was executed. Then all that larger part of the nation, among whom the Messianic hope was more feeble, were, not without many prophetic warnings and exhortations, allowed to be carried into a captivity from which they never returned. The smaller remnant were subjected to long and severe discipline, and they, too, were at last carried into the Babylonian captivity, from which—after two generations of exile—only the more earnest and devout part of them returned.

Soon after this the inspired record ceases, but the main facts of the history are well known. The nation was further purified by its terrible struggles with Antiochus Epiphanes. It became a kingdom

---
* Luke, xiv. 15.

more or less dependent upon its stronger neighbors, but still, as had been promised, preserving its autonomy until its everlasting King appeared, then losing forever its political existence. Its genealogies were preserved until it was made sure that the Christ was born, after the flesh, of David's line, and then those genealogies were so lost that there never again could be a recognition of the fulfilment of the promise. Their typical system of sacrifice and priesthood, sustained until fulfilled in the Antitype, were then overthrown forever. There is no single aspect of its history which does not present the Old Dispensation as preparatory for the New, as culminating in it, and as passing away when that had been revealed.

Turning now from history to the consciousness of the people, the same thing appears. For the evidence of that consciousness we naturally look to the poetry of the nation, and here we find the expectation of the fulfilment of the primeval promise deeply embodied in the thought of the people from the earliest song of the dying Jacob all down the ages of their history. Jacob looked forward to the continuance of Judah's blessing "until Shiloh come;"* and however modern critics have thought the traditional interpretation of this passage to be faulty, yet they must admit that it was the interpretation put upon it alike by the people and their prophets,† and embodied in the Targums, ‡ which is all that is required for our present purpose. Balaam's prophecy,

---

* Gen. xlix. 10.
† Ezek. xxi. 27, admitted to refer to Gen. xlix. 10 by Delitzsch, *Messianic Prophecies*, § 9. ‡ See Targ. Onkelos, Jonathan, and Jerus.

preserved in the sacred literature of the people, also admits of another explanation, but his declaration that "There shall come a Star out of Jacob, and a sceptre shall arise out of Israel,"* was in the popular apprehension, as shown in the Targums of Onkelos and Jonathan, a distinct foretelling of the Messiah. The song of Hannah at the birth of Samuel, looking forward to the universal kingdom of the Lord, saying that He "shall exalt the horn of His Anointed,"† receives its most natural explanation in the same expectation. Passing on to the time of David, the psalms ascribed to him are filled with the same hope that the great promise of an everlasting kingdom should be fulfilled to his posterity. It appears so constantly there in every form of direct prophecy and of typical utterances, and as the underlying basis of prayer and thanksgiving that it cannot be necessary to refer to particular instances. But it is important to note that the actual Davidic authorship of the psalms ascribed to him is of no consequence for our purpose. In fact, the more these psalms are ascribed to many authors, and the more their composition is ascribed to many ages, only the more widespread and long continued will this expectation appear. Beyond this time the expression of this consciousness becomes so interwoven with express prophecies that its further consideration falls more naturally under that head. Only it should be remembered that at the time of our Lord's coming the expectation of Him was not confined to prophets and to such individuals as Zecharias and Simeon

---

* Num. xxiv. 17. † 1 Sam. ii. 10.

and Anna, but that there were also others "that looked for redemption in Jerusalem."*

When Prophecy comes under consideration the only difficulty is in the selection from the abundance of material. I will refer only to a few passages in which the temporary character of the Old Dispensation and its absorption in the New, are especially set forth.

From the time of the palmy days of the monarchy may be selected the prophecy of Ps. cx. 4: "Thou art a priest forever after the order of Melchisedec." In describing the Messiah as a priest, and that after another order than Aaron's, the Psalmist looks forward, as is conclusively shown in the Epistle to the Hebrews,† to a total change of the priesthood, and hence necessarily of that whole Dispensation of which the priesthood was the most essential feature. The prophecies of Isaiah are too familiar to need citation. Yet passing mention must be made of his declarations, that the path to glory of the Lord's "Servant" lay through humiliation and that He would bear vicariously His people's sins.‡ These things were so at variance with all ideas of a temporal kingdom and of earthly aggrandizement that they could only point to a "kingdom not of this world," in striking contrast to the expectations of the more carnally minded Jews. As the period of the captivity drew near, the great prophet of the time was Jeremiah. It was his office chiefly to foretell woe and disaster; but through it all he looked forward to the return, and beyond it to that Mes-

---

* Luke, ii. 38. † Chaps. vii.-x. ‡ Isa. lii. 13–liii. 12.

sianic restoration of which the return from Babylon was the preparation and the type. So completely should the glory of the Old Dispensation be swallowed up and lost from sight in the higher glory of the New, that he could boldly say of the Ark, the very crown of all that was precious and sacred to the Israelite, "In those days, saith the LORD, they shall say no more, the ark of the covenant of the LORD: neither shall it come to mind; neither shall they visit it."* So utterly in the prophet's mind was the Old to be supplanted by the New. These words were spoken by Jeremiah "in the days of Josiah,"† that is, near the beginning of his prophetic activity. Again more than a generation later, in the reign of Zedekiah, the last king of Judah, he declares, " Behold the days come, saith the LORD, that I will make a new covenant with the house of Israel and with the house of Judah: not according to the covenant that I made with their fathers; . . . . but this shall be the covenant that I will make with the house of Israel; after those days, saith the LORD, I will put my law in their inward parts and write it in their hearts,"‡ and so on with clause after clause, bringing out the great spiritual change which, under the New Covenant, should pass over the relations of the people to their God. It was with these words ringing in their ears that the Jews passed away into the dreaded punishment of the Babylonian captivity. There two great prophets were raised up to them. Daniel, at the court of their conqueror, foresaw the succession of world-wide kingdoms culminating in

---

* Jer. iii. 16.   † *Ib.* vs. 6.   ‡ *Ib.* xxxi. 31–34.

that kingdom of God which " shall stand for ever," " Whose kingdom is an everlasting kingdom, and all dominions shall serve and obey Him." * This prophecy, it is true, blends together in one the beginning and the end of the New Dispensation, and takes into view that final triumph of the Messianic kingdom which, even to us, is still future. But he was not left without commission to proclaim specifically the beginning and the date of the beginning of this kingdom, and the full spiritual fruit it should bear in contrast with the types of old. "Seventy weeks are determined upon thy people and thy holy city, to finish the transgression, and to make an end of sins, and to make reconciliation for iniquity, and to bring in everlasting righteousness."†

The other prophet was Ezekiel, among the captives by the river Chebar. Parts of his prophecies are " hard to be understood," but perfectly clear is the Divine promise of the future He proclaims to the people, " I will give them one heart, and I will put a new spirit within you ; and I will take away the stony heart out of their flesh, and I will give them an heart of flesh ; that they may walk in my statutes, and keep mine ordinances, and do them ; and they shall be my people, and I will be their God." ‡ Again, at a later date, partly in the same words, but, if possible, still more clearly, he says, " Then will I sprinkle clean water upon you, and ye shall be clean : from all your filthiness, and from all your idols will I cleanse you. A new heart also will I give you, and a new spirit will I put within you :

---

* Dan. ii. 39–45; vii. 16–27. † Dan. ix. 24. ‡ Ezek. xi. 19, 20.

OLD TESTAMENT PREPARATORY FOR NEW. 73

and I will take away the stony heart out of your flesh, and I will give you an heart of flesh, and I will put my Spirit within you, and cause you to walk in my statutes, and ye shall keep my judgments and do them."*

The prophets of the return are few, and their writings brief; yet each one of them speaks upon the point under consideration. Haggai and Zechariah were engaged together in the effort to rouse the sluggish people into activity in the rebuilding of the temple. This was so manifestly the work to which they were called that we are surprised when they pause in their exhortations to look forward to that which shall be far better in the future; yet both of them do this with unhesitating voice. Haggai thus declares the divine purpose: "Yet once, it is a little while, and I will shake the heavens, and the earth, and the sea, and the dry land, and I will shake all nations."† And again: "I will shake the heavens and the earth; and I will overthrow the throne of kingdoms, and I will destroy the strength of the kingdoms of the heathen."‡ This "signifieth," as may be seen in the argument in the epistle to the Hebrews, "the removing of those things that are shaken, as of things that are made, that those things which cannot be shaken may remain."§ In Zechariah the things of the future are largely set forth by symbolical actions, but these actions are sufficiently explained to make their meaning clear. The high-priest is clothed in filthy garments and put upon his

---
* Ezek. xxxvi. 25–27. † Hag. ii. 6, 7.
‡ *Ib.* 21, 22. § Heb. xii. 27.

trial; he is then acquitted and clothed, and a fair mitre set upon his head. The meaning of this is declared to be that God "will bring forth His Servant the Branch," and "will remove the iniquity of that land."* A little further on and the high-priest is crowned with a double crown to show: "Behold the man whose name is the Branch. .... He shall bear the glory, and shall sit and rule upon His throne, and He shall be a priest upon His throne." † Such union of regal and priestly authority implied a revolution in the arrangements of the Old Dispensation, and was to be accomplished in that coming One whose title, "the Branch," had already been recognized in the older prophets. In the following chapters the change from the Old to the New covenant is described as so great that the accustomed fasts of the former shall be changed to "joy and gladness and cheerful feasts." ‡ Then Zion is told to "Rejoice greatly," for "Behold, thy king cometh unto thee: He is just, and having salvation; lowly, and riding upon an ass." § In that day a great change is to pass over the people, "and he that is feeble among them at that day shall be as David; and the house of David shall be as God;" and then shall be poured upon them "the spirit of grace and of supplications, and they shall look upon Me whom they have pierced." ‖ In the closing chapter of his prophecy, in figures strikingly like those of his predecessors, Joel and Ezekiel, he describes the great changes which must come over the Old Dispensa-

---

* Zech. iii. 3-5, 8, 9. † *Ib.* vi. 11, 13.
‡ *Ib.* vii., viii. 19. § *Ib.* ix. 9. ‖ *Ib.* x. 8, 10.

tion to transform it into the New, when "the LORD shall be King over all the earth," and everything, even the meanest, shall be "holiness unto the LORD."*

Malachi, the last of the prophets, and separated from those nearest to him by about three-quarters of a century, takes up the same strain. He declares that the New Covenant shall burst the narrow bounds of the old Jewish nationality, and "from the rising of the sun even unto the going down of the same my name shall be great among the Gentiles."† He describes the great purification which must be effected,‡ and the coming of "the Sun of righteousness with healing in his wings;" and promises that a forerunner shall be sent to prepare men for "the coming of the great and dreadful day of the LORD." §

Thus, whether one looks at the circumstances and promises connected with the calling of Israel, at its history, at the consciousness of the devout among its people, or at the express declarations of its prophets, he sees in all the same thing. The Old Dispensation was designed to prepare the way for the New. It was understood to be temporary, and to seek its consummation in the coming kingdom of the Messiah. In everything it looked forward to the future.

It is unnecessary to say how constantly the same view of the relation between the Old and the New is expressed in the latter. It is not a relation of contrariety, but of designed development; not of de-

---

* Zech. xiv. 9, 20, 21. † Mal. i. 11.
‡ *Ib.* iii. 2, 3. § *Ib.* iv. 2, 5.

struction, but of fulfilment. "Old things are passed away; behold, all things are become new;"* but it is by the bringing in of "a better hope" which had been in view from the outset.

Another feature of the relation between the two Covenants grows out of that which has just been considered, and should never be lost sight of in connection with it. Christianity was a New Covenant, and a Covenant embracing in its scope all mankind; yet it was made with God's people of old. This was the often-repeated promise in the time of the temporary Dispensation; and this was constantly recognized by the teachers of that which came in its place. It was on David's throne that David's descendant should sit.† "Out of Zion shall go forth the law, and the word of the law from Jerusalem." ‡ The Lord promised that He would make His new covenant "with the house of Israel, and with the house of Judah." § And so throughout the promises and prophecies of the Old Testament. Israel was God's chosen people, and the very object of their choice was that they might be the depositary of His promises, and the channel through which His redemption should be given to mankind. Correspondingly, the Gospel opens with tracing back to Abraham the genealogy of Christ.‖ When He came He was hailed with hosannas as "the son of David."¶ He taught the woman of Samaria that

---

* 2 Cor. v. 17.
† 2 Sam. vii. 13-16; Ps. lxxxix. 3, 4; cxxxii. 11, etc.
‡ Isa. ii. 3; Mic. iv. 2, etc.   § Jer. xxxi. 31.   ‖ Matt. i.
¶ Matt. xxi. 9; ix. 27; xv. 22; xx. 30, 31; xxii. 42, etc.

"salvation is of the Jews,"* and told His disciples that, so far as His immediate mission was concerned, "I am not sent but unto the lost sheep of the house of Israel."† When He chose His twelve Apostles and sent them forth, it was with the command, "Go not into the way of the Gentiles, and into any city of the Samaritans enter ye not; but go rather to the lost sheep of the house of Israel."‡ Even after His resurrection, when such restrictions were removed and He had given them the broadest charge, "Go ye into all the world and preach the Gospel to every creature,"§ they could so little understand His meaning, they were so convinced that the Gospel must first be spoken to the Jews,∥ that for years they went about, "scattered abroad" by persecution, "preaching the word to none but unto the Jews only."¶ After the Divine promise had been evidently fulfilled, after the Church had been founded and organized, and the New Covenant had been established with the believers among the people chosen of old, came the vision to Cornelius and to St. Peter,** by which the admission of the Gentiles to the already established Covenant was proclaimed. Even after this, it was still a considerable time before the Gospel was freely preached to them, and when it was, and great numbers believed, it was only as the result of a solemn council held at Jerusalem that the Gentiles were declared exempt from the observance of the ceremonial Mosaic law. In the very act of making this declaration St. James

---

* John, iv. 22.   † Matt. xv. 24.   ‡ Matt. x. 5.
§ Mark, xvi. 15.   ∥ Acts, xiii. 46.   ¶ Acts, xi. 19.   ** Acts, x.

declared to the council that this admission of the Gentiles was in accordance with "the words of the Prophets," and in fulfilment of the promise of God's new covenant with His people, and he applies to it the prophecy of Amos,* "After this I will return, and will build again the tabernacle of David which is fallen down; and I will build the ruins thereof, and I will set it up: that the residue of men might seek after the Lord, and all the Gentiles, upon whom My name is called." † Soon after the Gentiles far outnumbered the Jews in the Church, and there arose the danger, then as now, that men might think the Gospel an altogether new revelation, unconnected with that which had gone before. This led to the masterly argument of St. Paul in his Epistle to the Romans, ‡ in which he shows that "God hath not cast away His people whom He foreknew;" but that their partial and temporary rejection for their unbelief was in accordance with His dealings with them all along the course of their history, and that His promise was fulfilled through that remnant who had accepted His offered salvation.

Thus from whatever point the Old and the New Covenants are examined, it is seen that the New was cradled in the Old, and sprang out of it by a long designed and Divine evolution; but it is always to be remembered that the Old, though fulfilled with the coming in of the New, has not lost its value. Its lessons still remain for our instruction. Still to us, as to the Romans, the Corinthians, or the Galatians of the first century, the teaching of the Gospel

---

* Amos, ix. 11, 12.   † Acts, xv. 16, 17.   ‡ Rom. ix.–xi.

plants itself upon the teaching of the Scriptures that went before, and to appreciate the force of the reasoning of our Lord and of His Apostles we need to understand the facts, the institutions and the laws upon which that reasoning is founded. As the chosen people were gradually fitted for the new Covenant by their law, their prophecies, and the experiences of their history, so must our minds still be prepared to understand the Gospel revelation by the study of that which went before. In the Providence of God the two have been indissolubly joined together as the parts of one great work for the salvation of man in the restoration of his lost holiness and communion with God; and although the latest revelation may alone suffice to the humble seeker after truth, yet he can only understand its reasonableness and fully enter into its force through a knowledge of those earlier revelations which prepared its way.

The teaching of the Old Dispensation has naturally been considered as embodied, at least in its practical effects, in the lives of its heroes; and it is urged that these not only fell far below the Gospel standard, but that, acting it is said under the impulse of "the Spirit of the Lord," they did very abominable things, and were praised by the highest religious authority of the times for acts which are abhorrent to the Christian. It were too long to discuss each particular case; it is only possible to select those which have occasioned the greatest difficulty, and have been thought to array the morality of the Old Testament in opposition to that of the New. As examples, therefore, may be taken the deceit practised by Abraham in regard to Sarah, the stratagem by which Jacob obtained the birthright of his brother, the conduct of some of the Judges, and the horrible sins of David, the "man after God's own heart." The principles involved in the discussion of these will apply to all other instances.

But while discussing the lives of particular men, the general method of the Divine dealing with all men needs to be kept in mind. It is not in accordance with the plan of Infinite wisdom and love to *make* men holy by an act of Almighty power. All grace is indeed from God; every good thought and holy inspiration is from His Spirit. But His method is that of education, not of compulsion. He takes men as they are, puts new motives and desires into their hearts, and helps their weak endeavors to draw near to Himself; but He does not destroy their own responsibility, or lift them bodily into a higher state without their own exertion. Consequently we must expect to find in the saints of any period the knowledge, the ideas and the customs of that period as the groundwork of their lives; and from this they rise, not altogether and at a bound, but little by little, as far as they are enabled by God's grace to receive and act upon the higher spiritual ideas obtained by the closeness of their communion with Him.

The leading characteristic of Abraham was faith in God, and it was expressly on this ground that he was rewarded and blessed. His sin in the case of his

dealings both with Pharaoh* and with Abimelech,†
consisted in a failure of trust in God under circumstances of apparent danger, and a resort to equivocation as a means of safety. The sin, in any other
man of those times, would pass almost unnoticed;
in Abraham's case it was exposed, and he was put
to shame. The difficulty alleged is that he was left
unpunished while the innocent monarch against
whom he had offended suffered, and was reproved
for his sake. This statement of the case is not accurate. It is a mistake to suppose that Abraham
himself did not suffer for his sin in the exposure
and shame, and in being driven forth again to his
nomadic life; while the penalties inflicted on Pharaoh and on Abimelech were not of the nature of
punishments but of warning, and for the protection
of one in training to become the father of the
chosen people. What was done to them was simply
to prevent their coming athwart the Divine plan for
the salvation of man, now beginning to be developed. It is a perversion of the story to represent it
as the reward of the guilty and the punishment of
the innocent. It was really a dealing gently with,
though still punishing, the occasional fall of a pure
and noble man, and the bringing of sufficient pressure to bear upon those who were unconsciously
committing a great wrong, to show them the danger
in which they stood, and force them to respect the
bearer of a Divine commission, though overtaken, at
the moment, in a fault.

Neither in the case of Abraham, nor in that of

---

* Gen. xii. 12.   † *Ib.* xx. 1.

Jacob and the others which follow, does the Scripture narrative expressly state that the sufferings which followed the sins were the punishment for their commission. It simply narrates the facts as they occurred, leaving the moral to the intelligence of the reader. The punishments themselves, like most of those which follow wrong-doing in our own day, were for the most part of the nature of what we call "natural consequences" of evil; that is, they were consequences which came about under the immutable moral laws which God has ordained, and which show Him to be always, under all dispensations alike, the righteous Governor, not of one people, but of all the world.

Of Jacob's sin we have a much fuller account, and therefore the explanation is correspondingly easier. The birthright had been promised to him before he was born. His brother, in a bargain concluded with characteristic impulsiveness, had formally conveyed it to him and sealed the conveyance with an oath.[*] It is quite unnecessary to defend Jacob in the making of this bargain; the transaction is simply recorded in the narrative without comment. Only it is to be noted that by it Esau was absolutely estopped from claiming the blessing which he afterwards tried to gain. But, apart from this, it was certain from the beginning that if God's words were true Jacob must become the heir of the promise made to his fathers; but Rebecca would not wait for the vindication of God's faithfulness. She contrived a way to secure the coveted blessing by a

---

[*] Gen. xxv. 33.

miserable fraud, and Jacob weakly yielded to her commands. The consequence to her was a life-long separation from her favorite son; to him, exile from home, the wrath of his brother, danger of his life, and all the woes of the following forty years. He was certainly severely punished for his sin, and if that sin was allowed to be the means of securing his father's prophetic blessing, it was but what is continually seen in the world, where God overrules human wrong to the furtherance of His own purposes. The sin was punished; the blessing was given through the sin but not because of it. It had been promised from the first, and would certainly have been secured to Jacob without the punishment had the sin not intervened. The blessing, indeed, far outweighed the punishment, and there is something repugnant to our ideas in the bestowal of such a blessing on the occasion of such a sin; but this is because of the great advance in all our spiritual conceptions brought about by the progress of revelation since Jacob's time. Take the book of Genesis as the sole measure of religious knowledge, imagine ourselves with no ideas of right beyond those which nature supplies, and which might be gathered from that book, and it will be plain that He who sees the heart might justly overlook much which we have been taught to recognize as very evil, and so might reward that striving to draw near to God which was so far in advance of the mass of Jacob's contemporaries.

In times of Israel's great need and suffering for their unfaithfulness, the Judges were raised up by the Spirit of the Lord to deliver His people from their oppressors. We are not to think of them as prompted by the Spirit to the performance of each particular act recorded of them, but only as roused to the deliverance of their people, and selecting such means as seemed good to their own human judgment guided by such religious knowledge as they had. There are surely too many instances all around us of earnestly religious men and women using most injudicious and sometimes questionable means for the accomplishment of their purposes, to allow us to suppose that the choice of those means is determined by the Spirit who animates those who use them. There are too many instances of sin and wrong among those of a generally holy life to suppose that each and every act of a true believer in God is necessarily in accordance with God's will. What happens now, happened also then. The Judges were animated from on high by a pure and noble purpose; they chose the means for its accomplishment under such knowledge of right and wrong as they could have in those early days, and with such feeble adherence even to these ideas of right as belonged to untrained spiritual children. Their acts were often wrong when they did not know it, and Ehud's assassination of Eglon,* and Gideon's cruelty to the men of Succoth and Penuel,† doubtless may have been done with a clear conscience. Yet there was a marked difference in the Divine blessing upon the works of the various Judges as well as in the results effected by them. The sensual and

---

* Judg. iii. 18–23.   † *Ib.* viii. 13–17.

pleasure-loving Samson worried and annoyed the Philistines and inflicted many injuries upon them; but for all his mighty strength Israel was scarcely the better for his life, nor was the supremacy of their enemies broken by all he did. On the other hand, his contemporary Samuel, by his devout life, by his unwavering trust in God and devotion to His will, brought the nation to an unwonted state of prosperity, and prepared the way for the reigns of David and Solomon. Then, as now, *character* formed upon a close adherence to what was known of the Divine will, was a more important factor than any outward gifts. In those times of ignorance men were dealt with gently, for responsibility is ever proportioned to knowledge; but still the highest standard attained was the most abundantly blessed. There was much also done in accordance with the ordinary customs of the times, which seems to us harsh and cruel, but which did not then seem so either to those who did, or to those who suffered, these things. When Joshua made "the captains of the men of war" put their feet upon the necks of the captive kings before he slew them,* he only followed the ordinary custom of war, and impressed his captains with a vivid sense of the weakness of their foes, treating them as he would have been treated by them. When his successors cut off "the thumbs and the great toes" of Adoni-bezek, they only did what Adoni-bezek claimed to have himself done to "threescore and ten kings."† These things show how greatly our moral ideas have been elevated by the progress

---

* Josh. x. 24.   † Judg. i. 6, 7.

of revelation; but they show no other opposition between the Old and the New Dispensations than that which must of necessity always exist between the less and the more perfect. The Divine will was always the same; but men, both then and now, are mercifully judged according to their opportunities of knowing that will.

There is one case of which these considerations do not at first sight seem a sufficient explanation— Jael treacherously assassinated Sisera under the cloak of proffered hospitality.* In the song of the prophetess Deborah she is praised for this act as " blessed above women," and the details of the treachery and murder are especially enumerated. † The difficulty here is not so much with the act itself, which may readily be explained on the same principles with those already discussed, as with this commendation of it in all its detail. The suggestion is worse than useless that Deborah was not here speaking under the guidance of inspiration; for she was the chosen Prophetess of Israel, and uttered this song officially, and it is recorded in the sacred books without any intimation of disapproval. If it is not to be received as inspired, it would be difficult to determine on any reliable marks of inspiration for a large part of the Old Testament canon. The true explanation is undoubtedly that Deborah rightly commends Jael for her zeal on behalf of God's people at great personal risk to herself; and she speaks of the means used simply as the ordinary means of the time, neither she nor Jael having any conscious-

---

* Judg. iv. 18–21. † *Ib.* v. 24–27.

ness of their inherent wickedness. Constantine may have been guilty of great error and wrong in interlocking the church with the state; but we nevertheless commend his act, because, in his position and with his knowledge, it was a great and noble deed in behalf of truth and purity; and so far as his motives may have been right, we feel sure that he was commended above. So Jael did what was in her eyes a most brave and noble deed for God; and Deborah commended it; but it does not follow that the deed itself is to be looked upon otherwise than with abhorrence from the standard of a higher knowledge. Fearful indeed would be the condition of man if he could obtain his heavenly Father's approval only when he rises above his knowledge of the Divine will. God commends and blesses us when, like Jael, we bravely do and dare on His behalf according to the light He has given us; and such efforts, however mistaken in themselves, must always meet the approval of His prophets.

David lived some centuries later, and is shown by his life and his writings to have had far higher and clearer knowledge of the truth. The one characteristic of his life was an earnest desire to submit himself in all things to God's will and to be wholly guided thereby in all the affairs of life. But he was a man of strong natural passions and of excessive family affection. He was raised from being an obscure shepherd boy to the throne of Israel. He was a bold and successful warrior in a rude and barbarous age; a wise governor under most difficult circumstances; and a great statesman when his own people were disunited, and all the nations around bitterly hostile. His later life is checkered with fearful sins—sins not only against the standard of Christian morality, but which were flagrant and outrageous even according to the standard of his own time. Two remarks are here to be made : in the first place, David was long and severely punished for his sin. Not only was the child of his guilty passion taken from him, but from that time forth to the end of his life he was under a cloud of sore domestic afflictions, and all the woes denounced by the prophet Nathan * fell upon him in full force. The Divine displeasure was both pronounced in word and carried out in deed. In the second place, the depth of his repentance, when his sin was brought home to him, was proportioned to the enormity of his guilt. The annals of literature furnish no more deep and true outpouring of a penitent heart than is given in the fifty-first Psalm. If the Christian be overtaken by a fault as great in him, with his higher knowledge and fuller privilege, as David's was in his time and under his circumstances, he can express his sorrow and humiliation before God in no better language than that which David has supplied. Whether, therefore, we look at the manifestation of the Divine abhorrence of sin, or at the repentance for its commission, the case of David makes no jar in the moral unity of the two dispensations. There was vast progress in the knowledge of the Divine will from the one to the other ; but that will itself was always unchangeably the same.

---

* 2 Sam. xii. 11, 12.

The general relation of the Old Dispensation to the New, as shown in the conduct of its heroes, is the same as seen in every other aspect. In both is the same righteous God ever leading man, as he is able to bear, towards His own infinite holiness; but ever dealing with him according to his spiritual capacity and knowledge. From Jacob or Deborah to our own day there has been a vast progress in the knowledge of the Divine will, and consequently in the embodiment of that knowledge in action; but so far is the highest present standard below the infinite holiness of God, that in a future state, when we "shall know even as we are known," it may be more surprising to us that the Holy Spirit could dwell in us and help us as we are now, than it now seems to us that He could have loved and borne with those who were the best examples of virtue in the days of old.

LECTURE IV.

THE RELATION OF THE PRECEPTS OF THE LAW TO THE GOSPEL.

THE general relation of the Old Dispensation to the New having been discussed in the last lecture, and the conduct of its heroes examined in the light of Christian morality, it remains to speak of the relation of certain definite precepts of the Law to the Gospel.

This relation is set forth in a summary but comprehensive way in St. Paul's Epistle to the Galatians. He shows that, "The Scripture.... preached the Gospel before unto Abraham," that the law "was added because of transgressions," that "if there had been a law given which could have given life, verily righteousness should have been by the law," and that "the law was our schoolmaster to bring us to Christ." The essential points of this teaching have already been called to mind in the earlier lectures: that the principle of man's acceptance with God through trust in Him, was already made known before the giving of the law; and that the law was added because man required a preparatory training before he could become fit for the full reception of this principle. The most important elements of that training in the institution of the priesthood and the sacrificial system must be reserved for future consideration. At present some of the detailed precepts of the law, as examples of the whole, are to be considered, and their relation to the Gospel examined.

These precepts may be arranged, for convenience, in several classes, as national, educational, typical, and directly preparatory. Such classes, however, cannot be kept distinct from one another, but will be found to overlap and intermingle. Any single precept, with that multiformity of purpose which characterizes all the Divine works, may belong to more than one class, sometimes even to all of them. Still it is only by means of some such classification, however imperfect, that the different relations between them and the Gospel can be conveniently considered.

The examination may be begun with that class which seems at first sight most diametrically opposed to the Gospel, the precepts given to promote national separation and exclusiveness; and first, of those relating to food. That these precepts were national and given for the especial purpose of separating the Israelites from other nations needs no argument. No such distinctions were recognized in the original gift to Noah, " Every moving thing that liveth shall be meat for you ; even as the green herb have I given you all things;"* and it was determined by the Council at Jerusalem that they were no longer obligatory on the Gentile converts. †
Further, it is plain that, however they may have sprung from, they were not limited and determined

---

* Gen. ix. 3. † Acts, xv. 28, 29.

by the use of animals in sacrifice, since a large number, as notably the roebuck and hart, several kinds of birds and fishes, and many of other orders, were allowed for food which were not permissible in sacrifice.* But the point not always sufficiently observed is the extent to which these laws interfered with any intimate social intercourse between the Israelites and other nations. It was just such an interference as that which must always arise between a people enjoying with a good conscience perfect freedom in regard to food, and one hedged about on every side by very peculiar and apparently arbitrary enactments. Difficulties in their intercourse will continually arise in the most unlooked-for way and on the most unexpected occasions. The fact may be illustrated in modern times by the indignation of the Sepoys in India at the idea of being called upon in the ordinary round of military duty to use cartridges prepared with animal fat. In ancient times Daniel and his companions preferred to restrict themselves to an exclusively vegetable diet rather than incur the risk of defilement by eating of the royal food of Nebuchadnezzar.† No Hebrew could sit at the table of a foreigner without danger of finding forbidden kinds of fish and flesh and fowl set before him. Even those which were allowed would probably have been killed in an unlawful way, and the whole food prepared with ingredients, or with the neglect of precautions, which would make his participation a violation of the law. In consequence no Hebrew could safely become a

---

* See Lev. xi.; Deut. xiv. † Dan. i. 8–16.

guest at a Gentile table, and a great restriction was thus imposed on all social intercourse.

The bar thus formed was more than doubled by the laws of defilement and purification. The thirsty Hebrew traveller might not knock at the door of a stranger without fear that the vessel of water had become defiled and defiling by the accidental falling into it of the dead body of a fly or some other insect.* Some defilements rendered not only the persons immediately affected unclean, but every bed on which they rested, every saddle on which they rode, every seat on which they sat, communicated defilement to whoever touched them.† How could the Israelite, if he mingled with those who had no knowledge of such laws, be sure that he might not at any moment unconsciously incur defilement? His only safety must be in holding himself aloof from the heathen altogether. The laws of defilement were extremely intricate, and interwoven with all the affairs of the daily life. If the dead body of any creeping thing fell upon "any vessel of wood, or raiment, or skin, or sack," it must be put into water, and any meat upon which this water might fall was unclean, and any earthen vessel into which such body fell must be broken.‡ Dry sowing seed was not made unclean by such contact, "but if any water be upon it" then the defilement took place.§ How could an Israelite go in and out among people who knew nothing of such laws without continual defilement?

---

* Lev. xi. 32-34. † *Ib.* xv. 5-10; 19-23; 26, 27.
‡ *Ib.* xi. 32-35. § *Ib.* 37, 38.

Why should such precepts have been given, and what is their relation to the broad and universal principle of acceptance with God by faith, already announced to Abraham, and promised as the future religion of mankind? The answer to these questions is included in St. Paul's statement that the law "was given because of transgressions." The function of the law as a schoolmaster is here shown more in its negative office of restraining from evil, than in its positive work of leading to the good. The people had always shown a strong tendency to mingle with the surrounding nations, to adopt their customs and to give themselves up to their idolatries. It was absolutely necessary to prevent this in order to keep alive among them the knowledge of the true God and the sense of their duty to Him. To us the means used for this end may seem excessive; historically, they were scarcely sufficient for their purpose. To us they may seem almost puerile; to the people of the time, these detailed precepts were better suited than the teaching of principles which they could not yet understand. In still earlier times the great judgments of the expulsion from Paradise, the flood, the confusion of tongues, had failed to restrain the evil tendencies of man. Now, the peculiar nation, chosen to be the depositary and guardian of the sacred oracles, must be kept free for a time from contaminating influences, and to this end must be placed under laws which should make all intimate intercourse with others difficult. They were children who required to be separated from bad companions until their principles were fixed.

This, then, is the relation, and a most important relation it was, of this class of laws to the Gospel:—they were "added because of transgressions" to prevent the people from wandering away from their destined purpose. They were thus "shut up unto the faith which should afterwards be revealed."*

Another large part of the detailed precepts of the law may be classed as educational. Children require to be taught by rules rather than principles. They cannot understand the latter until they have been first trained by obedience to the former. The preparatory rules may or may not be of permanent obligation; they may be of such a character that their observance is necessarily involved in the principle itself, or they may be mere temporary and accidental exemplifications of it under existing conditions. In either case, it is the principle which is permanent and important; the rules, as rules, pass away when they have served their purpose. This relation of the law to the Gospel is very clearly brought out in the promise of the new Covenant by the prophet Jeremiah: "This shall be the covenant that I will make with the house of Israel; after those days, saith the LORD, I will put my law in their inward parts, and write it in their hearts; and I will be their God, and they shall be my people. And they shall teach no more every man his neighbor, and every man his brother, saying, know the LORD: for they shall all know me, from the least of them unto the greatest of them."† Under the Old Dispensation an expert was required to thread the maze of special precepts

---
* Gal. iii. 23. † Jer. xxxi. 33, 34.

and teach his neighbors what they might and might not do on the various occasions of life; under the new, a principle is implanted in every heart, and each one is responsible to his own Master for its application.

In several instances the rules given under the law are cited in the New Testament, and the underlying principle is brought out in its application to Christian duty. Thus St. Paul cites more than once* the precept, "Thou shalt not muzzle the mouth of the ox that treadeth out the corn,"† and shows that the principle it was designed to teach was a regard for the laborer, especially the spiritual laborer, allowing him to receive benefit and support from his work. So strongly does he consider this educational purpose to have been from the first the main object of the rule that he does not hesitate to say, " Doth God take care for oxen? or saith He it altogether for our sakes? For our sakes, no doubt, this is written." This does not mean, as is sometimes asserted, that God does not care for the lower animals whom He has created; but only that the object and paramount purpose here was the teaching of a principle by means of this definite and special rule. There are many such rules which the New Testament writers have had no occasion to explain, and which we must study in the light of the examples they have given. There are a number of precepts teaching the principle of simplicity, harmony, and congruity in all our conduct. This could be taught of old only in its application to particular acts, and those acts

---

* 1 Cor. ix. 9; 1 Tim. v. 18. † Deut. xxv. 4.

were often in themselves quite indifferent, so that, when the principle itself had been learned, the rules, no longer of value, would fall away like the husk from the fruit. Thus the precepts are given, "Thou shalt not let thy cattle gender with a diverse kind: thou shalt not sow thy field with mingled seed: neither shall a garment mingled of linen and woollen come upon thee;"* "Thou shalt not plough with an ox and an ass together,"† and others of the same kind. No man can fail to see that such precepts, as particular commands, are out of date and have ceased to be of force under the Gospel; and no thoughtful consideration of them, in connection with the times and people to whom they were given, can refuse to recognize their great value as a well chosen form of object teaching, and thus an education for a higher system.

Some of these rules belong both in this educational class, and also in another having for its object restraint from the ways of the heathen. There is a precept three times repeated which has to some seemed unmeaning: "Thou shalt not seethe the kid in his mother's milk."‡ The kid so prepared was a choice dish of the heathen eaten in connection with some of their idolatrous feasts. The Israelites must be charged to keep altogether clear of these. But it seems also to have had a higher educational object. From a merely utilitarian point of view there could be no harm done either to the kid or its mother. The kid was already dead and past all consciousness;

---

* Lev. xix. 19.   † Deut. xxii. 10.
‡ Ex. xxiii. 19; xxxiv. 26; Deut. xiv. 21.

the mother knew not what became of the milk after it had once been drawn. But to human sensibilities there was something revolting in thus making the mother in any way instrumental in the destruction of the offspring; and by forbidding the act, God would teach that such finer sensibilities are not to be violated. We are not called upon to contravene our reason; but there are many situations in life when either our reason fails to guide us at all, or at least fails in the promptness required for instantaneous action, and in these we are to be guided by what are sometimes called instincts of right, by susceptibilities which cannot be submitted to the test of our coarser and more slowly acting reason. Many laws were given to train the people in restraining their natural avarice and greed. Here belong the frequent injunctions against receiving any interest upon money from a brother Hebrew;* and also many minor precepts, such as those forbidding the owner to glean his fields and his vineyard,† and such minute directions as, "If a bird's nest chance to be before thee in any tree or on the ground, whether they be young ones or eggs, and the dam sitting upon the young or the eggs, thou shalt not take the dam with the young: but thou shalt in any wise let the dam go, and take the young to thee."‡ All these laws have doubtless other objects, as kindness to the poor, consideration for animals, and the like; but in these regards also they are educational.

The arrangements for the magnificence of the

---

* Ex. xxii. 25 ; Lev. xxv. 36, 37 ; Deut. xxiii. 19, etc.
† Lev. xix. 9, 10 ; Deut. xxiv. 21. ‡ Deut. xxii. 6, 7.

tabernacle, for the reverence with which it was to be treated, for the gorgeous robes of the high-priest with the plate upon his forehead, "Holiness unto the Lord," whatever other objects they may have served, were thoroughly educational, designed to teach reverence and awe for the Majesty on high. Another lesson taught by the tabernacle is beautifully brought out in New Testament interpretation. The Holy of holies was separated from the outer sanctuary by a vail through which none might ever pass save only the high-priest on one day in the year in the midst of solemn sacrifices: "the Holy Ghost thus signifying, that the way into the Holiest of all was not yet made manifest, while as the first tabernacle was yet standing."* The whole ritual of sacrifice, of purifications and the like, whatever the further office, was designed to educate the people in the sense of their own sinfulness and of the holiness of God—an education always needed by man, and pre-eminently necessary as a foundation for the teaching of the Gospel. This education was carried out in little matters as well as in great. The very fringes the people were required to wear upon the hem of their garments, the mottoes from Scripture they were told to have ever before their eyes, were intended to separate them from other people, expressly on the ground that they were called to be a people holy to their God. The elaborate arrangements for personal cleanliness, and for the cleanliness of houses and garments and the like, were not merely for purposes of health in a hot country, but

---

* Heb. ix. 8.

to teach the lesson of inward purity, of which all this was the symbol and shadow.

Another class closely connected with the foregoing, may properly be called typical. The subject of typology is a large one, which will be treated by itself, and for the present there is no question of resemblances, real or imaginary, between the Old and New Testaments, nor of what are known as prophetic types; but simply of precepts in which something was required setting forth in sensible form some truth or principle afterwards to be more clearly and spiritually revealed. The New Testament refers to many instances of such typical teaching, and perhaps no part of its use of the Old Testament has been more misunderstood.

As instances of this class of precepts may be taken some of the lesser commands in regard to the sacrifices. The provision that all victims must be "without blemish" (with only a partial exception in the case of mere thank-offerings), while it had its higher typical import, was also designed to train the people to a recognition of the Divine character. To One perfect in purity and holiness, only that which was "spotless and without blemish" might be offered. In the requirement that the oil of the sanctuary should be of the best and taken from the first flow of the olives, the same principle was involved, and also it was taught that the return to the Giver of all should be made from the choicest of His gifts. In the laws of the sweet incense, forbidden to the people in their houses and for any other use than worship, there was brought out in addition the separation between the service of God and the pleasures of ordinary life. The educational and preparatory character of other details in the laws of sacrifice is easily seen by any careful reader. One other instance may be given in connection with the sin offering. In general it was required that this offering should be an animal, and the principle is broadly laid down that "without shedding of blood is no remission." * But there might be those too poor to command even this offering. Yet the principle must be set forth that every one stood in need of, and must present a sacrifice for his sin. Therefore there was allowed and required in such exceptional cases an offering of fine flour. † Herein two points were typically taught: first, that all were sinful and must receive an atonement; secondly, that the lesser principle (set forth in the form of the offering) must yield to the greater (set forth in the universality of the requirement). This latter teaching man has even now but imperfectly learned. Our Lord often insists upon it, especially in regard to the observance of the Sabbath; here the direct command was by no means to be neglected, and yet He shows that this must give way to higher obligations. He illustrates this by allowing acts of necessity on that day, quoting in justification the Old Testament precept, "I will have mercy and not sacrifice," ‡ and by performing on the Sabbath miracles of mercy; and also by alleging the precepts of the law itself, requiring the priests on the Sabbath to violate the letter of

---

* Heb. ix. 22. † Lev. v. 11–13.
‡ Matt. ix. 13 ; xii. 7 ; Hos. vi. 6.

the law in fulfilling its higher purpose of the worship of God.* He also shows how David directly violated the law in the eating of the shew-bread,† and was guiltless, because the ordinary definite precept must give way when a higher necessity, and one unprovided for, arose. This typical teaching of the law is involved in every class of its precepts. Several instances will incidentally be mentioned in the treatment of the priesthood and of sacrifices.

We may pass on to another class of precepts, those which were directly preparatory for the Gospel. These are of two kinds: first, commands which are absolutely the same as those of the Gospel, such as "Thou shalt love the Lord thy God with all thine heart and with all thy soul and with all thy might,"‡ and "Thou shalt love thy neighbor as thyself."§ It was hardly to be expected that many of the ancients should understand the force of such commands or very seriously seek to fulfil them; yet they were placed in the law that there might be this full declaration of the Divine will for the few who could enter into its meaning; and also for those who were incapable of this, that they might at least know of the existence of a standard higher than they had yet attained. In both ways they were a preparation for the Gospel, as showing that the law

---

* Matt. xii. 6 ; Num. xxviii. 9, 10.

† Mark, ii. 25, 26, and Lev. xxiv. 5, 6, 9. That David's flight from Saul was on the Sabbath—another violation of the law—is shown by the fact that Ahimelech says the shew-bread had been replaced with hot bread on that day. 1 Sam. xxi. 3-6.

‡ Deut. vi. 5 ; x. 12 ; xi. 1, 13, 22 ; xix. 9 ; xxx. 6.

§ Lev. xix. 18, 34.

itself, though it could not yet much insist upon them, recognized the principles of the Gospel.

Much more common are precepts of a different kind, in which a standard of duty is enjoined above that to which the people were accustomed, but still falling so far below the Gospel requirements as to seem to us faulty. This class of commands has been mentioned in a former lecture as especially giving occasion to unfounded cavils. When it is impossible to raise a people to the highest standard, it is plainly the dictate both of love and of wisdom to lead them on towards that end as far as they can bear. When Moses, " for the hardness of their hearts " suffered a man to give his wife a writing of divorce and put her away, he certainly taught something which, however sanctioned by the laws of some modern states, was very far below the morality of the Gospel. Yet in reality, so far from opposing that morality, he was leading the people towards it as far as was then practicable. Before the law, the husband was accustomed to consider himself as the absolute and arbitrary master. If the wife displeased him, he had nothing to do but to send her away, perhaps in a mere fit of temper. The mere existence of this right of repudiation increased the absolute dependence of the wife upon the husband, and tended to reduce her to the condition of a slave, and to degrade the family relation in many ways. But the right was too highly valued by the husband to allow of its abrupt and total abolition. Moses, therefore, required that for a divorce, a legal and formal document should be given, which implied time and consideration. Many other checks and restraints were imposed, and divorce seems never to have been common among the Hebrews, or at least, there is scarcely any mention of it in their history. In every way a large advance was made from the previous customs of the people.

The same things are to be said of the laws of slavery mentioned in a previous lecture. It is worth while to recall them for a moment to mark how great was the amelioration in this matter introduced by the Levitical code. We are familiar enough with the absolute power of the master over the slave among the nations of antiquity, and know how frequently this power was abused. A very different state of things prevailed among the Hebrews. In this, as in some other matters, the law was different for themselves and for foreigners; because not only were they still unprepared for the idea of the universal brotherhood of man, but in order that they might become so, it was important to preserve for the present a sharply marked nationality. Of foreign slaves there is little especial mention in the law, although they come under the general precepts of justice and kindness and consideration applying to all slaves alike. The power of the master was in many ways circumscribed, and the rights of the slaves, as men, were recognized, so that their condition was greatly bettered, and the institution assumed quite a different aspect from that which it bore among the heathen. But the most important point was that any foreign slave, by becoming a proselyte and submitting to circumcision, entered into the condition of a Hebrew slave with all his rights and advantages. These rights were such as practically to transform Hebrew slavery into a mere form of contract labor for a certain term of years. At whatever time the Hebrew became a slave, in the seventh or Sabbatical year he was to go free.* He might have been in servitude six years or only one year; in that year he was free, and his master in manumitting him was bound to make ample provision for his immediate necessities.† The only exception to this was in the free choice of the slave, who might, after his experience up to the Sabbatical year, then elect to make his condition permanent.‡ In this I do not speak of the actual state of the people; but of what the law required. The Sabbatical year we know was utterly neglected down to the time of the captivity,§ and it is likely that the mitigations of slavery which depended upon it, were also neglected. But the question is not how far the people observed the law, but what the law was in itself, and what was its intended effect in preparing for the Gospel.

This is perhaps enough to say of particular precepts of the law in detail. Many others might be treated in the same way; but they will be found nearly all to come under one or more of the four heads enumerated: national, educational, typical, and directly preparatory. In all of these classes it has been seen that the law was, and was designed to

---

* Ex. xxi. 2; Deut. xv. 12; Jer. xxxiv. 9, 14.
† Deut. xv. 13, 14.   ‡ Ex. xxi. 5, 6; Deut. xv. 16-18.
§ 2 Chron. xxxvi. 21.

be "our schoolmaster to bring us to Christ." It gave such precepts as were needed by the people to lead them towards the higher revelation of the Gospel and prepare them for its reception. No objection to this can be based upon the fact that only a small part of the people actually did embrace the faith of Christ. This was their characteristic course with every revelation that had ever been made. A thousand years was required to bring them to a tolerable observance of the Mosaic law, and even then this was accomplished only by the rejection of the great mass of the nation. They showed the same disposition towards all their inspired teachers. "Which of the prophets," St. Stephen asks of his contemporaries, " have not your fathers persecuted? and they have slain them which showed before of the coming of the Just One."* It seems probable, from the incidental notices in the book of Acts, that as many of the people embraced the faith of Christ in Apostolic days as ever returned from the Babylonish captivity.

Another point in the relation of these precepts of the law to the Gospel is the recognized insufficiency of the former to salvation. The law did not, and could not secure to man the righteousness he needs for acceptance with God. St. Paul is explicit upon this matter. He writes, " If there had been a law given which could have given life, verily righteousness should have been by the law." † Yet in this its weakness, it did what it could by inculcating acts of kindness towards the poor, of considera-

---

* Acts, vii. 52. † Gal. iii. 21.

tion for the dependent, of mercy and love to the stranger and the afflicted, to teach the habits required by the Gospel and mould the character into the pattern acceptable to God.

Leaving for future consideration the more important matters concerning the priesthood, there are yet sundry minor provisions which do not affect the essential character of the institution and which may claim attention in this connection. The selection of a hereditary class of men to fulfil its functions may seem at first sight quite at variance with the arrangements for religious teachers under the Gospel, and to lead to an entirely different conception of their office. The latter objection is well founded, and it will appear farther on that the prototype of the Christian teacher is to be found rather in the prophet than in the priest. Possibly the setting forth of this distinction may have been one of the incidental objects in making the ancient priests hereditary; but there were others of a more immediate importance. The custom of inheritance of office in the priesthood was already familiar to the people among other nations, and especially among the Egyptians; but to the Israelites it concurred with the general principle of heredity on which the Mosaic legislation was founded, and which kept constantly before their minds the fact that their national existence depended upon an heredity whose central point was the future Redeemer of the world. It is plain also that by means of this arrangement the powerful influence of hereditary associations and traditions was brought to bear in keeping up among the priesthood, however corrupt, the recognition of Jehovah during long periods of Israel's apostasy and sin. Without this one great bar would have been wanting by which Israel was "shut up unto the Gospel."

To the small family of Aaron, who alone might execute the functions of priests, were afterwards added as assistants and servants the whole tribe of Levi, both that the position and dignity of the immediate ministrants in the Divine service might be increased, and also that this service itself might be celebrated with the perfection, and with the elaborateness of ritual, and later of musical accompaniment, which so greatly served to impress its majesty upon the people, and which could only be carried out by the assistance of numbers.

In regard to both these bodies, the smaller Aaronic family, and the large tribe of Levi, two lessons were to be taught of difficult combination, and yet in their principle important for all ages: First, that as the especial ministrants of the sanctuary and devoted to the immediate service of God, they were separate from other men; and secondly, that as men they were fellow-citizens with their brethren and stood, before God and before the laws, upon precisely the same footing as other men. The first point was emphasized by cutting them off from an inheritance of the land with the others, and giving them cities for residence scattered among all the tribes; by appointing for the priests, though not for the Levites, a peculiar dress when engaged in their holy functions, and this dress marked by a symbolical purity and cleanliness; by requiring, as a condition for entering upon the discharge of their functions, a high standard of physical perfection; and by imposing upon them alone the duty, as the representatives of God, of consuming the flesh of the sin-offerings and certain other offerings devoted to God. There were also many other provisions, partly concerning the priests alone, partly relating to the whole tribe of Levi, having the same object, such as the strict injunction that none but they should bear the ark and the vessels of the sanctuary, that they should proclaim the feasts, should abstain from the ordinary signs of mourning, should be restricted in their marriage, and many other statutes. By all this legislation it was declared that those devoted to the immediate service of the sanctuary were separate from other men, and placed under many obligations. On the other hand, what is commonly known as "ecclesiasticism," so fully developed in the mediæval church, was utterly discountenanced in the Sinaitic legislation. When the priests came out of the sanctuary they were not merely allowed, but required to put off their distinctive dress; they were amenable to the same laws, both penal and civil, and were tried by the same courts as their brethren, and this fact in itself placed them, in all their ordinary life, upon the same footing with other men; it was necessary for their support that the Levites should receive tithes from the other tribes, but that in this respect also they might be assimilated to their brethren, the Levites themselves must pay tithes to the priests—cut off by their duties from other means of livelihood; and above all, from the humblest Levite to the high-priest himself, they must all offer sacrifices and sin-offerings for themselves. Thus both objects were attained and both principles were taught. In so far as the authorized ministrations before God were concerned, they were separate from others, called to be and symbolically made, "holy, harmless, and undefiled;" beyond this they were men, fellow-citizens with their brethren of the commonwealth of God, with the same duties and the same responsibilities.

The consideration of these incidental matters shows how all the detailed precepts of the law had for their object the preparation of the people for the Gospel, by keeping them separate from heathen contamination, by educating them through rules up to the principles afterwards to be revealed, by typical setting forth of truths they could not yet receive in full clearness of revelation, and finally by training them in habits of conduct and elements of character directly preparatory for the Gospel. Thus with that harmony and perfection which marks all the Divine works, was the leading principle of the Levitical law carried out in detail, and in small matters as well as in great, "the law was our schoolmaster to bring us to Christ."

LECTURE V.

SACRIFICE.

THE earliest records of our race, sacred and profane alike, represent man as seeking acceptance with God by means of sacrifice. It does not matter whether this was originally done by immediate Divine command, or whether the human mind itself perceived the fitness of the rite; in either case, the sacrifice was from the first accepted, and as soon as laws were given, was regulated and required. Before that time there is little to be said about sacrifice. It had two general forms, the whole burnt-offering, as in the sacrifices of Abel,* of Noah,† of Abraham,‡ and frequently among the nations of the world; and of what were afterwards called "peace offerings,' in which only a part of the victim was consumed upon the altar and the remainder used by the worshippers in a sacrificial feast, as in the case of Jacob and Laban,§ and very often in the sacrificial feasts mentioned by classical writers. In addition to these, a thank-offering was customary, which the worshipper simply consecrated to God as a recognition of the blessings received from Him.

Nothing is anywhere said of the especial meaning

---

* Gen. iv. 4, 5. † *Ib.* viii. 20.
‡ *Ib.* xxii. 13. § *Ib.* xxxi. 54.

of either of these kinds of sacrifice. Left to infer this from the nature of the sacrifices themselves, it is generally considered that both kinds, as under the law, had more or less of a propitiatory character, but the whole burnt offering more particularly signified entire consecration to God; and the peace offering, the desire to hold communication with Him, and to sanctify to Him the events of ordinary life. The idea of propitiation is nowhere distinctly brought out, but may reasonably be supposed to inhere in the sacrifices of the patriarchs, both because it was the prominent idea in sacrifice among the heathen, and because it was expressly recognized and made prominent in the sacrificial system of the law. The sacrifices of Cain and Abel have sometimes been considered sin offerings, and may have been so; but there is no evidence of this in the narrative except by giving to the word *sin* (ver. 7) the sense of *sin offering*, a technical sense never elsewhere used until the giving of the law, some thousands of years later than the time of Abel. Still another use of ancient sacrifice was as the solemn seal of a covenant, first between God and man, as in the case of Abraham,* and afterwards probably between man and man.† Whatever may have been the immediate purpose in these various kinds of sacrifice, there is a plain recognition in all of them that man is separated from God, and that in approaching Him it is necessary in some way to remove the intervening bar of human sinfulness. At the same time it is plain that there could be no real

---

* Gen. xv. 9–21.   † See Gen. xxi. 30–32; Heb. ix. 16, 17.

power in the blood of bulls and goats to atone for moral transgressions, and this fact was emphasized by the constant repetition of the sacrifices. Along with this there was the constant remembrance that final victory over the power of evil had been promised to the woman's seed. Sacrifice was always, therefore, typical. It taught the sinfulness of man and the necessity of doing away with that sinfulness in order to his acceptance with a God perfect in holiness. Yet the means used were manifestly inadequate to the purpose, and there was the promise that the purpose should be accomplished. Hence they were a constant showing forth of something not yet revealed. We have no means of knowing how far their nature was understood in the earliest times; but after the establishment of the commonwealth of Israel, from Samuel and David down, it is clear that the prophets looked upon sacrifice as only the outward form of approach to God, and regarded the inward disposition of the heart as essential.

When the time of the Sinaitic legislation is reached, the whole institution of sacrifice is systematized and arranged by express Divine command. It is to the institution as thus ordered that the references of the New Testament are chiefly made; and it is on this, as the only system of which we have much definite knowledge, that we must rely as giving us the sacrificial bond of connection between the two Covenants. That it may be distinctly before the mind, it will be well briefly to review the main points of the Levitical sacrificial system.

First of all, there was one peculiar sacrifice, the Passover, which was instituted before the giving of the Sinaitic law, and which does not fall into its classifications, but which was recognized and preserved in it as one of the most important and significant of all its institutions. When the Passover was first commanded there was no established priesthood, no sanctuary, and no altar, and it was provided for a momentary and pressing emergency. Later all these things were changed; yet it was to be most carefully observed during all the generations of Israel. The head of each family was to offer the victim and to sprinkle its blood upon the side-posts and the lintel of the door of his house. Thus each man acted as the priest of his own house in accordance with the call to the whole people to be "a kingdom of priests and an holy nation.* After the erection of the tabernacle and the establishment of the priesthood, no change occurred in this respect,† and this priestly function of every Israelite in connection with the Passover was maintained as a significant mark of their original vocation of which they had proved themselves unworthy. Several modifications of the original institution were afterwards introduced; the Passover must be slain only in the place of the central sanctuary;‡ "a holy convocation" should be kept on the following day; and others which were in part provided for at the original institution, but which were impracticable on the occasion of its first observance, immediately followed as it was by the march from Egypt. More

---

* Ex. xix. 6.   † Num. ix. 3, 4.   ‡ Deut. xvi. 2–8.

important was the change introduced in the time of Hezekiah, when, on account of the general uncleanness of the people, the Passover was slain by the Levites and the blood sprinkled by the priests.* This was repeated in the time of Josiah,† and according to Jewish authorities, became the common practice in later ages.‡

The Passover has a peculiar interest in the relation of the Old and New Testaments, both because at its celebration the Lord's supper was instituted, and thus the continual rite of the Old Covenant replaced by the continual sacrament of the New; and because the Apostles especially point to it as a type of the one sacrifice on Calvary: "Christ, our Passover, is sacrificed for us."§ This, therefore, is a meeting point and bond of connection between the two dispensations. Wherein is it so? In the first place the original Passover was the turning point in the deliverance of God's people from Egyptian bondage. There had been long preparation and a severe struggle with Pharaoh; but this marked the decisive point. Now, when this is said typically to point forward to the deliverance of God's people from the bondage of sin into the liberty of the Gospel, the saying is liable to be misunderstood. Certainly the people were not directly taught by this to look forward to the vicarious death of Christ upon the cross; for they never had this idea, nor was there any reason that they should. But they

---

* 2 Chr. xxx. 15-19.   † *Ib.* xxxv. 11.
‡ See Lightfoot, *Ministerium Templi*, c. xii., Works, I., p. 727, ed. Fran. 1699.   § 1 Cor. v. 7.

were taught some other things which in the Divine plan for man's salvation necessarily involved this. They knew that they were the people of whom should be born the world's Redeemer, and that their deliverance from Egypt was a step in their foretold national history leading to this end. They recognized that at the moment of the institution of the Passover a great judgment was impending upon the land from which they were to escape by the use of Divinely appointed means. In all after ages they observed it in memory of these facts. But was that memory only a recollection of the past, or did it also set forth, whether they understood it or not, the things of the future? Certainly the latter at every point. The deliverance from Egypt was not the triumph over the power of sin; but it was a step towards the accomplishment of that promised triumph; and the commemoration of this step, like that of every stage of an unfinished work, necessarily joined the thought of past progress with the hope of its completion. The deliverance in the one case as in the other, could only be brought about by the intervention of the Divine power, and was effected in a way which human sagacity could not have foreseen. The people were taught by the Passover the same lesson of faith, of entire dependence upon God, which is required for the appropriation of the Christian means of salvation. Finally, the means used was sacrifice, " for without shedding of blood is no remission," and this use of the sacrifice must be the personal act of each representative Israelite. The connection then of the two Dispensations in and through the Passover does not lie in any external resemblance, though there was enough of external resemblance to point the thought to the deeper inward connection; but in the two facts that the same essential truths are taught in the one as in the other, and that the one was a step towards the other. In both exemption from impending danger is obtained by the use of the Divinely appointed means; in both deliverance from a terrible condition is reached by simple trust in God and the use of the appointed means; in both the forfeiture of life is the necessary condition of pardon and of the favor of God, and the means provided must be personally used by each and every man. Certainly these main points in the sacrifice of Christ for man's redemption were set forth to the people of that time as clearly as they well could be by any sensible symbol. Therefore, as in the Lord's supper "ye do show forth the Lord's death until He come," so not without reason is it considered that in the Passover, which preceded it and on which it was founded, there was a showing forth of the same sacrifice in type and symbol.

The sacrifices under the law may be arranged in four general classes, with some subdivisions. There are also a few special institutions not included in any of these classes. It is worth while to call to mind the chief characteristics of these, even at the risk of repeating what is very familiar. The ancient whole burnt offering was perpetuated, and became the regular daily morning and evening sacrifice. It was also required in the great feasts, and might be offered by any one at any time. The victim might be selected from any of the sacrificial animals, but must always be a male, except in the case of birds, where no distinction of sex was recognized.* The special provisions of the law in regard to this offering were: that the offerer must lay his hand upon its head, must kill it, and that the priest must sprinkle its blood upon the altar, and prepare and burn its flesh. The *minchah*, called in our version *meat offering* or oblation, was an unbloody offering ordinarily accompanying the animal sacrifices, though in some special cases, as in the offering of the first sheaf of the harvest on the morrow after the Passover,† it was presented alone. Its usual material was fine flour, oil, and these two combined in cakes of various kinds, incense of two kinds, *frankincense*—the simple exudation of a shrub, which was used by the people and burnt in the court of the tabernacle—and *incense* or *sweet incense*, compounded of the frankincense and of various spices, and which was burnt only within the sanctuary. There was also the drink offering, of wine or "strong drink," which was used only as an accompaniment of the other sacrifices. Most of these were probably used as offerings before the giving of the law, and they were without any separate expiatory significance. The single case where an expiatory offering of fine flour was allowed comes under the sin offering.

The peace offerings of the earlier ages were continued and systematically arranged under the law. They were the most common of all the sacrifices,

---

* Lev. i. 3, 10, 14. † *Ib.* xxiii. 10.

and formed the basis of all the religious feasts of old. The victim might be of either sex, and of any kind of sacrificial animal except birds, which were too small for the purpose. The blood was sprinkled on the altar, the fat burned there, a portion given to the officiating priest, and the rest consumed by the worshipper in a feast with his friends. The thanksgiving, the vow, and the voluntary offerings were subordinate varieties of the peace offering. The law was so far relaxed in regard to the last two that they might be eaten also on the second day,* and for the last that a victim might be accepted having a deficiency or redundancy of parts.† In the peace offering, as in the other sacrifices, the offerer must personally present the victim ‡ and slay it, after having laid his hand upon its head. The idea of propitiation was less prominent in this than in the other classes of animal sacrifices; yet that it was not altogether wanting is shown by the sprinkling of the blood upon the altar. It naturally became one of the most common sacrifices, and was sometimes offered in enormous numbers, as at Solomon's dedication of the temple.§ In this and similar cases the provision that the offerer must personally lay his hands upon the head of the victim and slay it himself was doubtless neglected; but even then it was probably done to a few of the victims as representatives of the whole. The peace offering was always preceded by the sin offering when both were offered on the same day. It was especially the sacrifice of communion with God, and the means of expressing

---

* Lev. vii. 16, 17.   † *Ib.* xxii. 23.   ‡ *Ib.* vii. 29.   § 1 Kings, viii. 63.

thanksgiving for His mercies or supplication for His favors.

The sin offering, including the subdivision of the trespass offering, was peculiar to the law, and was the most distinctive feature of its whole sacrificial system. It must be offered by every Israelite individually when he had sinned, from the high-priest down, and also in a very remarkable form for the whole people collectively. The offerer presented and slew the victim as in other cases, but there was a difference in the treatment of the blood. This was ordinarily to be put upon the horns of the altar in the court of the tabernacle,* but when the offering was for the high-priest or for the whole congregation it was to be brought into the sanctuary, and both sprinkled before the veil and put upon the horns of the altar of incense.† On the great day of atonement it was further carried by the high-priest into the holy of holies and sprinkled upon the mercy seat itself.‡ The disposition of the flesh of the victim depended upon this treatment of a portion of the blood. In all cases the rest of the blood was poured out at the foot of the altar, and the fat and kidneys, except with the bullock and the goat on the day of atonement, were burned upon the altar. The rest of the body was to be consumed by the priests in a holy place; but if a portion of the blood had been brought within the sanctuary, the flesh must be carried without the camp and there burned. The bullock and the goat of the day of the atonement must be so burned whole with their skin and all that

---

* Lev. iv. 25, 30.   † *Ib.* 6, 7, 17, 18.   ‡ *Ib.* xvi. 14, 15.

belonged to them. In all cases the priest is expressly "to make an atonement for the offerer"; and the word thus translated means literally "a covering"—by the sacrifice there was effected a covering up of the sins of him who offered the victim. This victim was in all ordinary cases the same, and was a she-goat,* the cheapest of all domestic animals and easily within the reach of almost every one. It was only varied where it could be done without violation of the principle and where the conspicuousness of the sinner required that the atonement for him should be especially marked. For the high-priest, or for the whole congregation collectively, the victim was a bullock,† on the day of atonement a bullock and two goats; for a ruler, it was a he-goat. ‡ Correspondingly for those too poor to afford the regular offering, a pair of turtle doves or two young pigeons; § in case of extreme poverty, fine flour might be presented. ‖ With this necessary allowance for exceptional cases, the sin offering was always the same and of the victim which could be most easily procured. It is especially important to note that no variation in the value or number of the victims was allowed in view of the greatness of the sin. For the most heinous and the lightest offence the offering was the same. Yet the offering was only permitted for what are called "sins of inadvertence;" for "presumptuous" sins, or sins "with a high hand," *i. e.* those done intentionally and with purpose to brave the Divine wrath, no sacrifice was allowed.¶

---

* Lev. iv. 28. † *Ib.* iv. 3, 14. ‡ *Ib.* iv. 23.
§ *Ib.* v. 7. ‖ *Ib.* v. 11. ¶ Num. xv. 30.

The trespass offering was a variety of the sin offering provided for transgressions which involved not only sin but harm to another, whether to God in the things of His sanctuary, or to a neighbor. In this case, in addition to the offering, which must in all cases be a ram, compensation must be made for the harm done with the addition of a fifth part as a fine.*

Under the same general head of the sin offering must be placed the peculiar sacrifice of the red heifer, to which allusion is made in the Epistle to the Hebrews.† A red heifer, which had never been yoked, was to be slain by the high-priest without the camp. After sprinkling her blood "directly before the tabernacle" he was to burn her whole body with "cedar wood and hyssop and scarlet," and the ashes were to be gathered up and preserved. When there was occasion, some of this was to be mingled with water constituting a water of purification to be sprinkled upon the unclean.‡

By far the most important of all the sin offerings was that on the great day of atonement, the only day of fasting prescribed by the law. The high-priest was first to offer a bullock for himself and for his house, and bring its blood within the veil to sprinkle it before and upon the mercy seat.§ He was then to do the same with a goat for a sin offering for the people.‖ After this he was to take of both to put upon the altar to hallow it and the tabernacle.¶ Finally, he was to take another goat,

---

* Lev. v. 14—vi. 7.   † Heb. ix. 13.   ‡ Num. xix.
§ Lev. xvi. 11-14.   ‖ *Ib.* 15-17.   ¶ *Ib.* 18-19.

which had been presented to the Lord at the same time with the first, and selected by lot,* confess over him the sins of the people and send him off "by the hand of a fit man into the wilderness." † This goat is the one known in our version as "the scape-goat," but in the Hebrew simply "the goat for Azazel," whatever that may mean. The bodies of the other goat and of the bullock, after their fat had been burned upon the altar, ‡ were to be burned without the camp. § In all cases the man who burned the body of the sin offering and led away the goat became thereby unclean and was obliged to wash his clothes and bathe his flesh. ‖

There were a variety of offerings, such as those for the cleansed leper and others, which do not require special mention. But there is one thing important to be observed in regard to all sacrifices: although they had, and could have no intrinsic efficacy for the forgiveness of moral sin, they yet did atone for mere legal and ceremonial defilements. ¶ They had therefore a certain absolute value.

Before speaking of the relation of this sacrificial system to the New Testament, it will be well to look for a moment at its treatment in the later ages of the Old Dispensation. The key-note of this was struck by the Prophet Samuel in his address to the vainglorious Saul, recognizing the obligation of sacrifice, but pointing to something still more important: "Behold, to obey is better than sacrifice."**
Very similar is the utterance of David, the pupil of

---

* Lev. xvi. 7, 8   † *Ib.* 20–22.   ‡ *Ib.* 25.   § *Ib.* 27.
‖ *Ib.* 26, 28.   ¶ See Heb. ix. 13.   ** 1 Sam. xv. 22.

the prophet and the successor of the king : " Sacrifice and offering thou didst not desire; mine ears hast thou opened : burnt offering and sin offering hast thou not required. Then said I, Lo I come, in the volume of the book it is written of me, I delight to do thy will, oh my God." * For while this utterance is prophetic, it yet expresses the Psalmist's own inspired view of the comparative value of sacrifice and obedience. The philosophic Preacher counsels : " Keep thy foot when thou goest to the house of God, and be more ready to hear than to give the sacrifice of fools." † The words of the earliest group of prophets whose writings have been preserved to us — Amos, Hosea, Isaiah, and Micah — are very clear. Amos says : " Though ye offer me burnt offerferings and your meat offerings, I will not accept them : neither will I regard the peace offerings of your fat beasts....But let judgment run down as waters, and righteousness as a mighty stream." ‡ Hosea : " They sacrifice flesh for the sacrifices of mine offerings, and eat it ; but the LORD accepteth them not ; now will He remember their iniquity,"§, etc. Isaiah is very bold and saith (at the beginning of his prophecies). " To what purpose is the multitude of your sacrifices unto me ? saith the LORD : I am full of the burnt offerings of rams, and the fat of fed beasts, and I delight not in the blood of bullocks, or of lambs, or of he-goats.... Wash you, make you clean ; put away the evil of your doings," ‖ etc. And again (at the very end): " He that killeth an

---

* Ps. xl. 6–8. † Eccl. v. 1. ‡ Amos, v. 22, 24.
§ Hos. viii. 13. ‖ Is. i. 11.

ox is as if he slew a man; he that sacrificeth a lamb,
as if he cut off a dog's neck; he that offereth an oblation, as if he offered swine's blood; he that offereth incense, as if he blessed an idol."* Micah
asks, "Wherewith shall I come before the LORD,
and bow myself before the high God? shall I come
before Him with burnt offerings, with calves of a
year old? Will the LORD be pleased with thousands of rams, or with ten thousands of rivers of
oil? shall I give my firstborn for my transgression,
the fruit of my body for the sin of my soul? He
hath shewed thee, oh man, what is good; and what
doth the LORD require of thee, but to do justly, to
love mercy, and to walk humbly with thy God." †
In the period just before the captivity, Jeremiah
says to the people, "Your burnt offerings are not
acceptable, nor your sacrifices sweet unto me." ‡ A
certain school of critics would fain find in such utterances a struggle against the whole sacrificial system
before the Levitical law had yet been established;
but this cannot be, since we find the same thing in
Malachi, long after, even on their theory, the Levitical system had been established. The last of the
prophets still speaks in the same strain with those
who had gone before. Having exposed some of the
iniquities of the people, he continues: "The LORD
will cut off the man that doeth this, the master and
the scholar, out of the tabernacles of Jacob, and him
that offereth an offering unto the LORD of hosts,
and this have ye done again, covering the altar of
the LORD with tears, with weeping, and with crying

---
* Is. lxvi. 3. † Mic. vi. 6–8. ‡ Jer. vi. 20.

out, insomuch that He regardeth not the offering any more, nor receiveth it with good will at your hand."*

These sacrifices had been divinely commanded, and at times the people were sharply reproved for their neglect,† or carelessness in their offerings;‡ but the prophets contended against an unworthy and perfunctory performance of the service of the Lord, because they "draw near me with their mouth, and with their lips do honor me, but have removed their heart far from me." § And even Malachi looks forward to the time when "from the rising of the sun even unto the going down of the same my name shall be great among the Gentiles, and in every place incense shall be offered unto my name, and a pure offering;" ‖ and when the "sons of Levi" shall be purified "that they may offer unto the LORD an offering in righteousness. Then shall the offering of Judah and Jerusalem be pleasant unto the LORD, as in the days of old." ¶ Doubtless, these expressions are to be interpreted of the antitypes of the Gospel; but it may be doubted whether the prophet himself understood the figurative character of his expressions, and at all events, the clothing of his predictions in the language of these sacrificial types shows that he looked upon the sacrifices themselves as good.

The prophets, then, must have regarded the sacrifices as divinely commanded and capable of being

---

* Mal. ii. 12, 13. † See Hag. i. 9–11; Mal. iii. 8.
‡ Mal. i. 6–7. § Isa. xxix. 13; cf. Matt. xv. 8.
‖ Mal. i. 11. ¶ *Ib.* iii. 3, 4.

so used as to constitute an acceptable service to God; but as having no intrinsic value for the forgiveness of sin, and utterly worthless when dissociated from the true service of the heart. In considering, therefore, their relation to the New Testament, we must take them in the light in which they are presented by the inspired teachers of the Old Dispensation, and not in the mere bare and outward letter of the law. Looking, then, upon the sacrifices, when used in an earnest and devout spirit, as the means provided under the Old Dispensation for approach to God and communion with Him, for the forgiveness of sin and for the outward sustenance of a holy life, what is their relation to the Gospel? Much, every way. First, because they brought home to man the consciousness of sin. This must ever be the starting-point in the drawing near of fallen man to an all-holy God. Therefore, in that full setting forth of the way of salvation, the Epistle to the Romans, the first chapters are occupied with the abundant proof of the universal sinfulness of man. When the Israelites are compared with the heathen, there can be no question that this sense of sinfulness was far more vividly preserved among the former, and the chief means whereby this was accomplished was the sacrificial system. Sacrifices were also practised by the heathen, but the same effect failed to be produced in anything like the same degree, by reason of the very different light in which their sacrifices were generally regarded. In the very forefront, then, of the relations of the Old Covenant, through its sacrifices, to the

New, should be placed the awakening and keeping alive of the sense of sin and of the need of forgiveness.

The holiness of God, standing over against the sin of man, was set forth in every possible form of symbol and of direct statement both in the laws of sacrifice and in the ordinances of the tabernacle and of the priesthood, which were parts of the sacrificial system. It is only necessary to compare the grossness and often the licentiousness of heathen worship with the Hebrew ritual to see how utterly different must have been the ideas of the Being worshipped conveyed to the mind of the worshipper. In the one He was a Being of enormous power indeed, but swayed by all the passions and even the sensual indulgences of man, and with opposing deities of whom he was jealous. In the other He was the sole and Almighty Ruler, who could be approached only in the recognition of His absolute purity and holiness. As there is no more powerful spring of conduct than the character of the Being to whom we are responsible, so there was no more important preparation for the Gospel than in the nature and attributes of God as set forth in the sacrificial system. Place the gods of Homer or of the later Greek poets by the side of the Jehovah of Israel, and none can fail to recognize the difference which must have resulted in the religious ideas of the people trained under the two systems.

A word may be said in regard to the unity of God as declared in the sacrificial system, because this has been misunderstood and misrepresented. In the legislation for the wilderness this was emphatically taught by the single altar to which all sacrifices must be brought, and where alone sacrificial worship could be accepted. Similarly, when the people were on the eve of their entrance upon the promised land, the command was given over and over again, in every form of emphatic repetition, that they should not be like the heathen whom they replaced, but should have one central sanctuary in "the place which the LORD shall choose to place His name there," * to which they should bring all their offerings and tithes, to which the Levites should resort for their service, and which should constitute the visible centre of their worship and of their nationality founded upon that worship. The critics allege that this is in itself proof of the late origin of these commands, since, in flagrant contrast with them, the history shows sacrifices offered with the Divine approval at a great variety of places, as at Gilgal and Ophrah, Shiloh, Bethlehem, Gibeon and Ramah, Carmel and Jerusalem, and on other heights. Without stopping to notice that the commands objected to are found only in Deuteronomy (which the critics suppose to be earlier than the Levitical legislation),†

---

* Deut. xii. 5, 11, 14, 18, 26 ; xiv. 23–25 ; xv. 20 ; xvi. 2, 6, 7, 15, 16 ; xvii. 8, 10 ; xviii. 6 ; xxvi. 2 ; xxxi. 11 ; Josh. ix. 27.

† The critics meet this difficulty by supposing that Deuteronomy, belonging, as they think, to the age of Josiah, was written at a time when the conflict about one exclusive central sanctuary was fresh, and therefore naturally inserted these laws, while "the middle books" were composed when the controversy had long been settled, and the necessity of inserting such provisions was forgotten. This explanation is singular and itself needs explanation, since, on the supposition of the critics, the very object of the Levitical legislation was to embody the results of the successful struggles of the priestly party.

it is sufficient to remark that the whole difficulty arises from a simple misapprehension. The source of authority is not Himself limited by the restraints He sees fit to impose upon the people. Unquestionably He limited them to a central sanctuary; but the foundation of this limitation was the manifestation of His presence. If now, in the disorders of the times, when the ark was separated from the tabernacle, or when the northern kingdom had revolted and cast off His worship, He in mercy vouchsafed to manifest His presence and to authorize sacrifices in other places than the one He had appointed, there is the same sanction for these other places as for the one. Yet this sanction was temporary and to meet an occasional necessity. When the people established a permanent worship in such places they were severely reproved. Nevertheless, even in this deviation from the letter of the law, the principle of the unity of God was always most firmly insisted upon; no sacrifice was ever countenanced except in such places as the one Jehovah had sanctioned.

The next point to be noted in the sacrificial system is the importance everywhere attached to the "shedding of blood." Although, as already said, this principle was of necessity waived in the sin offering of extreme poverty, yet it was generally true, and strikingly true, that "almost all things are by the law purged with blood; and without shedding of blood is no remission." * This was common, also, to the sacrifices of other nations, and expressed

---

* Heb. ix. 22.

the universal conviction of mankind that the forfeiture of life was the necessary penalty of sin, and therefore the condition of man's forgiveness. It was something, however, to have this established by the revealed will of God, placing it upon a basis of authority and certainty. Herein is perhaps the most important point of all in the relation of the two Dispensations. God is not only merciful, but righteous. He loves man and would receive him to Himself; but, that He may be consistent with Himself, His outraged law must be vindicated, and vindicated by that suffering which is the eternally established penalty of sin. Under the law it was only possible that this should be set forth in type and shadow; but those types were made as significant and instructive as the nature of the case allowed.

United with this, and giving force to its teaching, was the provision that the sacrifice must be the personal act of the worshipper. No proxy, no vicarious confession and worship were allowed. The offerer must himself lay his hand on the victim's head and slay it. It need not be said how fundamental to all religion is this personal relation between the sinner and his God. It is a principle continually violated in all false religions and in some corruptions of the true. It can hardly be necessary to guard this remark by saying that it does not apply to unconscious infants brought by circumcision or by baptism into the fold of God's Church of covenanted grace; nor to intercessory prayer for others. In both cases, by God's appointment, the influences of the Holy Spirit may be won for those we love; but the issue of those influences, the reconciliation of the sinner to his Maker, must finally depend, by an immutable law of congruity, upon the condition of his own heart.

The character of the offerer was another essential condition of all acceptable sacrifice. It has already been noticed that no offering was allowed for sins done "with a high hand." They were provided only for those who, through weakness, inadvertence and temptation, had "been overtaken in a fault." The offerer must recognize his sin; must seek reconciliation with God, and desire an atonement for his transgression.

Yet, even thus, under the law, atonement was only to be obtained by the intervention of the appointed priest. He it was, and not the worshipper, who must sprinkle the blood upon the altar. This was one of the innumerable ways in which the law taught "that the way into the holiest of all was not yet made manifest." Sinful man can never draw near to God except through a mediator; and while the one true and only Mediator was not yet revealed, these appointed types must stand between man and God, to set forth the necessity of this bridge over the otherwise impassable chasm. The separation between sin and holiness is not less than between the finite and the Infinite. In both the terms are incommensurable, and can only be brought into relation by a mediator. It is common to talk of the "boundless goodness" of God, as though He were ready to receive and have mercy upon all, without regard to character or to the use of His appointed means; but a higher authority has said, "No man cometh unto the Father but by Me;"* and this necessity of a mediator in all our approach to God was typically set forth in the requirement of an intervening priest to make the atonement.

A further point taught by the sacrificial system was the equality of all men before God. This has been mentioned in a former lecture, as set forth in various ways under the law; but most emphatically was it declared in requiring offerings for sin from all, and as far as the nature of the case allowed, the same offering from every man, and precisely the same ritual in every case. The law recognized no difference between the powerful and the weak, the rich and the humble. Only official responsibility in the one case, and extreme poverty in the other, allowed necessary difference in the victim. Equality was as strongly asserted as it could be.

The same fact shows that in the Hebrew sacrifices the idea was totally excluded of a *quid pro quo*, of a compensation offered to God for the sin committed against Him—an idea very prominent in the heathen sacrifices, where the victims were increased in number and value as the sin to be atoned for rose in greatness, even to the extent of offering human victims. Among the Israelites nothing of this kind was allowed. The peace offerings. designed for a sacrificial feast, might be indefinitely multiplied as occasion required; but for the sin offering only that which the law prescribed could be sacrificed. In

---
* John, xiv. 6.

this fact, that the same single victim * must atone alike for the greatest and the smallest sin, it was plainly shown that it was not in the victim itself to atone for the transgression. The heathen idea, that by this means an equivalent was offered to God, and He must, therefore, in common justice, forgive the sinner, was entirely excluded. Forgiveness remained among the Hebrews the free and gracious act of God; sacrifice was His appointed means of seeking this blessing. Why He should have appointed it, and how it was efficacious, were questions they may not have raised, and certainly could not have solved; but that the power was not in the value of the sacrifice itself was plain, when all sins of every degree had the same atonement.

Finally, the insufficiency of sacrifice itself for the forgiveness of sins was shown in two ways, both of which are pointed out in the argument in the Epistle to the Hebrews. In the first place, there was a constant repetition. This might possibly be alleged as required by the constant repetition of the sin. The worshippers were forgiven, but sinning again, needed a fresh atonement. Even this would show that the sacrifices were only effectual as against some particular sin, and not against that which most sorely presses upon man, his sinful condition, the alienation of his heart from God. But a perfect atonement, even in this limited sense, would be too much to allow to them. " The law .... can never with those sacrifices which they offered year by year continually make the comers thereunto perfect. For then

---

* Lev. iv. 28.

would they not have ceased to be offered, because that the worshippers once purged should have had no more conscience of sins. But in those sacrifices there is a remembrance again made of sins every year." * And then the contrast is drawn between these and Him who "after He had offered one sacrifice for ever, sat down on the right hand of God.... For by one offering He hath perfected forever them that are sanctified.† The recognized insufficiency of the sacrifices of old taught plainly the need of the sufficient Sacrifice, and the primeval promise made sure that it would come.

The other way in which the insufficiency of the sacrifices was shown was of a different kind, and one which perhaps appealed only to the more thoughtful and devout. It was in the inherent want of congruity between the means and the end; in the want of any relation between the life of the brutes and human transgression. "It is not possible," the Apostle argues, "that the blood of bulls and of goats should take away sins." ‡ Something further and more was needed; and it was because the people did not see this, but were disposed to trust implicitly to their sacrifices, that the sacred writers of old spoke of them in the terms which have been quoted. It is true that they simply require that the sacrifices should be offered in an honest and good heart, in humble submission to God and earnest effort to do His will. And it is also true that the saints of old who offered their sacrifices in this spirit, were accepted and forgiven. But this was not on the ground of

---
* Heb. x. 1–3.   † *Ib.* 12–14.   ‡ *Ib.* 4.

the sufficiency of the sacrifices; it was because they had faith in God's promises, and sought His forgiveness in the way of His appointment, although that way was obviously inadequate and derived its only efficacy from the Divine command. If in any way the Divine righteousness was to be vindicated in the forgiveness of the sinner, if any true atonement was to be made for sin, it must evidently be in some way not yet revealed.

After this somewhat full statement of the purpose and design of the sacrificial cultus, its place in the relations between the Old and New Dispensations is apparent without further discussion. The sacrifices were educational in that they set forth the purity, the majesty, and the holiness of God and the sinfulness of man. They taught man that he could draw nigh to his Maker only through the forgiveness of his sin, and that this forgiveness must be obtained by the sacrifice of life and the intervention of an authorized mediator. They were preparatory in showing that personal act and personal character were the necessary conditions of forgiveness, and he who was forgiven and brought into communion with God must needs live a life in accordance with God's will. Above all they were typical, in that they bore upon their very forefront the impress of their own insufficiency, and thus pointed forward to some means yet to be revealed when the "Seed of the woman" should come to crush the power of evil. There is no meaning in the sacrifices of old except in the light of the cross; and we gain much help in understanding Christ's sacrifice by the illustrations furnished in these typical offerings. Through them we are enabled to recognize Him as "the Lamb of God that taketh away the sin of the world." *

---

* John, i. 29, 36.

LECTURE VI.

THE PRIESTHOOD.

PRIESTHOOD and sacrifice are correlative terms. There may indeed be sacrifice without an appointed priesthood, as in all things the function is more general than the organ especially set apart for its discharge; but as we are taught in the Epistle to the Hebrews, there can be no priesthood without sacrifice,* since otherwise the office, having no object to serve, would cease.

During the early ages of mankind we have seen that sacrifices were offered, and yet there was no other appointed priest than the head of the family, in this, as in all other things the representative of those dependent upon him. As the family developed into the tribe, the two offices of prince and priest were not at first separated but remained united in the same person, as in the instances of Melchisedec† and of Jethro; ‡ so also Balak, as king of the Moabites, joined with the Prophet Balaam in offering sacrifices for his people. § When the tribe had further developed into a considerable nation, it became manifestly impracticable for the monarch, with his many occupations, actually to officiate as

---

* Heb. v. 1; viii. 1, 2. † Gen. xiv. 18.
‡ Ex. iii. 1; xviii. 12.   § Num. xxii.–xxiv.

the one universal priest of his nation, and therefore, as in Egypt, a permanent order of priests was established with a high-priest for each particular deity, but yet the monarch remained at the head of the whole hierarchy, the great high-priest of the whole kingdom.

In Israel, the ancient Church of God, the case was different. There was no king in the original constitution of this commonwealth, and, as we have seen, there was at first no priesthood. The people were to be under the direct government of God, and were to be "a kingdom of priests. and an holy nation." * Accordingly in the first sacrifice that was appointed, the Passover, each head of a family was made the officiating priest. They miserably failed to fulfil their high vocation, and although the institution of the monarchy was deferred for some centuries, it became necessary that the people should at once have some one, as they had desired, to stand between themselves and God, and accordingly the Aaronic order of priests was consecrated. This continued ever after a separate and distinct order, from whose functions—nothwithstanding the assertions often made to the contrary—the monarchs were emphatically excluded, and any attempt upon their part to assume them was most severely marked by the Divine displeasure. † Thus came about the first instance in history of the separation of the functions of the priesthood and the monarch, of Church and State. Later, for a time in the period of the Maccabees, the supreme civil and ecclesiastical offices

---

* Ex. xix. 5.   † 1 Sam. xiii. 10–14 ; 2 Chron. xxvi. 16–21.

were united in the same person; but this was because the priests, through stress of circumstances, temporarily absorbed the royal prerogative, not by reason of the kings assuming priestly functions.

With the Sinaitic legislation a distinct order of priests were divinely appointed. Two points are especially to be noted in regard to them: first, that their appointment was directly from God Himself.* This fact is everywhere insisted upon and was essential to the value of their office. They were in no sense appointed by the people, and had they been so, they could not have acted authoritatively as mediators between God and the people. It has already appeared that the Levitical sacrifices had no intrinsic efficacy for the forgiveness of moral sin, but derived their whole value from the Divine appointment, and the same thing is to be said of the priesthood. The priests themselves needed atonement, and were obliged to offer for their own sins; yet by the prescribed unction they were constituted acceptable intercessors and mediators for the people. All was from God; and while this gave assurance to the people in their daily worship, the priest's own imperfection showed that the true reconciliation with God by the restoration of holiness to man had not yet been manifested. The Seed of the woman who should bruise the serpent's head could only be typified, not realized, by the Levitical priests. Yet this very imperfection in another way secured for them a qualification which the author of the Epistle to the Hebrews urges as essential, that the high-priest

---

* Comp. Heb. v. 4.

THE PRIESTHOOD.

should be able "to have compassion on the ignorant and on them that are out of the way; for that he himself also is compassed with infirmity."* It was essential, then, to their office that they should have authority, and to its rightful discharge that they should have sympathy with those for whom they ministered.

The fundamental object of their office was, as repeatedly declared, "to draw near to God," † on behalf of the people. They were to do this chiefly by offering sacrifices for the forgiveness of sins, and they thus sustained a distinct mediatorial character between God and His people. This appears in every part of the law concerning them. The golden plate inscribed "holiness unto the Lord" which the high-priest wore upon his brow, was expressly declared to mean that he should "bear the iniquity of the holy things which the children of Israel shall hallow," ‡ and the flesh of the sin offerings was given to the priests "to bear the iniquity of the congregation, to make atonement for them before the Lord."§ The ritual of the sin offering in the case of the whole congregation, of the ruler, and of one of the common people closes with the declaration, "and the priest shall make an atonement for them and it shall be forgiven them." ‖

From this primary and essential duty of the priests naturally followed many others of a secondary character. They had the care of the sanctuary,

---

* Heb. v. 2.   † Lev. vii. 35; x. 3; xxi. 17; Num xvi. 5, etc.
‡ Ex. xxviii. 38.   § Lev. x. 17.
‖ Lev. iv. 20, 26, 31, 35; v. 10, 13.

the especial charge of the copy of the law, of the instruction of the people, and many other things, which all grew out of their primary office, and need not here be considered. But it is important to bear in mind that their one essential function, that for which their office was instituted, was to stand as mediators between God and the people, and to make atonement for their sins by means of sacrifice. Of course, from the very nature of these sacrifices, and from their own nature, too, they could do this but symbolically, and they were appointed until the great and true High-Priest should come, Who by His one all-sufficient sacrifice " hath perfected forever them that are sanctified." *

This brings us at once to the relation between the old and the new Dispensations as involved in the priesthood. The priests, like the sacrifices, were types of Christ; that is, they set forth, in imperfect and insufficient acts, that which He alone could really accomplish. This whole relation is so fully wrought out in the Epistle to the Hebrews, that it cannot be necessary to dwell very much upon it. Only there are certain features of Christ's priesthood in relation to the Levitical, and also in relation to the general functions of all possible priesthood, brought out in that epistle, which it is desirable to have clearly in mind.

The first of these is its superiority to the Aaronic priesthood. This is shown by various satisfactory proofs, familiar to us, of which only one is especially connected with the present subject, viz.: That the

---

* Heb. x. 14

Aaronic priesthood was temporary, while that of Christ summed up in itself all other priesthood, and is everlasting, so that there neither is nor ever can be any other priesthood in the original sense of that word. The declarations on this point are very specific. His perpetual priesthood results from the whole comparison drawn between Him and Melchisedec, and from the statement that "He is able to save them to the uttermost that come unto God by Him, seeing He ever liveth to make intercession for them;"* and that He is a Priest "after the power of an endless life;" † and again, that He "is consecrated for evermore," ‡ and that He is "a priest for ever." § That His priesthood is a finality necessarily results from this argument; for He being a perfect and eternal High-Priest, how can there be occasion for any other? It is not, however, allowed to rest here. We know that, as is urged in this epistle, ‖ there can be no priest without he "have somewhat to offer," or, as it has already been expressed, priest and sacrifice are correlative terms, so that there can be no priest without a sacrifice. If there be one point which, more than any other, the Epistle to the Hebrews labors to make clear and emphatic, it is that Christ's sacrifice was complete and perfect, offered once for all and admitting of no other. "By one sacrifice He hath perfected forever them that are sanctified;" ¶ He "needeth not daily, as those high-priests, to offer up sacrifice....; for this He did once, when He offered up Him-

---

* Heb. vii. 25. † *Ib.* ver. 16. ‡ *Ib.* ver. 28.
§ v. 6; vii. 21. ‖ viii. 3. ¶ x. 14.

self;"* "He entered in once into the Holy Place, having obtained eternal redemption for us;"† "now once in the end of the world hath He appeared to put away sins by the sacrifice of Himself;"‡ "we are sanctified by the offering of the body of Jesus Christ once for all;"§ "this man, after He had offered one sacrifice for sins for ever, sat down on the right hand of God." ‖ To quote all the passages having the same significance, would be to quote a considerable part of the epistle. The whole is admirably summed up in the teaching of our own Church in her communion office, saying of Christ's death upon the cross, "Who made there (by His one oblation of Himself once offered) a full, perfect, and sufficient sacrifice, oblation and satisfaction for the sins of the whole world."

If, then, the priesthood of old could only be typical because it lacked power to be more, that of Christ, because it was all-sufficient and effective, was complete and final. As there can be no sacrifice beyond His, so there can, in the nature of things, be no further priesthood. He has accomplished all that was to be done; there is nothing for another to do, nor, if there were, is there any other who has power for its doing.

Just here it may be well to make a moment's digression lest the Christian use of the term *priest* for the officers of the Church, and of sacrifice in connection with its chief sacrament, should seem to militate against the position here taken. As early as the time of Cyprian, that is in the middle of the third

---

* Heb. vii. 27. † ix. 12. ‡ ix. 26. § x. 10. ‖ x. 12.

THE PRIESTHOOD.

century, the distinctive Greek word for *priest*, ἱερεύς, came to be applied first to the Bishop, and then to the Presbyters. This was natural, since in all the communities in which Christians lived the title of those who conducted religious services was universally "the priest," and they assimilated the name, just as, in an opposite way, the rabbis in Jewish synagogues now are popularly called "ministers" or "clergymen," and this was the more readily done because the religious minister throughout the Old Testament Scriptures was the priest. But the name did not carry with it the thing signified by the name, and not until the theology of the Church had become deeply corrupted was it ever imagined that the function of the Christian priest was to offer propitiatory sacrifice.

Similarly the name "sacrifice" came to be associated with the eucharist, as with every other outward act of devotion, with prayer, and thanksgiving, and alms, and perhaps still more readily with this as the memorial of the one great Sacrifice, offered once for all; but with no thought that this sacrament was a sacrifice in the strict and proper sense of the word, as an atonement for sin. But naturally and easily as these terms came to be thus used, it is not to be forgotten that even such a use of them is most scrupulously avoided throughout the New Testament. Frequently as the term ἱερεύς is used of the Levitical priests, often as it is applied to our Lord, and sometimes to the whole body of His followers, it is never once used, nor any derivative or cognate word, of the Christian ministry. They are called *presbyters, prophets, teachers, leaders* (ἡγούμενοι), *ministers, bishops* or overseers, but never priests.* So, also, often as the word "sacrifice" is used, whether of the bloody sacrifices of old or of the figurative sacrifices of alms and prayer and praise, and often as the Lord's Supper is mentioned, directly or in allusions, the two terms are never brought together, nor is the chief sacrament of our religion ever described in sacrificial language.† The inspired writers were deeply impressed with the all-sufficient and final character both of our Lord's sacrifice and of His priesthood. If another use of terms has since come into vogue, and if, through stress of circumstances, any of us be led to adopt this later usage, care needs to be exercised lest with the terms should come back the idea of atonement which, once perfectly accomplished, can never be repeated.

To return: but a word more need be said of the relations of the two Dispensations as shown in the Priesthood. It is evident that the earlier was preparatory for the later, and the later was the designed completion of the earlier; but it is particularly to be noted that this is true, not merely in a chronological,

---

* In Rom. xv. 16, St. Paul speaks of himself as ἱερουργοῦντα τὸ εὐαγγέλιον in order that there might be an acceptable προσφορά of the Gentiles. But this word is derived not from ἱερεύς, but from ἱερός, and would be accurately translated "making a sacred service." Besides, the whole passage is highly figurative, and even if referred to priestly service, could be so only in the same sense in which the Gentiles are called "a sacrifice."

† Heb. xiii. 10—"we have an altar"—has sometimes been referred to in this connection; but the context shows that whether θυσιαστήριον be here taken of the cross or of Christ, it cannot refer directly to the Eucharist.

but also in a logical sense. It is not merely that the Levitical priests were before Christ in point of time; but the essential nature of the priesthood, in obtaining the forgiveness of sins and the reconciliation of man to God by an authorized mediatorship founded upon the sacrifice of life, was so set forth in their prescribed functions, that only by a careful and thorough study of these can we reach any true idea of the priesthood of Christ. And Christ's priesthood is one of the chief points of the New Testament teaching. It remains, therefore, that the Levitical law was not only to the Jews a temporary and typical substitute for the Gospel and a preparation for Christianity; but its study continues in all ages to be to the Christian the indispensable means of understanding the fundamental teaching of the New Testament. On the other hand this teaching of the New Testament throws back its light over the institutions of the Old, and shows to all who have eyes to see that these could not have been of mere human invention and development; but rest on the command of Him who saw the end from the beginning, and ordained all in harmony for the purpose of leading fallen man as fast and as far as he was able to bear, in the way of eternal salvation.

The supreme function of the Jewish priesthood was on the great day of Atonement, when the high-priest, sheltered by the cloud of incense from the golden censer, passed within the veil and presented the blood of his sacrifice before the Mercy-seat. This was the culmination of his symbolical work of atonement; for that did not end with the sacrifice, but was continued and completed in the presentation of the blood before the symbolical dwelling-place of the Most High. These things, like every part of the sacrificial system, had their significance, and pointed to truths which should be fulfilled in the substance when the shadow had passed away. For it is to be remembered that while the great sacrifice of our Lord's priesthood was accomplished once for all, so that there can be no other sacrifice in the proper sense of that word; yet it is declared He "abideth a Priest for ever" and "ever liveth to make intercession for" us.* The consequences of His sacrifice are permanent. The intercession based upon that sacrifice continues forever as the ground of our hope of salvation, and can be offered in its priestly significance only by Him who was Himself the sacrifice which He offered once for all for our redemption. He is our only and our perpetual Priest.

---

* Heb. vii. 25.

LECTURE VII.

THE KINGDOM OF GOD.

THE form of government among the people of the Old Dispensation has an important bearing upon the relations between that dispensation and the New, as furnishing the language embodying the ideas of the Messianic kingdom, both in prophecy and in the Gospel. All government must have originated with the family,* and as the numbers of the family multiplied, this naturally developed into the clan or tribe with its chieftain, and then into the nation with its monarch. In Israel this natural development was greatly modified. Abraham, indeed, can hardly be refused the title of the Sheikh of a tribe when he could muster for war three hundred and eighteen " trained servants, born in his house," † indicating a clan of not less than fifteen hundred, whose multitude of tents spread far over the fields where he sojourned. Abimelech, king of the Philistines, made a treaty with him on equal terms, ‡ and the Hittites recognized him as "a mighty prince among us." § His son and grandson succeeded probably to his wealth and position, and a large body of retainers would thus

---

* See Maine's *Ancient Law*. † Gen. xiv. 14.
‡ *Ib.* xxi. 22–32. § *Ib.* xxiii. 6.

have gone down with the flocks and herds of Jacob and his sons to the land of Goshen. But there the tribe, or rather the collection of tribes, developed into a nation under extraordinary circumstances. They were a servile people, and when Moses appeared as their deliverer and lawgiver, it was under a special and temporary Divine commission. He made no attempt to become the founder of a dynasty, and his sons were simply ordinary Levites among their brethren. It was necessary that there should be a general to lead the hosts of Israel in the conquest of the land, and accordingly Joshua, chosen from another tribe, was selected to be in so far the successor of Moses. But this also was a merely temporary appointment, and at Joshua's death the tribes of Israel were left with no visible earthly head, to live under the immediate government of God. Everything in their national polity was made to symbolize the fact that they were a kingdom under an invisible and Divine King. The bond of unity among their tribes, that which alone constituted them a single nation, was their common and united worship of Jehovah and obedience to His laws. In so far as they neglected this, they fell apart into a mere collection of independent and sometimes warring tribes. In all grave questions of national concern they were to ask the counsel of their invisible Governor by the Urim and Thummim worn by the high-priest. The very tenure of their land was not in fee simple, but as tenants of the one Lord, to whom the soil belonged, and to whom they were to render its first fruits and tithes. So Israel started on their national existence as a kingdom under the direct and immediate government of an invisible and Almighty King.

But as Israel had failed of its high vocation to be unto God "a kingdom of priests," and it had become necessary to consecrate a special order of priests; so also they failed in the other part of their vocation to be "an holy nation."* For some centuries temporary expedients were made use of to bridge over the difficulty. During the whole period of the Judges no other permanent form of government was given them than that to which they had been called, the immediate and direct government of Him who had chosen them to be His people; and when they fell away from Him and were punished for their sin, and then turned again to Him in penitence, special deliverers were raised up from time to time, always, however, as the human agents of the invisible King, and responsible to Him for the exercise of their powers.

At last the people tired of this uncertain and variable condition and asked an earthly king, that they might be "like all the nations." † It was a faithless request, and God declared that in making it, "they have rejected Me, that I should not reign over them." ‡ Yet, while they thus put aside the higher condition designed for them, the lower one which they sought was better suited to their necessities, as long as they persisted in their sinfulness. God, therefore, granted them a king, not as an absolute earthly monarch, but as holding his office only on the condition of obedience to His will, and

---

* Ex. xix. 6. † 1 Sam. viii. 6–20. ‡ *Ib.* viii. 7.

of being His earthly representative. Israel was still to be a theocracy; only the form and the instrument of the Divine government was to be changed. Their real King was still the invisible Monarch on high; the earthly king was chosen and anointed by His command, and always held responsible to Him. The first monarch, Saul, was accordingly set aside for disobedience, and another chosen who should be "a man after God's heart." During the following reign the idea of the theocracy was made prominent, and David constantly sought to order the affairs of the kingdom as directed from on high. The earthly glory of the kingdom of Israel reached its zenith under Solomon, and was then arrested, for he, intoxicated by his power, prosperity and wealth, more and more aimed to change the theocracy to a worldly empire. As soon as the end of its existence was forgotten, the kingdom itself was doomed, and under his successor was broken in two. Ten of the tribes revolted and set up for themselves a petty state, given over to idolatry, and this, after a short checkered existence, became a prey to the more powerful heathen kingdoms around. It was at last destroyed utterly, and its people carried into captivity by Assyria, and it appears no more upon the page of history. The smaller southern kingdom always retained, with more or less distinctness, the idea of the theocracy; the people believed that they were God's people, and that whoever might be their earthly king, he was but the servant of the Lord of Hosts. This belief was never wholly lost, though many of their kings were exceedingly wicked, and

THE KINGDOM OF GOD.

even idolatrous; but it became at last, to a great extent, degraded into a mere national superstition, overclouded with all ungodliness of living, and, therefore, the terrible chastening of the Babylonian captivity became necessary for the purification of the people. Then they were taught the lesson of the "stone cut without hands," which smote the image of all earthly power and sovereignty until it was "broken to pieces together, and became like the chaff of the summer threshing floors." *

Thus, under whatever form of government, and however unfaithful to their calling, Israel was never allowed to lose the knowledge of an invisible King, and of a kingdom which under His almighty sway must finally replace all earthly power. If they still thought of this under the forms of worldly glory and with the characteristics of a temporal monarchy, it was because their earth-bound minds could rise no higher; but the main fact of a kingdom which is God's, and which at last should embrace all the earth, was firmly planted in their minds, to be spiritualized and glorified by the teaching of the Gospel.

There was another promise made to Israel which combined with this expectation of a future universal kingdom under the invisible King, and did much to give it, in the minds at least of the more devout and thoughtful, a peculiar character. The nation had been originally selected as the special depositary of the promise that the Seed of the woman should "bruise the serpent's head,"† and Abraham had been called that in his seed all the families of the earth

---

* Dan. ii. 34, 35. † Gen. iii. 15.

should be blessed. As the promise of the future kingdom became more clear and definite in the mouths of the prophets, this other and earlier promise was ever blended with it, and especially was this the case after it was announced that the future King should be of the seed of David. There was not only, therefore, an expectation of a future universal kingdom, but that this kingdom should in some way heal the woes of earth and overcome the power by which man had been brought under the dominion of evil. Dazzled as the eyes of the carnally minded Jews were by their visions of the earthly glory of the Messianic kingdom, those who thought seriously upon the matter could not but perceive that a kingdom, foretold as a deliverance of mankind from the power of evil, must needs contain more than the elements of earthly greatness. Only a kingdom with spiritual power could fulfil that which was promised.

Still further: when we come down to the ages of prophecy, many of the predictions of the Messianic kingdom are of a distinctly spiritual character, impossible of fulfilment by any merely earthly empire. One cannot read Isaiah without observing how constantly from beginning to end, in the earlier and the latter part alike, the promise of the future is the promise of the forgiveness of sin and the establishment of righteousness. "I will .... purely purge away thy dross, and take away all thy tin .... Zion shall be redeemed with judgment, and her converts with righteousness," * is the key-note of the whole book. " In that day shall the Branch of the Lord be beau-

---

* Isa. i. 25-27.

tiful and glorious, ... when the Lord shall have washed away the filth of the daughters of Zion, and shall have purged the blood of Jerusalem from the midst thereof by the spirit of judgment, and by the spirit of burning." * In that beautiful prophecy of the "Rod out of the stem of Jesse," it is declared that "the Spirit of the Lord shall rest upon Him, ... the Spirit of knowledge and of the fear of the Lord;" and in consequence there shall be universal happiness and peace, "for the earth shall be full of the knowledge of the Lord as the waters cover the sea." † The promise of "the precious Corner stone" to be laid in Zion is always with the assurance, "Judgment also will I lay to the line, and righteousness to the plummet."‡ The future "king shall reign in righteousness;" "Judgment shall dwell in the wilderness, and righteousness remain in the fruitful field." § God declares to Israel, "I am He that blotteth out thy trangressions for mine own sake, and will not remember thy sins." ‖ And again, "I have blotted out as a thick cloud thy transgressions, and, as a cloud, thy sins." ¶ But to quote all the passages to the same effect in Isaiah would be to transcribe a large part of the book.** The latter part of the fifty-second and the whole of the fifty-third chapter are occupied with the prophecy of the removal of sin by the vicarious sufferings of the Lord's servant. ††

---

* Isa. iv. 2, 4.   † *Ib.* xi. 1–9.   ‡ *Ib.* xxviii. 16, 17.
§ *Ib.* xxxii. 1, 16.   ‖ *Ib.* xliii. 25.   ¶ *Ib.* xliv. 22.
** See *e. g.* Isa. xxvi. 2, 3, 12, 13; xxvii. 9; xxix. 19–24; xxxiii. 5, 14, 15, 24; xlii. 1–4, 6; xliii. 25; xliv. 22; xlv. 8; xlvi. 12, 13; lvii. 15–18; lviii. 6, 7; lx. 21; lxi. 8.   †† *Ib.* lii. 13–liii. 12.

And always the promise that "the Redeemer shall come to Zion" is qualified expressly or implicitly by the explanation, "unto them that turn from transgression in Jacob." *

Isaiah's contemporaries, Hosea † and Micah, speak in the same strain. "He will have compassion upon us; He will subdue our iniquities: and Thou wilt cast all our sins into the depth of the sea." ‡

Passing on to the later period of Jeremiah, the hope held out to the people of God was still the same. The promise of the new covenant is still, "I will forgive their iniquity and remember their sin no more;" § "I will cleanse them from all their iniquity, whereby they have sinned against me." ‖ Ezekiel declares, "I will put a new spirit within you, and I will take away the stony heart out of their flesh . . . . that they may walk in my statutes and keep mine ordinances." ¶ And again, "I will sprinkle clean water upon you, and ye shall be clean. . . . . A new heart also will I give you . . . . and I will put my Spirit within you, and cause you to walk in my statutes." ** His prophecy of the purifying waters from the sanctuary is familiar. †† Daniel foretells the "seventy weeks determined upon thy people . . . . to finish the transgression, and to make an end of sins, and to make reconciliation for iniquity, and to bring in everlasting righteousness." ‡‡ The prophets of the return from the captivity, to the last dwell upon the same hope. Zechariah says, "In that day

---

* Is. lix. 20. † Hos. xiv. 4. ‡ Mic. vii. 19.
§ Jer. xxxi. 34. ‖ *Ib.* xxxiii. 8. ¶ Ezek. xi. 19.
** Ezek. xxxvi. 25–27. †† *Ib.* xlvii. 1–12. ‡‡ Dan: ix. 24.

there shall be a fountain opened to the house of David and to the inhabitants of Jerusalem for sin and for uncleanness.* And Malachi declares that "the Messenger of the covenant" shall be "like a refiner's fire and like fuller's soap;" † and so crying is the need of this purification, that before the " Sun of Righteousness arise with healing in His wings," and "the coming of the great and dreadful day of the Lord," Elijah the prophet must be sent to "turn the heart of the fathers to the children . . . . lest I come and smite the earth with a curse." ‡

These teachings of the prophets are extremely frequent, and are associated and interwoven with all their promise of the Messianic kingdom. It was to be a universal empire under an invisible and almighty monarch, the abode of righteousness, and therefore all sin must be purged away from its citizens. Its Head should be manifested on earth as the Redeemer who should bruise the serpent's head, the Seed of Abraham in whom all the families of the earth should be blessed, the King of the house of David unto whom the people should be holy to the Lord in heart and life.

The people, therefore, showed no surprise at the preaching of John the Baptist, "Repent ye, for the kingdom of heaven is at hand." § However the idea of the kingdom may have been overlaid in the popular mind by gross and sensual expectations, underneath there ever lay the prophetic representations calling for true and earnest repentance as the kingdom was announced to be near. When our Lord

---

* Zech. xiii. 9. † Mal. iii. 1, 2. ‡ *Ib.* iv. 2–6. § Matt. iii. 2.

Himself took up the same words the people were prepared for them, and "the kingdom of heaven" or "of God" was no new idea. It is noticeable that our Lord, during His life on earth, never says that it has come, but always that it is near, has touched * you. More He could not say until the cross had been reared on Calvary, the bars of the tomb burst, and He had returned to the glory He had with the Father before the world was. Yet His coming brought the kingdom, and when His work was completed it was established forever, though but as the mustard seed, to grow and spread through the ages, or as the leaven to diffuse its influence little by little until the whole lump should be leavened. Most of His parables were spoken to illustrate the nature and character of that kingdom. Not a line of its features is at variance with the prophetic descriptions, but there is much to make these more distinct and to clear away popular misapprehensions. Still, while He lived on earth, these could not be entirely removed, and to the last moment even His chosen disciples showed the confusion yet remaining in their minds by the question, " Lord, wilt Thou at this time restore again the kingdom to Israel." † Our Lord had indeed taught them, in answer to a question of the Pharisees, "The kingdom of God cometh not with observation: neither shall they say, Lo here! or lo there! for behold the kingdom of God is within you ;" ‡ but they were not

---

* ἔφθασεν.   † Acts, i. 6.

‡ Luke, xvii. 20, 21. *Within*, and not *among*, is the right translation, both because of the proper meaning of ἐντός, and because our Lord never speaks of His kingdom as already established.

prepared to understand its spiritual character. It was not until after they had been enlightened by the gift of the Holy Ghost that they could teach "we must through much tribulation enter into the kingdom of God,"* that they realized that this kingdom "is not meat and drink; but righteousness, and peace, and joy in the Holy Ghost;"† "that flesh and blood cannot inherit the kingdom of God;"‡ that only by the cultivation of a proper character and life "an entrance shall be ministered unto you abundantly into the everlasting kingdom of our Lord and Saviour Jesus Christ;"§ and only then could they thankfully and exultingly feel that the promise was already fulfilled, and that God "HATH translated us into the kingdom of His dear Son," ‖ and exhort their fellow disciples, "wherefore we receiving a kingdom which cannot be moved, let us have grace whereby we may serve God acceptably." ¶ So far the description of the kingdom was common to both Dispensations; but this was necessarily set forth under the earlier in figures and images which the carnally minded perverted into the expectation of a vast temporal dominion, in which the chosen people should bear earthly sway over all the nations of the world. Not until the revelation of the Gospel could it be made entirely clear that the promised kingdom of the Redeemer was "not of this world," ** but should be established in the hearts of His disciples. Yet the prophets had all along taught the same truth as clearly as was practicable in their

---

*Acts, xiv. 22.   †Rom. xiv. 17.   ‡1 Cor. xv. 50.   §2 Pet. i. 11.
‖Col. i. 13.   ¶Heb. xii. 28.   **John, xviii. 36.

times. Certain differences in the representation were to be expected. Even in the New Testament the kingdom of God is set forth in somewhat different aspects by the various writers. St. Matthew delights to dwell upon it as the fulfilment and consummation of the Old Dispensation, given to the chosen people; St. Luke, as a universal kingdom, designed from the first for all mankind. Both aspects are true, and neither of them excludes the other.

The relation between the two Covenants in their presentation of the kingdom of God, was the same as has been observed in regard to everything else; there was one essential idea underlying both, and this idea was taught of old in such wise as to prepare for its fuller development and realization under the Gospel. The long promised victory over the power of evil should then be accomplished, and perfect peace and communion between God and man be restored.

In this, as in other matters, the prophets occupied a very peculiar and important position under the Old Dispensation. Their predictions of the future formed but a small part of their function. They were not recognized by the law as an established order, nor were their duties in any way prescribed. Nevertheless, they are found in every period of Israel's history, and under Samuel schools of them were established, which appear to have continued for centuries, since they are mentioned in the times of Elijah* and Elisha.† They were often especially

---

* 2 Kings, ii. 3, 5, 15. † *Ib* iv. 1, 38; vi. 1; ix. 1, etc.

divinely called to their office, sometimes from these schools, sometimes from the priesthood, as in the case of Jeremiah and Ezekiel, and sometimes from the common people.* Their duty was to declare, both to the kings and to the people, the will of God. This was communicated to them by special revelation when there was occasion; but sometimes, as in the case of Samuel's answer to the people asking for a king,† or of Nathan's approval of David's purpose to build the temple, ‡ they spoke from their own sense of right, and were divinely required to reverse their first opinion. In general, they were the spiritual counsellors of the nation, and the expounders of the revelations already made. They thus in so far foreshadowed and were the precursors of the Christian ministry, and " Prophets " became a common name of the religious teachers of the New Covenant; still they had no special spiritual care of particular portions of the people, and the "cure of souls" involved in parochial organizations is a special feature of Christianity. Yet, in the constant proclamation of the Messianic kingdom as a kingdom of righteousness, and of the necessity of repentance as a preparation for its coming, may be seen something of the importance of their office in the relation of the Old Dispensation to the New.

It is to be remembered that the kingdom of God, whether under the Old or the New Dispensation, is always represented in the Scriptures as based upon a Covenant between God and man. It is never re-

---

* Amos, vii. 14, 15.   † 1 Sam. viii. 6, 7.
‡ 2 Sam. vii. 3, 8-12; 1 Chron. xvii. 2, 4.

garded as a rule imposed by almighty power upon unconscious or unwilling subjects. The service which is acceptable to God must ever be a free-will service, and because it is a service of the heart and of the will, St. James describes it as "the perfect law of liberty," * and the Collect addresses God as one "Whose service is perfect freedom." † The very name by which the records of both Dispensations are known, and by which the Old is repeatedly called in the New, is "Covenant." We have long been accustomed to use the word "Testament," but "covenant" is the proper force of the original word, ‡ and conveys the idea sanctioned by God Himself. It was a "Covenant" which He made with Noah, § with Abraham, ‖ Isaac, ¶ and Jacob, ** and with their descendants at the giving of the law. ††

It is true that St. Peter at the council of Jerusalem speaks of this law as "a yoke upon the neck of the disciples which neither our fathers nor we were able to bear;" ‡‡ and St. Paul describes it as "the weak and beggarly elements," §§ and again as

---

* James, i. 25.
† Collect for Peace in the Book of Common Prayer.
‡ Heb. בְּרִית, Gr. διαθήκη.
§ Gen. vi. 18; ix. 9, 12, 13, 15, 16.
‖ Gen. xv. 18; xvii. 2, 9; Luke, i. 72; Acts, iii. 25; Gal. iii. 17.
¶ Gen. xvii. 19; xxvi. 3.
** Ex. ii. 24; vi. 4; 1 Chron. xvi. 17.
†† Ex vi. 4; xix. 5; xxiv. 7, 8; xxxiv. 27; Lev. xxvi. 9, 25, 42, 44, 45; Deut. v. 2; ix. 9; xxix. 1, 12, 14; Judg. ii. 1; Jer. xi. 1; xxxi, 31–33.
‡‡ Acts, xv. 10. §§ Gal. iv. 9.

the covenant "from the Mount Sinai, which gendereth to bondage,"* and still again, as "the enmity, even the law of commandments contained in ordinances."† Such must ever be the relation of the "schoolmaster" undertaking to continue his discipline over the full grown man who has passed beyond his pupilage. That which was good for the child becomes intolerable and prejudicial to the man. Nevertheless, there had been a time of childhood in the history of God's people, and that which was good for them then must afterwards be put away; and so the same St. Paul speaks of the "commandment which was ordained to life," although, through sin, it was "found to be unto death," and declares that "the law is holy, and the commandment holy, and just and good," and adds, "we know that the law is spiritual."‡

The relation therefore of the law to the Gospel was not one of contradiction, but of preparation. Opposition arose between them only when this relation was neglected and an attempt made to continue preparatory precepts and customs after their purpose and consummation had been revealed. The scaffolding, however necessary while the building was in progress, became unsightly and inconvenient when the edifice stood complete, and those who would still maintain it, mar the plans of the Divine Architect.

But the fact must be emphasized that the law, while it remained, was a covenant. Certainly the command was from God, and the people were bound

---

* Gal. iv. 24. † Eph. ii. 15. ‡ Rom. vii. 10, 12, 14.

to obey it, but this would be true of all mankind. St. Paul shows at length in his Epistle to the Romans* that there is a certain knowledge of the Divine Being and of His will among all men, and that they are guilty before Him in refusing their obedience to this. But the obligation of the chosen people was something more than that of the heathen. They had received a fuller revelation, a clearer knowledge of duty, and had entered into solemn covenant of obedience. This covenant, originally made by the fathers, was expressly renewed to each child of Israel in the sacrament of circumcision, and, in his maturer years, in the Passover and other institutions of the Mosaic economy. The difference in this respect between Judaism and Christianity was that the former was the exclusive privilege of a chosen nation, the latter is the universal blessing of mankind. But both were covenants. The kingdom of heaven is in the hearts of men ; and they who truly serve God, serve Him with a "reasonable service," † with a service of the heart and the affections which must ever be perfect freedom.

It remains to say a word upon the worship of the older church in its relation to Christian worship ; for worship, whether on earth or in heaven, must ever be one of the characteristics of the kingdom of God. In this a marked and blessed progress may be observed corresponding to the progress of revelation in all other respects.

Private worship in praise and prayer and confession has necessarily been essentially the same in all

---

* Rom. i, 18-32.   † *Ib.* xii. 1.

ages, except as modified by the indwelling of that "Spirit of adoption, whereby we cry Abba, Father,"* and by the clearer knowledge of the Father's will, and of the redemption that is in His Son. Of this private worship, there is no occasion to speak. But the public and collective worship of men has greatly changed. There is no record of any other social or public worship in the earliest times than in connection with the offering of sacrifices. When the places where these might be offered came to be limited to those which God should "choose to place His name there," or to a single place, as while the tabernacle was standing and again after the temple was built, such sacrificial worship must have been impossible to the great mass of the people except on rare occasions. When Israel became more strongly knit together as a nation and settled down to peaceful pursuits, the need of some more frequent common worship was likely to be felt. The Sabbath had been from the first enjoined as a day of rest from labor, and some of its hours were probably improved in the family and then in the neighborhood in recounting to the children the wonderful works wrought for the fathers. To this, after sacred poetry had been multiplied, would naturally be joined the chanting, in concert or responsively, the national hymns of prayer and praise. Such worship would have been usually in the open air and altogether informal and occasional.

It was not until after the return from the captivity that synagogues began to be erected, administered

---

* Rom. viii. 15.

with order and regularity, and a stated, non-sacrificial, worship instituted, with prayer, the reading of the sacred word, singing, and occasional exhortation. These synagogues were still in process of multiplication at the time of the Christian era.* In them much of our Lord's teaching was given,† and some of His mighty works were wrought.‡ They afforded an opportunity for the first promulgation of the Gospel by the Apostles, not only in Judea, but in all the cities of the Roman Empire where the Jews had congregated. Here also Gentiles were reached who had come in to attend the Jewish worship.§

The worship of the synagogue was naturally the prototype of that of the Christian Church. This was especially true of the Jews, of whom the Church was at first exclusively composed, and scarcely less so of the earlier converts from the Gentiles, who were chiefly gathered from those who attended the Jewish worship. Christian worship rested, not upon daily typical and imperfect sacrifices, but upon the one perfect Sacrifice accomplished once for all; and it was designed, not for a peculiar nation having an earthly centre, but for all mankind who should "worship God in spirit and in truth." It was therefore free from all local limitations, and hence it was assimilated to the synagogue rather than to the temple worship.

The worship of "the kingdom of God" under

---

* Luke, vii. 5.

† Matt. iv. 23 ; ix. 35 ; xiii. 54 ; Mark, i. 21, 39 ; Luke, iv. 15 ; John, vi. 59, etc.

‡ Matt. xii. 9-13 ; Luke, iv. 33-35, etc.   § Acts, xiii. 42-43.

both the Old and the New Dispensations has at once a retrospective and a prospective character; but in the Old, the retrospective element had respect to the preparatory stages of the history and teaching of the people of God, and the prospective to the coming of the promised Redeemer. In the New, the retrospective element is that which was prospective of old, and the prospective looks forward only to the perfect consummation of what has already begun. This change of that which was hoped for into that which has already been realized, involves a much larger development of present privilege and blessing. Already " God hath given to us eternal life, and this life is in His Son. He that hath the Son hath life."* We are already made members of the kingdom; we have already " passed from death unto life;" we already have "the earnest of the Spirit in our hearts;" † and that which is still future is not a wholly new life, but the development and perfecting of that which is already begun. Even now we are taught by the Spirit of adoption to call Him who rules on high, " Abba, Father." ‡

From the progress thus made results another change. The consciousness of the brotherhood of all who have received this Spirit in their hearts creates a new necessity for common prayer, and gives new zest and meaning to common worship. They who partake together of the same redemption, they who share the same life of the Spirit, they who have the same common hope, and are to worship

---

* 1 John, iv. 11, 12.   † 2 Cor. i. 22, cf. v. 5; Eph. i. 14.
‡ Rom. viii. 15; Gal. iv. 6.

hereafter before the same throne, have need also here in their earthly pilgrimage of a common worship.

The difference between the dispensations in this respect may be a difference of degree rather than of kind; still it is a very marked and real difference. As there was "life and immortality" of old, but it was Christ who, by abolishing death, "brought these to light;"* so there was a common membership in the Church of their fathers, but it is only under the Gospel that we are made to realize that "we, being many, are one body in Christ, and every one members one of another." † Of old, there was a strong community of feeling between all who were descended from Abraham; but it rested upon this natural descent, and was hardly extended even to "the proselyte of the gate," though he worshipped with the chosen people. Now, our common prayers, confession and praise, our common baptism and participation in the one bread, continually emphasize the fact that we are all one body in Christ, who is our brother. "For we, being many, are one bread and one body: for we are all partakers of that one bread." ‡ It is in view of the narrow nationality of the Old Dispensation that St. Paul teaches the unity and common brotherhood of all the members of the New: "Ye are .... fellow citizens with the saints and of the household of God, and are built upon the foundation of the apostles and prophets, Jesus Christ Himself being the chief corner-stone: in Whom all the building fitly framed together groweth into an

---

* 2 Tim. i. 10. † Rom. xii. 5. ‡ 1 Cor. x. 17.

holy temple in the Lord; in Whom ye also are builded together for an habitation of God through the Spirit." *

The worship, therefore, of the Church, the kingdom of God, brings out the same relation of progress from the Old to the New which has been seen everywhere. The extension and advance is so great that we are tempted to forget that its beginnings are to be found in the soil of the Old Dispensation. Christian worship brings out in strong relief the idea of Christian brotherhood. But, above all, we are brought nearer to God, and come to Him, not as the Almighty Ruler, the distant Sovereign of the skies, but in and through Christ we are taught to call Him "Our Father which art in heaven."

---

* Eph. ii. 19-22.

LECTURE VIII.

PROPHECY.

PROPHECY etymologically, and in the scriptural use of the word, means any utterance on God's behalf; but it will be treated here only in that more restricted sense which is confined to the prediction of the future.

True prophecy necessarily involves the supernatural and miraculous, and its existence is therefore denied by all who regard our religion as a mere human development. With such there need here be no argument; our differences with them must be discussed on a larger field. But many who profess to admit these things yet deny the existence of really predictive prophecies, and the controversy on this point, always more or less active, has been intensified through the discussions of the most modern so-called critical school. The first point must therefore be to establish the fact of prophecy. Its opponents have generally narrowed down the question to this statement: the existence of prophecy will be established by any instance in which any definite event, incapable of being foreseen by human sagacity, has been foretold at a time certainly before the event; but without such instance it cannot be admitted, for want of any sufficient proof of its existence. There is other and further proof of prophecy; but for the present this demand of its opponents may be accepted. It is not to be denied that there are difficulties in this, because the critics generally assume that the very existence of such a prophecy as they require is in itself proof of the lateness of the book in which it is contained, or at least of its interpolation. Yet, while they thus reject in advance all ordinary sources of proof, there remains an abundance which cannot be gainsaid. I select only three instances— which is three times as much as is demanded.

The first is the prophecy of Micah: "But thou, Bethlehem Ephratah, though thou be little among the thousands of Judah, yet out of thee shall He come forth unto Me that is to be Ruler in Israel, Whose goings forth have been from of old, from everlasting."* There is here no question of the date of the prophet as in the eighth century before the Christian era, and there is no suggestion of interpolation, since in view of the statement of the royal commission appointed by Herod, this, if possible, must have been too early to affect the argument. The interpretation was settled in the most public and formal manner before the fulfilment was known. In answer to the question of the Magi, "Where is he that is born king of the Jews?" the king appointed a commission of inquiry, composed of "all the chief priests and scribes of the people," and they replied, on the express ground of this prophecy, "in Bethlehem." † If the Gospel of St. Matthew be accepted as historically reliable, there

---
* Micah, v. 2. † Matt. ii. 1–6,

remains but one possible way of escaping the force of this prophecy. It may be said that as the Messiah was expected to be David's son (an expectation itself resting on previous prophecy), the prophet might have simply thought it probable that He would be born in David's town. This is not likely. David early left Bethlehem and made Jerusalem his royal city. So far as human sagacity could have foreseen, his great descendant would certainly be born there. But independently of this fact, there is another independent and seemingly contradictory prophecy which must be considered in connection with this. In Isaiah (ix. 1, 2) it is declared that the despised land of Zebulon and Naphtali shall be greatly honored and shall see a great light. This was fulfilled, and fulfilled only, by the long residence and mighty works there of our Lord. Here, then, are two prophecies, one of the birth of the Messiah at Bethlehem, the other of His residence in the outcast region of Galilee. It is inconceivable that human sagacity could have foreseen both of these things.

The other two instances I have selected because their fulfilment is not distinctly recorded in Scripture, and therefore there can be no possible question of an attempt to bring prophecy and fulfilment into accord. The first of them occurs in Jacob's dying benediction upon the twelve tribes.* The date of this has indeed been disputed, and some critics have assigned it to the time of David; but this has been done on purely internal grounds of such slight value as not to seem entitled to consid-

---

* Gen. xlix. 7.

eration. We assume that any fair examination of its contents shows that it must have been written before the settlement of the tribes in Canaan, which is all that is necessary for our purpose. Here, then, it is said of Simeon and Levi, " I will divide them in Jacob, and scatter them in Israel." There is no difficulty in regard to Levi. The prophecy, however, was fulfilled in a very different sense from that which the speaker expected. He describes this scattering as a punishment on these tribes for the sins of their fathers, and it is quite impossible that it could have been put in this way by a writer living after the selection of the tribe of Levi to the honor of ministrants of the sanctuary. Nevertheless, in his case the prophecy was literally carried out; Levi had no inheritance among the other tribes, but occupied cities scattered among them all. Only, in consequence of the noble stand taken by the members of this tribe in a critical rebellion in the wilderness, the curse was transformed into a blessing. About Simeon nothing is anywhere said of the fulfilment of the prophecy; but we have the following facts which show that it must have been fulfilled in accordance with its original intent. In the division of the land among the tribes the portion assigned to Simeon was at the extreme south, the southern part of the district originally given to Judah.* This territory was at the time sufficiently fertile, as is evidenced by the remains still existing there; † but is now a desolate wilderness, habitable

---
* Josh. xix. 1–9.
† See Palmer's *Desert of the Exodus;* Trumbull's *Kadesh-Barnea*

only by nomads. The change has been brought about by the destruction of the works for irrigation and the gradual drying up of the country; and this appears to have set in at an early date, since in the time of Saul and of David the region was inhabited by Amalekites and a few of the Kenites. Simeon is not at all mentioned in the account of the various campaigns in that region, and in part had already left it.* It is certain that a little later, when the kingdom was divided, Simeon, as a tribe, joined his fortunes with the "ten tribes," the northern kingdom, which would have been impossible if his territory had been separated from them by the whole breadth of Judah and Benjamin. He had then left his original inheritance and gone north. But where could he have gone? The whole land was already in the possession and occupation of the other tribes. He could only have been divided and scattered among them. Human sagacity could not have foreseen this, nor how precisely the same prophecy in regard to Simeon and to Levi should have been carried out in such totally different ways and with such opposite results.

The remaining prophecy to which I referred belongs to the New Testament, and was uttered by our Lord Himself. Formerly the doubt was urged whether it might not have been written after the event; but the result of searching criticism has been to establish a general conviction of its priority. The prophecy (Matt. xxiv. 15–22) refers to the destruction of Jerusalem by the Roman army, and contains a warning to escape from the horrors of its siege

---

* 1 Chr. iv. 31, 39–43.

and capture. It happened that after the investment of the city there was a temporary suspension of the siege, and the followers of our Lord, warned by this prophecy, escaped to the little town of Pella and were delivered. The Jews who did not accept His authority remained and suffered the woes He had predicted. Here again is a definite prophecy, understood and acted upon before the event.

There are also other reasons why we must either accept the fact of prophecy or else regard the prophets as conscious deceivers. Kuenen and his school have endeavored to show that the prophets did not conceive themselves as really foretelling future events, but merely as clothing their teaching in the form of prophecy for the purpose of impressing it more strongly upon the minds of the people. No one, however, can read the latter part of Isaiah, especially chaps. xlv.–xlviii., without seeing that the declaration beforehand of that which is to be hereafter is set forth as a proof of the omniscience and supremacy of God. It is the test which the Almighty has chosen, by which men may try His claim to their allegiance.

There are some prophecies, like those of Ezekiel, forming a series continued through a considerable space of time. The central point of this series in Ezekiel is the destruction of the temple and city of the Jews by Nebuchadnezzar. Some of his prophecies profess to have been uttered before this event and are filled with warnings in view of its approach; others are uttered afterwards, and are occupied with exhortations based upon its accomplishment. Many of these prophecies are distinctly dated. Is it conceivable that such a series, unless true, could be given without intentional deceit?

Again: there are great and broad prophecies, such as that of the coming of the Redeemer, which underlie the whole Old Testament economy, which human sagacity only foresaw in the most dim and vague way as it was enlightened by the tradition of the primeval promises, yet which have been fulfilled, and on their fulfilment rests the whole structure of our religion.

It may, therefore, be fairly considered as a settled point that the Scriptures are committed to the assertion that future events are therein predicted. This has been so understood by the vast mass of their readers in all ages; it is the express declaration, often repeated, of the New Testament writers concerning the prophecies of old; and it can only be set aside by a critical subtilty in plain violation of the dictates of common sense.

The next question, and the only other one which needs to be here considered, is, How were these prophecies given? To this the answer must be, in various ways. (1) By distinct utterances plainly declaring in so many words what was to be hereafter. Of this there are very many instances; but it is altogether immaterial whether the language of the prophecy be couched in terms of the future, or whether its character of futurity is left to be understood from the connection and the circumstances under which it was spoken. Of the former many examples will at once occur to the mind, as Mal. iv. 5 : " Behold I will send you Elijah the prophet, before the coming of the great and dreadful day of the Lord." Gen. xlix. 10: " The sceptre shall not depart from Judah, nor a lawgiver from between his feet, until Shiloh come," and many others. Of the latter, a marked instance is in Ps. cx. 1, where the words in their mere form give no indication of futurity, but the idea " The Lord said unto my lord " could only be realized in something far beyond any present experience.

(2) But it results from the essential connection between the Old and the New Dispensations that many other ways of foreshadowing the future must have been open to the preparatory covenant. Prominent among these must have been all those institutions and ordinances which were in their nature temporary, but given for the express purpose of leading men to their perfect and sufficient realization in the future. Among these the institutions of sacrifice and of the priesthood hold the most prominent place and have already been treated at length. They were necessarily and from their very nature prophetic, and are constantly so regarded in the New Testament. We must suppose these to have been prominent in that teaching of our Lord to the two disciples on the way to Emmaus, when, " Beginning at Moses and all the prophets, He expounded unto them in all the Scriptures the things concerning Himself." *

(3) Closely connected with this are those particular acts and events on the border-land between prophecies and types which have been fitly called prophetic types. In some of these there was a

---

* Luke, xxiv. 27.

direct teaching of the people to whom they were given of the truths afterwards to be more fully revealed in the Gospel. Thus by the manna in the wilderness Israel was taught "that man doth not live by bread alone, but by every word that proceedeth out of the mouth of God."* This may be called a prophecy in act of the support afterwards to be furnished from God to sustain His Church in its wanderings through the wilderness of the world. It is not to be supposed that the people of old could have understood the prophetic force of such acts, except in so far as they learned by them truths which were afterwards to be more clearly revealed. In some cases, as in that of Jonah,† there is no reason to suppose the event could have suggested to the people of the time anything in the future; and it becomes prophetic only when made so by being established in the New Testament times as a sign. There are few, if any other, instances of this class.

(4) All those parts of the Sinaitic legislation which were of an educational character were necessarily prophetic, in the same sense in which all education is prophetic, of the ends which it is given to subserve; only in this case the ends were divinely proposed and certain to be accomplished. The prophetic character in this case may not be distinctly recognized by those who are under the training, but is clearly seen when it has done its work, and may then be referred to in its true import.

(5) The same thing is true of a history leading

---

* Matt. iv. 4.   † *Ib.* xii. 39, 40; xvi. 4.

up to a fore-ordained end, declared from the beginning. As each stage of that history is unrolled in the course of time, it becomes prophetic of the end towards which it is leading. Its purport is clear in proportion as that end is distinctly seen; but its full prophetic value becomes obvious only in its consummation. Hence in this, as in some other methods, prophecy is only seen in its full value when looked back upon from the times of the New Testament, and it is plain that much might then be truly claimed as prophecy which had been only dimly, or not at all, recognized in that character while it was actually transpiring. This is necessarily true of secular as well as of sacred history. In both the guiding hand of the Lord of all is seen overruling all things to the accomplishment of His purposes. Could we, too, see the end from the beginning, we should see that, as each event advances one step towards the destined end, it is prophetic of that end; and this we can see, in looking back upon the past, in so far as the Divine purposes have been unfolded to our sight. In the prevalence of Greek culture and literature under the successors of Alexander, and in the wide subjection of the world to the sway of imperial Rome, we can see the preparation for, and therefore the prophecy of, an universal religion. This kind of prophecy is not unlike what are often described as the prophecies of nature. The earlier stages of creation were arranged to lead to the later, and were therefore prophetic of them. The so-called "comprehensive type" was prophetic of the several more specialized genera into which it should afterwards be divided. The bud is prophetic of the flower and the fruit. The embryo is prophetic of the child, and the child of the man.

(6) From the relations existing between the kingdom of God and the opposing world, always essentially the same, much that was declared of them at any one time must necessarily be true at all times. Hence, what was said of these of old, and of the actors in them, especially of David as the head of the theocracy, is prophetic of the Church of Christ and its Head; not prophetic in the sense that the words spoken of old had an immediate and direct reference to the future, but that this future reference is necessarily involved in the very nature of the case. Sometimes this future bearing was Divinely pointed out either at the time or afterwards, but still before the great fulfilment, and sometimes it was left to be manifested in the future. Thus the priesthood of Melchisedec did not, in the time of Abraham, necessarily convey the idea of anything beyond; but when, in the time of David, it was declared of his greater descendant, " Thou art a priest forever after the order of Melchisedec," * his priesthood became prophetic of that of Christ. On the other hand, the relation of the child of the bond-maid, Hagar, to that of the child of Sarah, which was by promise, did not in itself show that this relation should be repeated, but only that if such a relation should again occur, the same principles in regard to it would again have place.

---

* Ps. cx. 4.

The striking application given to this truth by St. Paul in his Epistle to the Galatians,* rests upon the fact that the same relation of heirship according to the flesh and heirship according to promise, had recurred in the Jewish and the Christian Church, and therefore that the application of the principle involved in the events of old became prophetic of the application of the same principle, which must always hold.

Such prophetic applications of the history of old are quite common in the New Testament, and although sometimes thoughtlessly made the ground of objections, are evidently perfectly legitimate, and the arguments based upon them are sound and forcible.

Having thus briefly sketched some of the more important forms of prophecy, we must now turn to the New Testament to observe how the prophecies are treated there before we can take up the relation between the two involved in prophecy. Little more will need to be said about the relation when the facts upon which it depends are fairly before us.

First of all, a small number of quotations in the New Testament which have occasioned much controversy, but which really have no bearing on the subject, must be wholly set aside in the present discussion. It is customary, and has been in all ages and among all people, to quote from the Bible or from any other well-known records of the past, passages which fitly describe events of the present, and

---
* Gal. iv. 21–31.

apply them, without any thought of suggesting that these present events were in the view of the writer quoted. How frequently have David's words at the death of Abner, "Know ye not that there is a prince and a great man fallen this day in Israel?"* been applied to the death of some great leader or ruler in our own day, and that oftentimes with the expression, "To-day are these words fulfilled." How many a stirring exhortation to progress in the Christian life has been addressed to those who have just sealed their baptismal vows, from the command to Moses, "Speak to the children of Israel that they go forward." † The application of such passages to our own time is justified, as I have said, by the common consent of devout men in all ages; nor is any one misled by the formula in connection with them, "these words are now fulfilled." Remembering that the New Testament writers were all devout men, familiar all their lives with the Scriptures of the Old Testament, we have no right to cut them off from such a use of the language of the sacred writers— which was common to all their countrymen. Of course such quotations cannot be used argumentatively, to show that any event or truth was foreseen, nor are they ever so used in the New Testament, as any fair interpretation will show. They serve only for illustration, or even for the mere expression of what the writer would say in the familiar words of the sacred books. Why the right of thus using them should be denied to the New Testament writers alone of all mankind, it is hard to understand. Pas-

---

* 2 Sam. iii. 38. † Ex. xiv. 15.

sages of this kind are comparatively infrequent. When they occur, they consist sometimes of a mere use of the words of the Old Testament, without any formula of quotation whatever, as when St. Paul writes to the Corinthians,* "Wherefore come out from among them, and be ye separate, saith the Lord, and touch not the unclean thing, and I will receive you," although this might be classed under the educational precepts mentioned below as having a prophetic character. Sometimes they are introduced with the remark " it is written," as in the First Epistle to the Corinthians: † "Death is swallowed up in victory. Oh death, where is thy sting? O grave, where is thy victory?" and sometimes they have the formulas "thus was fulfilled," or "that it might be fulfilled which was spoken," as when St. Matthew writes, ", Then was fulfilled that which was spoken by Jeremy the prophet, saying, 'In Rama was there a voice heard, lamentation, and weeping, and great mourning : Rachel weeping for her children, and would not be comforted, because they are not.' " ‡

Sometimes, in consequence of the deep underlying connection between the Old and New Dispensations, there are quotations of a doubtful character. They may belong to the class which has just been described, or they may be intended to bring to the light that underlying connection. A marked instance of this occurs only a few verses before the one last cited. Speaking of the sojourn

---

* 2 Cor. vi. 17, 18, cf. Isa. lii. 11.   † 1 Cor xv. 56, cf. Hos. xiii. 14.
‡ Matt. ii. 17, 18, cf. Jer. xxxi. 15.

of the Infant Jesus in Egypt, St. Matthew writes, "That it might be fulfilled which was spoken of the Lord by the prophet, saying, Out of Egypt have I called my Son."* No one can fairly deny the right of the Evangelist to have quoted these words simply as an apt expression of what occurred. Possibly this is all that is meant, but there may also have been a much deeper meaning in his words. There is no doubt that Hosea is here speaking not prophetically, but simply historically of the Exodus of the Israelites from Egypt. But with what propriety does God speak of this people as "My Son"? Because they were His Church, the Body of which the Only Begotten Son was the Head. Their sonship was because they partook of His Sonship. Hence it may well have been that St. Matthew, realizing this fact, felt that the words of Hosea became true in a fuller sense than he knew when the Son Himself incarnate was called out of Egypt.

For our present purpose we may put quite aside all such instances in which the quotation is either a mere use of the Old Testament for illustration, or a simple expression of the writer's thoughts in its language. Only such passages are to be considered as are plainly cited for their prophetic value.

Among these a large number consist of quotations from the Old Testament prophets of distinct expressions foretelling the things of the New. These are familiar and abound in almost every book of the New Testament. Once having recognized prophecy as a part of the Revelation of God, there is no diffi-

---

* Matt. ii. 15. cf. Hos. xi. 1.

culty with these. The prophets of old foretold the things that were to be; the Evangelists and inspired teachers of the Gospel recognized these predictions and told of their fulfilment. Only it is not to be supposed that the New Testament writers have cited all such prophecies. They have mentioned only those which came in their way—those of which the subject they had in hand naturally led them to speak. Others remain for our instruction. The very distinct prophecy of the seventy weeks to be fulfilled before the Messiah's coming, for example, is nowhere quoted; and so of many others. There is no treatise on the fulfilment of prophecy. Only here and there, as their fulfilment happens to be noted, is one and another of the utterances of old called to mind. It is moreover to be observed that the various writers differ much from one another in their habit in this respect, especially in view of the persons for whom they more immediately wrote. St. Matthew and the author of the Epistle to the Hebrews, writing for those always familiar with the older Scriptures, quote from them abundantly; while St. Mark, having in view rather Romans, little interested in Jewish literature, after the first few verses of his Gospel, does not from beginning to end make a single quotation of his own from the Old Testament; while St. John, with his deep spirituality, delights to cite prophecies which only become clear after some reflection upon the deeper meaning of the words uttered of old.

Next to these citations of direct prophetic utterances come the references to the institutions of the

Old Testament as declaring beforehand those of the New. The most prominent instances of this are in the Epistle to the Hebrews, and these are accompanied with a full and sufficient argument to show how and why they were prophetic. In regard to the sacrifices, for example, it is shown that since they were insufficient in themselves for the accomplishment of their purpose, and yet established the principle that "without shedding of blood is no remission" of sin, they necessarily made it manifest that there should be a sufficient sacrifice; and this having been so perfectly fulfilled in the offering of Christ "once for all," it was to His sacrifice and to His alone that they pointed. The Aaronic priesthood is treated in the same way, as looking forward to a better and enduring priesthood after the order of Melchisedec. But there are many other passages in the New Testament in which only passing allusion is made to the institutions of old, and which some writers would consider as merely illustrations. These institutions, however, were, on the basis of the principles just laid down, truly prophetic, and there can be little doubt that the Apostles meant to refer to them in this point of view. When St. Paul wrote to the Corinthians, "For even Christ our Passover is sacrificed for us; therefore let us keep the feast, not with old leaven, neither with the leaven of malice and wickedness; but with the unleavened bread of sincerity and truth," * his language might indeed be amply justified as simply an illustration of exceeding beauty; but remembering how deeply he

---

* 1 Cor. v. 7, 8.

had considered the whole prophetic character of the old Dispensation, one can hardly fail to see that he referred to the Passover in its necessarily prophetic bearing, and to its accompanying ritual as embodying in outward symbol a deep teaching of Christian truth. St. Paul, trained from childhood in the shadows of the old revelation, especially enlightened by the Holy Spirit to discern their meaning, and with a clear and bold reasoning faculty, is, perhaps, of all the New Testament writers, the one who most delights to bring out this kind of prophecy.

The prophetic character of single acts and events may be better treated under the head of typology; yet one illustration may be given here. Our Lord refers to the manna of old when speaking of Himself as "the living Bread which came down from heaven."* Certainly this was a very indefinite prophecy to the Israelites in the wilderness; yet it did teach them that God knew their wants and would provide for their needs. Now, when we find man's highest needs met by the gift of Christ, "Who is our life," we see that this indefinite promise of old is made definite in Him, and is thus prophetic of Him. Such prophecies, indeed, have only a secondary character. They do not stand out simply and by themselves, but require to be taken in connection with other circumstances, or explained by argument; yet they are by no means of little importance on this account, nor of small value in the links which bind the two Dispensations together in one vast plan for the salvation of men.

---

* John, vi. 48, 49.

The educational laws of the Mosaic legislation may be thought, at first view, a still more indistinct kind of prophecy. Yet since they set forth the will of God in such terms as the people of the time were able to understand, they must needs prophesy of what shall be the declaration of that will when more clearly revealed. Sometimes in the New Testament the prophetic character of such precepts is distinctly brought out, as in St. Paul's quotation of the law, " Thou shalt not muzzle the mouth of the ox that treadeth out the corn ;" * but more frequently the precept of old is simply cited in its higher application to the Christian, as in the quotation from Proverbs † in the Epistle to the Romans, ‡ " If thine enemy hunger, feed him; if he thirst, give him drink; for in so doing thou shalt heap coals of fire on his head." Such quotations are not infrequent throughout the New Testament, and are particularly apt to be made in the form of the Septuagint translation.

Beside the prophecies of history already mentioned, there is another kind: direct prophecies are given of a nearer historical future, which, when accomplished, becomes itself prophetic of a more distant future. Both kinds are used in the New Testament. To the former belong the story of God's care for the Church in the wilderness, the rest of Canaan, the deliverance from surrounding enemies, and the restoration from the captivity. All these, and many other experiences, were steps in the

---

* 1 Cor. ix. 9; 1 Tim. v. 18 ; cf. Deut. xxv. 4.
† Prov. xxv. 21, 22.   ‡ Rom. xii. 20.

working out of the great plan of the redemption of mankind, and just in so far as this was the case, became prophetic of that result. Some of these are referred to in the New Testament in this light, and others may be used by us in the same way. This prophetic purpose is sometimes made clear even in the older Scriptures. Thus, that the rest of Canaan was not the end of the promise, but only the means to a further end, is shown by the argument in the Epistle to the Hebrews * that the rest was still declared to be future, long after Canaan had been in the possession of the chosen people.† Yet only here and there is the argument thus developed; for the most part it remains to be worked out by those who attentively consider the declaration of God's purposes and the history of their fulfilment. To the other kind of historical prophecy belong all those predictions of the near future in terms which catch their glow and force from the more distant times to which they are the preparatory steps, and of which they therefore form a necessary part. Such are the glowing descriptions of the kingdom of Solomon in the 72d Psalm, in which the prophet looks through the immediate to the final and eternal kingdom of Israel. Such, also, are the prophecies of the Church of the restoration from the exile, which look to that Church not merely as it should be in the days of Shealtiel and Zerubbabel, but as it should grow from that stage of its progress into the Messianic kingdom, and even beyond, until it should at last develop into the heavenly Jerusalem, the Church triumphant above.

---

* Heb. iii. 15—iv. 13.   † Ps. xcv. 7, 8.

In studying such prophecies, and also those of the New Testament which sometimes similarly connect the beginning and the end, it is always to be remembered how feebly ideas of time have always been developed in the Oriental mind, and how much more engrossing and important has been that of purpose. It made but little difference *when* the Divine promises were to be fulfilled; the great question was *what* they should be. They realized that with God "one day is as a thousand years, and a thousand years as one day," and therefore they often describe in one breath, as it were, the preparatory stages and the ultimate result. We, from the character of our mental habits, attach more weight to the distinctions of time. Moreover, in an advanced stage of the preparation, we are able to separate the work more distinctly into its parts; they viewed it from beforehand as a whole. The New Testament writers lived between. They justly claimed such prophecies as fulfilled when the great, fundamental point of their fulfilment was accomplished, though much still remained to be done. At the Council of Jerusalem concerning the admission of the Gentiles to the Church, St. James claimed * the fulfilment of the prophecy, "After this I will return, and will build again the tabernacle of David, which is fallen down; and I will build the ruins thereof, and I will set it up: that the residue of men might seek after the Lord, and all the Gentiles, upon whom My name is called." † This was spoken by Amos with a primary reference to the restoration from the Babylonian cap-

---

* Acts, xv. 15.   † Amos, ix. 11, 12.

tivity; but that was only a step to its accomplishment. Its great fulfilment was when Christ laid down His life a ransom for all. Its realization began when the doors of His Church were thrown open freely to Gentile believers—the precise point of time when St. James cited its promise. From that day to this it has been in ever progressive fulfilment; but its end is not yet, and we still cite it as a promise and a prophecy which each successive generation sees more and more completely fulfilled.

Finally, there are passages cited as prophecies in the New Testament which have, on their face, as we read them in the Old, no prophetic character; but simply speak of persons and circumstances as they existed at the time. David, in the second Psalm, * asks, "Why do the heathen rage, and the people imagine a vain thing? The kings of the earth set themselves, and the rulers take counsel together against the Lord and against His Anointed." So far all this was true of David himself; and although the Psalm goes on with language which indicates in David a consciousness of a higher and a future reference, yet it is this first part of the Psalm which is quoted by the Christians and applied to the opposition of the Jews when Peter and John had been arrested, threatened, and unwillingly released by the Sanhedrim.† They did so with good reason; for David in his time was the head of the theocracy and represented the Church of God as opposed by heathen enmity. What was true of him in this capacity must necessarily be true in the same rela-

---
* Ps. ii. 1, 2. † Acts, iv. 13-26.

tion of his greater descendant, the true Head of the Church. What David then says of himself in such a relation is prophetic of Him who in a higher way stood in the same relation. Prophecies of this kind are frequently cited. They sometimes contain in their language evidence of their intended application to the future; sometimes their words relate directly only to the present. This does not matter. The prophecy is essentially in the thing and not in the mere words. There is no reason to suppose that the thoughts of the Psalmist went beyond himself when he wrote of them "that hate me without a cause;"* yet the beloved disciple did not err when he applied the saying to One against whom hatred was more causeless than against David.†

After considering these various kinds of prophecy as they are written in the Old Testament and as they are quoted in the New, nothing more need be said as to the prophetic connection between the two. It is plain that the inspired writers of the Old Testament understood sometimes very fully "that not unto themselves but unto us they did minister the things which are now reported unto you by them that have preached the Gospel;"‡ and it is correspondingly plain that the inspired writers of the New Testament looked upon Christianity as the outcome and designed fulfilment of the entire old Dispensation, and therefore upon that Dispensation as in every part more or less clearly prophetic. These facts are always to be recognized in the

---

* Ps. lxix. 4, cf. xxxv. 19.   † John, xv. 25.   ‡ 1 Pet. i. 12.

study of the use of the Old Testament in the New. There are amply enough of plain and express prophecies to give a firm basis for this more widely extended prophetic relation; but we should quite fail to enter into the spirit of the New Testament writers, if we did not recognize that they took this wider view, and freely considered everything in the older Dispensation and Scriptures that foreshadowed and led up to the things of Christ as essentially, and in its very nature, prophetic.

This broader use of prophecy appeals only to those who have already come to appreciate something of the relation in which the two Dispensations stand to each other. It is made use of in the New Testament only for the benefit of such. When prophecy is used argumentatively, to prove some proposition needing to be established in the mind of the hearer or reader, either only the more distinct prophecies in the narrower sense are used, or else they are accompanied by an exposition and argument showing their bearing upon the case in hand. We, as Christians, may well follow this inspired example. In our own private thoughts, and for our own edification, we may well use alike the history, the institutions, the precepts, and the sacred songs of old as setting forth in shadow the higher things of the present dispensation, and these, again, as showing us the still higher glories, yet to come, of the Church triumphant; yet care is to be taken that this be done in a reasonable and not in a merely fanciful and sentimental way, for it is always to be remembered that the Gospel appeals to our reason as well as to our feeling, and that we do but weaken and dishonor it when we appeal in its behalf to that which our reason cannot sanction. In argument, in establishing that which the hearer does not yet admit, we must confine ourselves to a narrower ground, and first establish on clear evidence the Divinely arranged connection between the two Dispensations on the basis of clear and express declarations before we can wisely go on to use those subtler prophetic indications which really fill the whole teaching of "Moses and all the prophets."

LECTURE IX.

TYPOLOGY.

I. *Its History and General Principles.*

THE treatment of the subject of typology must depend upon the definition of the word type. There has always been and still continues to be much confusion about its meaning, and it will therefore be well to begin with a short historical sketch. This would naturally start with the Christian fathers; but there is a difficulty in representing their views from the fact that they generally made little distinction between two very different things, *allegory* and *type*. This confusion still remains, and the first point therefore must be to make the distinction between them.

In allegory it is of no consequence whether the things narrated really occurred or are a fictitious story for the purpose of setting forth the truth to be taught. In Nathan's parable to bring home to David's conscience the enormity of his sin,* it is a matter of indifference whether a poor man whose one ewe lamb was seized by his rich neighbor, actually lived or whether the story was invented for its purpose. So also with our Lord's parables; it is unnecessary to suppose that the events narrated in them had really occurred, nor would the supposition

---

* 2 Sam. xii. 1-4.

that they were narratives from actual life add anything to the force of their moral teaching. This, then, is the first characteristic of allegory: it is independent of the real or fictitious nature of its narrative. The narrative may or may not be true; this does not affect its use. The other characteristic is that this narrative, real or fictitious, is used for the conveyance of a meaning of a different and a higher kind.

Types, on the other hand, presuppose, as essential, the reality of the facts, institutions, or circumstances on which they are based, or at least the conviction of their reality on the part of both the speaker and the hearer. Further, the type does not, like the allegory, involve a different sense; but only a different and higher application of the same sense. This will be explained and illustrated further on; for the present it must be assumed as a characteristic of the type in contradistinction to the allegory.

Both these forms of teaching, the allegorical and the typical, without much distinction between them, were largely employed by the Fathers, especially by the Greek Fathers, Clement of Alexandria and Origen. It is sometimes hard to tell whether they regarded the Old Testament narratives as literally true or not, and therefore whether they meant to treat them as allegories or as types. For illustration I quote a single instance from Fairbairn's *Typology* * of the treatment of the same narrative by Origen and by his master, Clement. The subject is Abraham's marriage to Keturah. Origen

---

* Bk. I., Chap. I., § I.

says this teaches "that there is no end to wisdom, and that old age sets no bounds to improvement in knowledge. The death of Sarah is to be understood as the perfecting of virtue; but he who has attained to a consummate and perfect virtue, must always be employed in some kind of learning—which learning is called by the divine word, his wife. Abraham, therefore, when an old man, and his body in a manner dead, took Keturah to wife. I think it was better, according to the exposition we follow, that the wife should have been received when his body was dead and his members were mortified. For we have a greater capacity for wisdom when we bear about the dying of Christ in our mortal body. Then Keturah, whom he married in his old age, is, by interpretation, *incense*, or sweet odor. For he said, even as Paul said, 'We are a sweet savor of Christ.' Sin is a foul and putrid thing; but if any of you in whom this no longer dwells, have the fragrance of righteousness, the sweetness of mercy, and by prayer continually offer up incense to God, ye also have taken Keturah to wife." * He goes on to show how many such wives may be taken, hospitality, care of the poor, patience, and every Christian virtue being a wife. On the other hand, Clement † finds this instruction in the narrative of Abraham's marriage successively to Sarah and to Hagar: " A Christian ought to cultivate philosophy and the liberal arts before he devotes himself wholly to the study of divine wisdom." The way he takes to make this out is the following: Abraham is the image of a per-

---

* Origen, Hom. vi. in Genes. † Clement, Strom. L. I., p. 333.

fect Christian, Sarah the image of Christian wisdom, and Hagar the image of philosophy or human wisdom (certainly a very ill-favored likeness!). Abraham lived a long time in a state of connubial sterility—whence it is inferred that a Christian, so long as he confines himself to the study of divine wisdom and religion alone, will never bring forth any great or excellent fruits. Abraham, then, with the consent of Sarah, takes to him Hagar, which proves .... that a Christian ought to embrace the wisdom of this world, or philosophy, and that Sarah, or divine wisdom, will not withhold her consent. Lastly, after Hagar had borne Ishmael to Abraham, he resumed his intercourse with Sarah, and of her begat Isaac; the true import of which is, that a Christian, after having once thoroughly grounded himself in human learning and philosophy, will, if he then devote himself to the culture of divine wisdom, be capable of propagating the race of true Christians, and of rendering essential service to the Church.

The Western Church, attaching more importance to the literal truth of the Old Testament narratives, was far less extravagant in the use of allegory, but still sought types everywhere, apparently guided only by the practical use that could be made of them at the moment. Abundant instances may be found even in writers of such power and good sense as St. Augustine. There was no careful examination of the principles on which such interpretations rest, and the example thus set was followed without reflection during the middle ages, so far as any attention at all was given to the Scriptures.

With the great awakening at the Reformation a reaction set in against this arbitrary treatment of the older Scriptures. The prominent writers of the Reformation period protested in no measured terms against what they called "the licentious system" of Origen and the allegorists; yet their minds were too much occupied with other matters to examine or determine the principles of typology, and notwithstanding their protests, not a little of the same vicious allegorizing and typical explanation may be found in their writings. On the other hand, there was at the same time such an excessive effort to establish what was called "the natural and obvious meaning" of Scripture that the real sense of the more enigmatical prophecies was often lost to view. The best writings of the period were characterized by a well-meant effort to develop the true sense of the sacred writings, but without any fixed principles to guide them in regard to typology, and consequently much uncertainty and more than doubtful interpretation.

In the seventeenth century arose what is known as the Cocceian school, though it began earlier than the life of Cocceius himself. Its chief exponents were Glass, in his *Philologia Sacra;* Cocceius, in his Commentaries; Witsius; and Vitringa. They rejected the Alexandrian theory of a double sense of Scripture, and yet reached nearly the same result by a system in which everything in the Old Testament in which any trace of resemblance could be discovered to anything in the New was considered as typical. For example: Cocceius understands Asshur's "going out and building Nineveh as a type of the

Turk or Mussulman power, which at once sprang from the kingdom, and shook the dominion of Antichrist;"* and the others look upon the withdrawal of Isaac from his father's house to the land of Moriah, as a type of Christ's being led out of the temple to Calvary; and Samson's meeting a young lion by the way and the transactions that followed, as a type of Christ's meeting Saul on the road to Damascus, with the train of events succeeding.†

This school of interpretation largely prevailed in England during the seventeenth and the beginning of the eighteenth centuries. Beautiful, but exceedingly fanciful illustrations of it may be found abundantly in the works of Jeremy Taylor. The obvious defects of this school were: first, that it furnished no fixed principles of interpretation; and, secondly, that it was based on no true idea of the connection between the Old and New Dispensations, between type and antitype, and thus led to a dwelling upon merely superficial and external resemblances, while the vital principles of the connection between the law and the Gospel were overlooked.

The positions of the Cocceian school were opposed by various scholars, and notably by Spencer in his *De legibus Hebræorum*, and by Dathe in his edition of Glass; but their opposition went so far, and even true types were so much discredited by them, that their views were not generally adopted. Gradually,

---

* *Cur. Prior.* in Gen. x. 11.

† Glass, *Philol. Sacr.* Lib. II. P. I. Tract II. Sect. 4. Vitringa, *Obs. Sac.* Vol. II. Lib. VI. c. 20. Witsius, *De Œconom.* Lib. IV. c. 6. For these references I am indebted to Fairbairn, *ubi supra*.

however, as from various causes the study of the Old Testament was more neglected, all typology fell into neglect. This may have been hastened by the extravagances of the Hutchinsonian school, which sought to find all truths, as well of philosophy as of science, concealed in the letter of Scripture. The cabalistic and extravagant character of this school, so far as it had any effect, could only increase the suspicion with which types were already regarded. Another school therefore arose, of which Bishop Marsh was the ablest exponent. Realizing that the existing extravagances in typical interpretation were dishonoring to Scripture and pernicious to religion in the opinion of sensible men, and seeing no other escape from these absurdities, he rejected all types except those expressly sanctioned in the New Testament. The earlier school sought Christ unwisely in everything contained in the older Scriptures, but had the redeeming point of really seeking Him; the school of Marsh unwisely did not seek Him there at all, and was the outcome of an essentially unchristian theology. In rationalistic hands this school finally denied all types, and interpreted those expressly sanctioned in the New Testament as mere accommodations to Jewish notions. Thus the true connection between the Old and New Testament was broken in the opposite way from the former school, and the words of Christ concerning the relation of the older Scriptures to Himself were made impossible. This school certainly offends less than the Coccean against good taste and common sense, and has less of extravagance to repel thoughtful men; but it is cold, and hard, and dry. It is at variance with the teaching of the forty days, and in opposition to the analogy of the Apostolic preaching and writings. If it were the only escape from the capricious extravagance of the opposite school, it might indeed be urged with some reason; since we must believe that the Holy Spirit did intend to convey some definite meaning in the Old Testament Scriptures, and not merely to set forth a row of hooks on which each man might hang his own fantasies. Yet it can never meet the wants of the devout student's heart, nor even satisfy the minds of those who duly weigh the use made of the Old Testament in the New; since it also fails to unfold the real and essential connection between them.

Is, then, the principle correct that we can only recognize as true types those for which we have inspired authority? Certainly not, for several reasons. First, from the analogy of prophecy. In this closely connected subject such a principle would be clearly wrong, and the same reasoning applies here. As in that case enough prophecies are interpreted to form a guide and model, and we are then left to interpret others in the same way (our Lord reproving the disciples because they had not done this), so in regard to types. Enough of them are treated in the New Testament to show the principles of their use, and it is intimated that many more are left untouched. In the Epistle to the Hebrews ordinary Christians are reproved for their dulness in apprehending them, as in the case of Melchisedec.* Secondly,

---
* Heb. v. 11, 12.

the types treated in the New Testament, though quite numerous, are of such a kind and are so selected as to leave the conviction that in the minds of the writers they were only instances selected for their immediate purpose from a storehouse of like material. In the Epistle to the Hebrews* this is expressly affirmed of the arrangements of the tabernacle, and it seems an unavoidable conclusion from the way in which types are cited everywhere. Clearly the types are there, if we can only determine with certainty where and what they are. This is the critical point, and Bishop Marsh urges with reason that Scripture itself furnishes the only possible means of distinguishing between the true and the falsely alleged type; that only by its means can we determine "that two distant though similar historical facts were so connected in the general scheme of Divine providence that the one was designed to prefigure the other." But it is not necessary that the teaching of Scripture should be confined to the particular types expressly cited. If we can discover the reason why those types were cited, and the principle of their application, we may surely accept other types which have the same reason and rest upon the same principle.

Meantime, to conclude the history of the matter, it can scarcely be said that there are at present any marked schools of typology remaining. Each individual writer or commentator follows, more or less, in the footsteps of one or other of the schools already enumerated; yet with the general advance-

---

* Heb. ix. 5.

ment in sound principles of interpretation, there is a growing recognition of the true principles of typology. It is not to be expected that every one will come to a perfect agreement in the application of those principles in detail to each particular case. Differences arising from temperament or from previous habits of thought will always remain, just as textual critics, having the same authorities and the same principles, will yet occasionally come to different conclusions in regard to some difficult and well-balanced reading. This does not matter. The main point is that some fixed principles of typology should be determined and accepted; and then slight differences in their application will be of very little moment.*

For this purpose it is necessary, first of all, to fix clearly the meaning of the word type, and this is so important that a somewhat full treatment of it may be excused. It is used in Scripture both in a more general and a more restricted sense. The primary meaning of the word, derived from τύπτω, is *a stroke*, and then *the impression left by a stroke, a trace*, or *print*. In this sense it is found in John, xx. 25, "Except I shall see in his hands the *print* of the nails, and put my finger into the *print* of the nails;" but it does not occur in the New Testament elsewhere in this meaning. From this sense it came naturally to be used in the classics (and so also in

---

* For a valuable discussion of the whole subject of types, see Fairbairn's *Typology of Scripture*, 2 vols. 8vo. The first part of Vol. I. treats of the general principles of Typology, and much of this historical notice is abbreviated from Book I.

the Septuagint) of the stamping of coin, of pictures, and of sculpture, and hence, also, of monuments, statues and images. Thus it is used by the prophet Amos,* and in the passage quoted from him in the speech of St. Stephen, "*figures* which ye made to worship them."† Closely akin to this is the meaning *pattern, model,* or *example.* It bears this sense in those passages which speak of Moses as building the tabernacle after the *pattern* shown him in the Mount;"‡ in the account of the letter of Claudius to Felix, written "after this *manner;*"§ in St. Paul's exhortation to Titus, "showing thyself a *pattern* of good works;" ‖ in his statement in recounting to the Corinthians the history of old, that "these things were our *examples,*" and that "all these things happened unto them for *ensamples*" ¶ (where the better text has the word in the form of an adverb); in his exhortation to the Philippians, "walk so as ye have us for an *ensample;*"** in his speaking of the Thessalonians †† as "*ensamples* to all that believe;" and of making himself "an *ensample*" unto them;‡‡ in his exhortation to Timothy, "be thou an *example* of the believers;" §§ and in the same way in St. Peter's address to the elders, "being *ensamples* to the flock." ‖‖ The word is found in only two other instances in the New Testament: in the expression, "ye have obeyed from

---

* Amos, v. 26.
† Acts, vii. 43. The same word is used by Josephus (Ant. I. 19, § 11) of the images of Rachel.
‡ Acts, vii. 44; Heb. viii. 5.   § Acts, xxiii. 25.   ‖ Titus, ii. 7.
¶ 1 Cor. x. 6, 11.   ** Phil. iii. 17.   †† 1 Thess. i. 7.
‡‡ 2 Thess. iii. 9.   §§ 1 Tim. iv. 12.   ‖‖ 1 Pet. v. 3.

the heart that *form* of doctrine which was delivered you,"* it is doubtful whether the same meaning of "pattern of doctrine," is to be retained, or whether there is here a further derived sense of "compend. of doctrine;" but the sense can only be one or the other of these. In the only remaining instance of the use of the word, St. Paul speaks of Adam, "who is the *figure* of Him that was to come."† In this passage the word will easily bear the sense we have had all along, "the pattern or example of Him that was to come;" or it may be taken in the more technical sense of type, "the one foreshadowing and setting forth Him that was to come." As, however, the latter sense is found nowhere else, the former seems required by the *usus loquendi*. The two senses are closely connected, and inasmuch as many things of old are spoken of as examples, and those same things did actually, in many instances, foreshadow the things to come, the transition is very easy from the meaning of types as simply examples to that of foreshadowing examples, though strictly the word is never so used in the New Testament.

There have come to be the two senses of the word in theological literature: (1), simply examples; (2), foreshadowing examples. The former sense was widely extended in common use until it came to mean nothing more than a mere reminder, anything that might suggest to the thoughts some religious fact or truth. Thus the early ecclesiastical writers speak of the masts and yards of a ship, or again of

---
* Rom. vi. 17. † Rom. v. 14.

the trunk and cross branches of a tree, as "types" of the cross. Of course, the word *type* here can have only the sense of something which suggests to the mind, something which by its external form brings up in the devout mind the thought of the cross. There is no limit to types in this sense, nor is it possible to make any systematic arrangement, or give any rational account of such types, which are co-extensive with the power of association in the human mind. Type was employed in this way in early Christian literature not only in regard to natural objects, but also in respect to the histories and institutions of Scripture. Everything in the Old Testament became a "type" which could in any way, however remotely, suggest to the mind any fact or truth of the Gospel. Exuberant fancy sometimes carried such reminders to a point where the laws of common sense seem to have been quite forgotten, and the effect produced on the ordinary mind was more ludicrous than devotional. When the seven daughters of Job are spoken of (as they were by Gregory the Great) as typical of the twelve Apostles, because the number *seven* is made up of the addition of three and four, and three multiplied by four makes twelve, we seem to be dealing rather with those conundrums used as the pastime of ingenuity, than with suggestion of religious or even worthy thought. Far short of such absurdity as this, there are great multitudes of more or less fanciful resemblances commonly spoken of as "types" in which there is no real connection of thought or purpose between the type and the antitype. Some minds greatly delight in these. The lintel and the side posts of the door upon which the passover blood was sprinkled, are suggestive to them of the form of the cross; the red color of the thread bound by Rahab in the window, brings to their minds the blood of Christ; and so of a great multitude of other details in the story of old. They are not disturbed by the remote nature of the resemblance in many cases, nor by the palpable evidence of a different object in others. Thus, in the two cases just cited, it is plain that the actual form, if any, determined by the points on which the passover blood was sprinkled, would be a triangle and not a cross; and the object of the red color of Rahab's thread in her window was evidently to make it conspicuous from a distance, that the conquering hosts of Israel might the more readily recognize and spare her house. Nevertheless, the tracing out and dwelling upon resemblances of this kind, has been in all ages and still continues to be a delight to many devotional minds, and must therefore be recognized as one of the ways in which the flame of devotion may be nourished. Only in this, as in other matters, it is to be remembered that the excessive cultivation of the fancy and the imagination is not unattended with danger. As continual reading of fiction nourishes a tone of day-dreaming and unreality, and tends to unfit the mind for the sober realities of life; so care must be exercised lest too much dwelling upon fanciful resemblances in Scripture confuse our perception of those which were divinely intended, and also lead us to seek in its records, like the Cabalists, rather fanciful lessons of our own devising than those serious facts and truths which the Holy Spirit designed to give for our instruction.

This may be enough to say of the so-called type looked upon in its lower and less important sense of a mere resemblance. It is plain that in this aspect it cannot be reduced to laws, but is simply a matter of each individual's sense of fitness and congruity, and can be restrained only by good sense and good taste within reasonable bounds. It has not to do with the real meaning of Scripture, but only with the exercise of the fancy and the imagination under the guidance of a devotional spirit.

Let us pass on, therefore, to the higher sense of the word as " a foreshadowing example," that is, an example in the Scripture of old having so much of the nature of prophecy that it foreshadows something corresponding to it in the Gospel. It is in this sense only that the word *type* will hereafter be used. One point, however, needs to be observed in advance. An example of old foreshadowing something in the Gospel did not necessarily make the thing foreshadowed known to the men to whom it was given. It may have helped to prepare them for it, without their being conscious of what they were prepared for; and we, in looking back over both the type and the antitype, may be able to see a connection between them which was not visible to those who could see clearly only the type.

When the question is asked, What is a type, and how is it to be recognized? the answer will be universally accepted that it consists in a resemblance by which the things of old gave indication beforehand of the things of the Gospel. The difficulty of the subject lies in the determination of the points wherein that resemblance is to be looked for. On this it will be necessary to dwell at some length, for it forms the key to the whole matter. The two fundamental canons on the subject are concisely and well set forth by Fairbairn substantially as follows:* (1) There must have been in the type the same great elements of truth as in the antitype, and in this unity of teaching the true resemblance between them is to be found; (2) In the older Dispensation this truth must have been exhibited in a form more easily understood by the men of the time to whom it was given than the antitype would have been.

The former of these canons is the more important, and its truth is easily seen on considering the relation between the Dispensations and the definition of a type as a "foreshadowing example." The earlier Dispensation could only have been preparatory for the later by means of the truths it taught, or at least by its forms in connection with these truths. The mere forms alone, apart from the truths conveyed by them, could not have been "foreshadowing examples," partly because there is sometimes no answering form in the antitype, as in the case of the smitten rock in the wilderness; and partly because when there is, as in the case of a king, the consideration of the mere form, apart from the truth in-

---

* Fairbairn, *Typology of Scripture*, Chap. ii., II., Vol. I., p. 50. Amer. Ed. 1867.

volved, has been so far from preparing men's minds for the antitype, that it has rather filled them with a false expectation of an exact repetition of the old form on a grander scale. It is clear, then, that the essential resemblance between the type and the antitype must be in the truth conveyed. This is the ground of the connection between them, and it is by this that we distinguish the true from the false type. That which conveyed to minds under the earlier Dispensation the same truth which was afterwards to be more fully revealed, helped to prepare them for the latter and became a "foreshadowing example," or a true type. Often, but not always, the recognition of the connection was helped by the resemblance in the outward forms in which the truth was embodied; but a mere resemblance in form, without any connection in teaching, is no type. To illustrate: the brazen serpent was a type of Christ, and was used by Himself in His conversation with Nicodemus as "a foreshadowing example" of His death for the salvation of men.* Wherein was it a type? It is not infrequently spoken of as if it consisted in the form of a cross on which the brazen serpent was suspended; but this is puerile, and where is the evidence that there was any cross in the case at all? The serpent may have been "set up" on a stone, or placed on a pointed pole (as the language in the narrative seems to indicate),† or in the crotch of a forked stick. And supposing— which is very unlikely—that there was a cross, what would it have taught, or how would it have prepared

---

* John, iii. 14, 15. † Num. xxi. 8, 9.

the Israelites for Christ and His death? As soon, however, as we look at the truth conveyed, all becomes clear. The Israelites, bitten by serpents, were in danger of death; God commanded a means of safety which had no apparent natural efficacy to the end proposed. The brazen serpent was set up, and whoever trusted in God's word and used His appointed means by looking at it was saved. So our Lord told Nicodemus that He "should be lifted up," that whosoever trusted in Him should not perish, but should have eternal life. The outward resemblance expressed in the words "lifted up" was a help to the perception of the underlying truth, but did not in itself constitute the type. The Israelites were here taught in an elementary way and in a particular concrete instance, suited to their understanding, the same truth afterwards to be taught by the sacrifice of Christ. They were not told of that sacrifice by the brazen serpent; but their minds were in some degree prepared for it by the lesson they then received.

The type and the antitype thus stand in an intimate mutual relation to one another. It may often happen that we gain a better understanding of the antitypes from the consideration of the foreshadowing types; for the writers of the New Testament constantly assume a knowledge of these on the part of those whom they addressed. This is pre-eminently the case in regard to the great types of the sacrifices and the priesthood. Much of the New Testament language would be very obscure without a knowledge of these, as they were ordained in the

Jewish polity. On the other hand, the types would often be still more obscure, and their full purpose misunderstood, without the light thrown back upon them by the antitype. There must have been in them a primary and direct teaching to the men of the age in which they were given, or else they would have been of no use or value at all; and that teaching necessarily lay more upon the surface; while to us, on the contrary, the typical teaching has become of more importance.

It follows from these things that the resemblance between the type and the antitype must have been designed; for the object of the one was to prepare the way for the other, not by mere outward resemblance, but by teaching the same fundamental truth.

If, by the consequences of Adam's sin visited upon all his posterity, God taught that the members of our race are all effected by the acts of their federal head, Adam therein becomes a type of Christ; because the same truth in a higher and fuller and better development is still involved in the relation of the Christian to his Master. This truth, of the existence of a federal as well as an individual relation of man, is indeed everywhere in nature and in history, and thus, in a certain sense, every one who stands in a federal relation to others may be spoken of as a type; but as no other man can ever possibly represent that relation so strongly as the one from whom we are all descended, so no other can, in this respect, be so strong and clear a type of Christ. But Adam does not hereby necessarily become a type of our Lord in other respects. He is a type just in so far as the same elements of truth appear in his history as reappear still more clearly in that of Christ. To refer to one more illustration much inferior in its typical character, but which was yet a favorite with many of the early Christian writers. They speak of Eve as a type of the church, because she was formed from Adam, even as the church is derived from Christ. Here it cannot be denied that there is a real type, because the same truth of a derived and dependent life appears in either case; and yet every one must feel that the type is of a lower kind, because the life in the case of Eve was merely the physical, animal life, while the church draws from Christ its highest spiritual life. That which is of most importance in the antitype is altogether wanting in the type. Such an instance, therefore, while it cannot be altogether denied the character of a type, yet jars upon our sense of congruity and fitness almost as the "ambiguous middle" in logic jars upon the reason. The frequent use of such very imperfect types has a tendency to confuse our appreciation of Scripture teaching. The very prominence of the superficial resemblance is in danger of concealing the want of correspondence in the deeper and more essential truth.

It will at once be seen that the application of this canon cuts up by the roots a vast mass of fanciful types. They may remain types in that looser meaning of the word, which consists of a mere reminder founded upon some outward resemblance; but they can be no longer considered types in the sense of "foreshadowing examples;" because they do not contain the same elements of truth as the antitype. David's guilty murder of Uriah may be spoken of as a type of the Christian's putting his sins to death; but it is plain that there is no real connection between them. To use such a type one must shut his eyes to the real meaning of Scripture and the lessons it was given to teach, and occupy his attention with its mere words. Yet while this is an extreme instance, there are many others, less repulsive perhaps, but equally devoid of any true and living connection between the alleged type and the antitype.

The second canon in regard to types, laid down above, that "in the Old Testament the truths must have been exhibited in a form more level to the comprehension, more easily and distinctly cognizable by the minds of men," is also necessarily involved in the nature of the case, and is included in what has already been said. The preparatory would be of no use, there would be no occasion for its being given at all, unless it were more easily apprehended than that for which it is designed to prepare the way. The progress of revelation must ever be on an ascending scale, and especially the great transition from the Old Dispensation to the New must be marked by a rise in the fulness and completeness of the revelation of spiritual truth. Of course, it is not meant by this canon that the full truth shall be made more clear by the type than by the antitype; for this would be the very reverse of the fact. But the lesson actually taught by the type to the men of the time must have been clearer to their minds than the full truth which it typifies would have been to them. Thus in regard to the flood: It was a true type of baptism, because it contains a resemblance teaching the same fundamental truth—the destruction or death of sin, and the salvation of God, with its blessings bestowed upon a new life; but the men of the old world could not have read these truths in the simple rite of baptism. They needed to be taught by such a tremendous and sensible Divine interposition as the deluge. In the same way the passage of the Red Sea is called a baptism unto Moses;* that is to say, the relation into which the Israelites thereby entered to Moses as the prophet of God, was a true type of the relation into which the Christian enters by baptism to Christ. In either case there is a complete surrender of the individual's life and safety into the hand of his divinely appointed leader, and a giving of allegiance to him in the very act of accepting the salvation he offers.

In these instances it is plain that there may be many and different types of the same antitype. Truth is many sided, and it is often impossible that it should be fully set forth in all its varied aspects in any one type. On the other hand, it is also true that one and the same thing under the Old Dispensation may be typical of more than one under the New. For the type may embody within itself more than a single truth, and each part of it will thus have its corresponding truth, in the later Revelation. Thus to take an illustration from the sacrifices: Two goats, one to be slain and the other to

---

* 1 Cor. x. 2.

be sent into the wilderness were necessary on the Day of Atonement, because it was impossible that one victim could set forth the necessity of death for the forgiveness of sin and also the bearing away of sin out of sight and knowledge. On the other hand, the ordinary whole burnt offering both typified the first of these truths, the necessity of the shedding of blood for the forgiveness of sin, and also that of entire consecration to God's service.

It seems hardly necessary to say that in view of these principles nothing in a later dispensation can be considered as typical of anything in an earlier, and nothing which teaches a truth plainly can be looked upon as typical of that which obscurely sets forth that truth in a figure. Both these principles are violated by such interpretation as that of Wordsworth which makes the crystal sea in heaven typical of baptism on earth * This is a violation of every principle of typology.

It is easy to see that the connection between the type and the antitype must be where it has been placed, in the truth conveyed rather than in the mere outward resemblance between the objects set before the mind, for both a negative and a positive reason. Negatively, a partial and incomplete representation of an object would necessarily have tended to preoccupy the mind with the representation itself, and thus to unfit it for the representation of the reality. The preparatory would have been more difficult to understand in its essential meaning than the complete ; just as an outline sketch is more dif-

---

* Wordsworth, *Lect. on the Apocalypse.* Lect. IV. p. 101.

ficult to understand than a full picture. Even as it is, this difficulty has always attended the use of types. As a matter of history, the carnally minded Jews went astray from this very cause. They recognized the preparatory and typical character of their Dispensation and looked forward to the Messiah; but they looked to objects and not to truths. Especially in regard to the ritual types: they looked for the perpetuity of the temple and its sacrifices and the universal establishment of the whole Mosaic law. Consequently when these types were fulfilled in the revelation of the truths which they were designed to set forth, they were strongly disposed to cling still to the shadow as necessary to the substance. It was only with difficulty, after much discussion, and when the Divine will had been very clearly made known that the believing Jews, of whom the Christian Church was at first exclusively composed, could be induced to admit the uncircumcised believers* to their fellowship on equal terms. This mistaken looking to the outward object, instead of to the essential truth contained in the type, was one of the great stumbling-blocks in the way of the reception of the Gospel by the Jews. It has been the same thing under Christianity. Among the uncultured especially, the sensible images by which the Scriptures have sought to set before the mind the truths of the future world have too often been taken literally as the actual description of objects, and so have led to expectations of the future altogether false and unworthy. The errors of the Chiliasts rest

---

* See Acts, xv. etc.

upon the same misapprehension. They sought the meaning of the type in the mere outward object instead of in the underlying truth, and so interpreted spiritual things sensuously. It is a general tendency of the human mind always leading to more or less serious error.

The positive reason for the statement that the connection between the type and the antitype is in the truth conveyed rather than in any merely outward resemblance, needs but to be stated. It is at once seen from this point of view how the mind, by the imperfect teaching of the type, was led up towards the truth of the Gospel and prepared for its reception, when it should be revealed in the fulness of time. Types thus fall into their place in harmony with all other parts of the preparatory Dispensation, and become one of the many ways in which "the law was our schoolmaster to bring us to Christ."

Having thus far spoken of the general principles of typology, I propose to examine these in their application to various classes of types; for the types, like the prophecies of whose nature they partake, may be arranged in several kinds or classes. The examination of these different classes separately will conclude this discussion of typology.

LECTURE X.

TYPOLOGY—Continued.

II. *Special Classes of Types.*

In the last lecture the general principles of typology were considered; we have now to examine the application of those principles to particular classes of types. It is not necessary to make an exhaustive classification of these; but only to take up the more prominent and important kinds as sufficient examples of all.

I.

I begin with Ritual or Legal Types; in other words, with the symbolical institutions of the Mosaic Dispensation.

It is to be remembered that the typical character of these, however important in itself, and however it may have been the reason for their existence, is yet in a certain sense secondary. If they are prophetic symbols, they must have been first of all symbols; they must have been outward, sensible representations of divine truth in connection with an existing dispensation. They must have had a primary value to the men of the time when they were given. While looking back upon them in the light of the antitype we are apt to overlook too much their significance in the time to which they belonged and to dwell too exclusively on their connection with the future. The first point, therefore, is to enquire what they were designed to teach the men of old. If we do not find that they taught anything to them in the same line of truth, so to speak, as that with which we are disposed to connect them, then their typical significance in this respect fails. For example, during the first great battle of the Israelites with Amalek in the wilderness when Moses held up his hands in the attitude of prayer, Israel prevailed; when he let them fall, their enemies were too strong for them.* This may truly be called an example, or if you please, a type of the value and efficacy of intercessory prayer; but when it is cited as a type of the cross, because Moses with his outstretched arms exhibited the form of the cross, the supposed typical significance altogether fails, since there was nothing to suggest to those who saw it the teaching of the cross or to prepare them for the reception of its especial doctrine.

To bring what has been said to bear directly upon that class of types contained in the symbolical institutions of the Mosaic legislation, let us look first at their great central type, the sacrifices. Each of these had its special typical significance. They have already been treated so much at length that it is not necessary to enlarge upon them. Let us select then the sin offering, in several respects the most important and the most significant of them all. Was this

---

* Ex. xvii. 11, 12.

really typical of the sacrifice of Christ; in other words, did it set forth in sensible and easily understood image the same great truths afterwards to be more clearly and fully revealed by our redemption upon the cross? Setting aside minor matters, three points are obvious: first, the recognition of sin. We see in the Psalms and in the Prophets the effect of this teaching, in strong contrast with the literature of most other nations, in the recognition of sin in its true character. Where else can be found that cry of the penitent, "Wash me thoroughly from mine iniquity, and cleanse me from my sin. For I acknowledge my transgressions, and my sin is ever before me. Against thee, thee only, have I sinned and done this evil in thy sight."* Surely in the sin offering the type and the antitype are bound together in the truth conveyed, and the former becomes a most important preparation for the latter.

The second truth conveyed by the sin offering was that of the surrender of life in consequence of transgression. The typical significance of this is plain. God's love for the sinner and His righteous wrath against sin were both alike to be taught. Simple and unconditioned forgiveness might have expressed the one, but would have given no manifestation of the other. The abhorrence of sin must be shown at the same time with the forgiveness of the sinner. By the shedding of blood as the condition of the atonement this was made as clear as was possible in a type, and thus man was prepared for

---

* Ps. li. 2-4.

the vindication of God's righteousness in the death of His Son upon the cross, that thereby we might be reconciled to Him and our trespasses be forgiven. Yet it was far from teaching that Christ's sufferings were a compensation for our sins, an equivalent rendered to God for our misdoing; on the contrary, His atonement appears as the vindication of the righteousness of God, manifested to the whole universe, while at the same time in his infinite love He extends free forgiveness to all that trust in Him.

The third great truth taught by the sin offering is already involved in what has been said—God's acceptance of a vicarious substitute. To this men made small objection as long as the teaching of the Old Testament was fresh in their minds; but in our own day, when men have drifted away from this, such vicarious substitution has become to them one of the stumbling-blocks and offences of the Gospel. I do not know that other evidence is needed, both of the typical and preparatory character of this Mosaic institution, and at the same time of the importance to us, even in the full noonday light of the Gospel, of keeping alive and fresh this preparatory teaching of the dim ages of antiquity.

There are many other typical elements in the sin offering, but these are subsidiary; the great outlines of its teaching have been here recapitulated. They remain forever true, though the type in which they were once embodied has passed away, to be repeated no more.

In the same way all the other institutions of the Mosaic legislation might be treated at length, and it would be seen that in all of them the typical value consists in the truth conveyed rather than in their outward resemblance to the antitype. Thus the great lesson of the priesthood was the necessity of an authorized mediator to stand between man and God. " No man taketh this honor unto himself, but he that was called of God as was Aaron."* Thus were the minds of men prepared for the coming of the true Mediator, with the perfect authority of the Son of God Himself, Who by His greater and more perfect sacrifice, offered once for all, " hath perfected forever them that are sanctified." And the same teaching is still needed for us to show that the object and work of the priesthood having been fully and finally accomplished, and " eternal redemption " having been obtained for us, there can be forever no priest for us, other than He who has gone "into heaven itself, now to appear in the presence of God for us," † where " He is able also to save them to the uttermost that come unto God by Him, seeing He ever liveth to make intercession for them." ‡

These may serve as sufficient examples. All other typical institutions may be examined in the same way, and the conclusion will be reached in all that what constitutes the type, what formed the ground of the connection between the type and the antitype, so that the one prepared the way for the other, was the truth which it taught.

---

* Heb. v. 4.   † *Ib.* ix. 24.   ‡ *Ib.* vii. 25.

II.

The next general class of types is the historical. Two considerations suggest beforehand that such types will be found in Scripture : First, since the Old Testament as a whole was preparatory for the New, and both were parts of one general Divine plan, we should expect that its history would be so ordered, and the inspired record of that history would be so written, as to bring out, in their elements at least, truths which were afterwards to be fully revealed in the Gospel. Secondly, since this purpose is plainly impressed upon the institutions of the Mosaic economy, we should expect the history to be in harmony with them and to concur in the same general design. In the nature of the case the connection between type and antitype must be somewhat less close in history than in expressly established religious symbols. The latter are more exclusively Divine; the former are more affected by the play of human action. Still, both are under the Divine control, and if the relation of the type to the antitype is less close, it is nevertheless the same in kind.

The actual existence of such types is shown by three considerations: (1) There are many narratives of the Old Testament typically interpreted in the New, and in these examples we may observe the same sort of resemblance and limits of resemblance as have already been found in the symbolical institutions. (2) Numerous and varied historical types in the earlier dispensation were highly important to the accomplishment of its great object, the preparation of mankind for the Gospel. The symbolical and directly religious institutions met the needs of the people on one side; but there would have been a great defect in their training if they had not found the same lessons impressed upon their minds by their history, which they were so often exhorted to recall and to teach to their children and their children's children. (3) The Old Testament itself gives clear indications that much of its history was so related to a higher future ideal as to stand to that ideal in the relation of a type.

A short development of each of these points will be all that is necessary to be said on the subject of the historical types.

(1) Some of the principal narratives of the Old Testament typically treated in the New are the story of Adam and Eve, of Cain and Abel, of the Flood, of Melchisedec, of Abraham, Sarah and Hagar, Isaac and Ishmael, of Moses, of the Exodus from Egypt, the Passover, the passage of the Red Sea, the giving of the manna, the water from the rock, the brazen serpent, and other things in the wilderness, of David, Solomon, and the prophet Jonah. Some of these have already been mentioned in the general discussion of the subject; but it is as true of the historical type as of the typical institution, that it may foreshadow more than one truth according as it is looked at from different points of view. Thus the story of Adam and Eve is used by our Lord to show that monogamy was God's original design for man and

that divorce is generally unlawful.* By St. Paul it is used in a variety of ways: to the Corinthians he speaks of it as setting forth the proper relation between man and woman,† and again, in another aspect, to Timothy as setting forth the same relation.‡ Of Adam alone he also speaks at length to the Romans as a type of Christ in his federal headship of the human race,§ and again, to the Corinthians in his great chapter on the resurrection ;∥ in the same passage also he makes Adam, in contrast with Christ, a type of the natural and earthly body as contrasted with the spiritual and heavenly.¶ All these different truths were set forth by this same story, and therefore in all these respects it was truly typical of the things to come. Alike many-sided was the teaching of the flood. Mention has already been made of the passage in which St. Peter refers to it as a type of baptism ;** but it is also used by our Lord as a type of the end of the world in that, in the one case as in the other, the Divine warning of the coming calamity is neglected, and men continue in their accustomed ways until the sudden destruction bursts upon them ; †† again, in the Epistle to the Hebrews, Noah is referred to as an example or type of faith, showing forth in his conduct the true nature of faith in all ages ; ‡‡ once more, St. Peter makes the deliverance of Noah teach the general truth of God's delivering the righteous and over-

---

* Matt. xix. 4-6; Mark, x. 6-9, cf. 1 Cor. vi. 16.
† 1 Cor. xi. 8.   ‡ 1 Tim ii. 11-14.   § Rom. v. 12-19.
∥ 1 Cor. xv. 21, 22.   ¶ *Ib.* ver. 44-46.   ** 1 Pet. iii. 20, 21.
†† Matt. xxiv. 37-39 ; Luke xvii. 26, 27.   ‡‡ Heb. xi. 7.

throwing the ungodly;* and finally, in a very important passage,† he sets forth the flood as a type of the final destruction of the world. In this last instance the type is of especial value to us as showing the nature of that final destruction; for the Apostle says that the world shall be destroyed by fire as it has already been by the flood,—that is the world as inhabited by man, and there shall be new heavens and earth in the one case as in the other, thus showing that nothing is affirmed as to the continued existence of this terraqueous globe.

It were too long thus to dwell in detail upon all the Old Testament narratives typically treated in the New. Several others are brought out in different relations as different truths were contained in the lessons of the same story. Others are mentioned but once, or if more than once, only in connection with the same truth. Thus Rahab is spoken of both in the Epistle to the Hebrews‡ and in that of St. James.§ Both writers treat of the same typical act; but one as teaching "a working faith," the other "a faith working." It is plain that the New Testament writers take up and treat the histories of old embodying the lessons they were at the moment engaged in enforcing; and had they been treating of other subjects, they would have referred to other stories which enforced such other truths as they wished to teach. The types of the Old Testament are not therefore exhausted by the treatment of the New. Rather these are but examples showing us

---

* 2 Pet. ii. 5.   † *Ib.* iii. 5–7.
‡ Heb. xi. 31.   § James, ii. 25

how to make use of types, viz.: by developing the lessons of truth taught through them to the men of their time, and bringing these to bear upon the fuller revelation of the Gospel. There are even instances of types, declared to be such in the Old Testament, which are not mentioned in the New. That in which a truth was taught of old, whatever it be, is a type of that wherein the same has been taught also " in these last days."

There are two points in which these historical types generally may seem defective: (a) The outward resemblance may sometimes be faint, as in the case of Ishmael, the son of the slave, a type of the Jew, and of Isaac, the son of promise, a type of the Christian;* or the external resemblance may even at first sight seem to be inverted, as in the case of the destructive waters of the flood typifying the saving waters of baptism.† This belongs to the nature of symbolical representation of truth. Our Lord himself, in a parable, likens God to an unjust judge; ‡ and St. Paul uses the simile of grafting the wild olive upon the good tree.§ Such instances are not infrequent because the object is to set forth some truth which is found in the main point of the parable, or figure, or type. The accessories, the likeness or unlikeness in minor points, is unimportant and is passed by. Perhaps the fact may be best illustrated by a false type, such as representing Abel, a feeder of flocks, as herein a type of the Good Shepherd. In this there is a sufficiently close

---

* Gal. iv. 22–31.   † 1 Pet. iii. 21.
‡ Rom. xi. 16–24.   § Luke, xviii. 1–8.

external resemblance, but the one throws no light upon the other; there is no great common truth taught, and the earlier in no way prepares the mind for the latter. Certainly there are other ways in which Abel may in some degree prefigure Christ, as in his faithfulness, his innocent death at the hands of the guilty, etc.; but, simply as a shepherd, he is only a type in the same way as every other shepherd; there is nothing peculiar to Abel. Types of this kind are never used in the New Testament. What is there sought is not external resemblance, but identity of moral truth.

(*b*) The other defect in the historical types to which I referred, is a want of correspondence in the proportion between the truth set forth by the type in the system to which it belongs, and the proportion between the truth in the antitype and its system. Generally speaking, this must be the case, and necessarily results from the fact that an imperfect system of truth cannot be proportioned in the same way as a more perfect one. Thus Joshua, in the strength of the Lord, leading the people to the conquest of Canaan, is a type of Christ leading those who trust in Him to the victory over their spiritual enemies; but in the one case, the conquest itself is the prominent feature, in the other, this is secondary, and is a consequence of the union of the believer with Christ. This difference of proportion is necessary in all forms of preparatory teaching. Even in direct and explicit commands, the precept, "Thou shalt love thy neighbor as thyself," * belongs

---

* Lev. xix. 18; Matt. v. 44; xix. 19; xxii. 39, and parallels; Rom. xiii. 9; Gal. v. 14; James, ii. 8.

both to Leviticus and to the Gospel; but in the one it was inconspicuous; in the other it has become the great law of intercourse between man and man. In types, however, this disproportion is especially marked. Man needed to be impressed with the majesty and terribleness of the Almighty by the thunders of Sinai, before he could understand the unutterable love of the Gospel. So great was the change, that the New Testament puts the one in contrast with the other: "Ye are not come unto the Mount that might be touched".... "but ye are come unto Mount Zion."* There are, indeed, a few of the most important both of the prophecies and of the types of old which correspond in their proportion, simply because they are the most important to the proportion of the similar things under the Gospel. Thus the prophecy of Christ's first coming occupies in the Old Testament a similar place to the prophecy of His second coming in the New. The great type of sacrifice was the leading feature of the Mosaic legislation, just as the antitype, the sacrifice of Christ, is the great fact of the Gospel. But this correspondence of proportion, for the reasons just given, can only hold in regard to those matters which occupy the very first rank. In regard to others, the type and the truth it teaches cannot occupy the same proportionate place in the elementary and in the perfected system. We cannot set truth before the mind of the child in the same proportion as in maturer years; the elements of truth must first be thoroughly taught, but there

---

* Heb. xii. 18, 22.

comes a time when, as we are exhorted, "leaving the principles [or elements] of the doctrine of Christ, let us go on unto perfection."*

(2) The next consideration mentioned as showing the existence of historical types was the importance of them to the accomplishment of their great object, the preparation of mankind for the Gospel. This follows from the position of the Israelites as belonging to a preparatory Dispensation. Living, as they did, in the midst of symbolical institutions, much of their life—in other words, of their history—would naturally have taken on a symbolical character. There must have been a harmony between themselves and the dispensation to which they belonged, in so far as they were true to their vocation either consciously or by the overruling hand of Him who shaped their destiny. Hence there would have been a correspondence between their history and that of the truths taught in an elementary way in their religion, and this is the same thing as to say that their history was typical.

The New Testament refers to many instances of such typical teaching in the history of old. Thus St. Paul writes, " Moses put a veil over his face, that the children of Israel could not steadfastly look to the end of that which is abolished. But their minds were blinded: for until this day the same veil remaineth untaken away in the reading of the Old Testament; but even unto this day, when Moses is read, the veil is upon their heart; nevertheless, when it shall turn to the Lord, the veil shall be taken

---

* Heb. vi. 1.

away."* This is not a mere illustration; it is a bringing out of the typical force and meaning of an Old Testament transaction. Moses put the veil over his face when he came down from his prolonged and close intercourse with God on the Mount, because "the skin of his face shone," and the people "were afraid to come nigh him."† This incident, immediately and directly, showed two things to the people: first, that man was elevated and glorified by close communion with the Almighty; and secondly, that they themselves were as yet unfitted for such communion. Nevertheless, they had both the Divine declaration that they should be a "kingdom of priests"‡ to their God, and the primeval promise that the head of the serpent, the power of evil, should be bruised by the woman's seed.§ Thus their present state was shown to be abnormal, and they were taught that there must be some way, not yet manifested, by which man could be brought near to God.

At an earlier date Abraham was promised a child in whose posterity all the nations of the earth should be blessed. After remaining childless until all human possibility of the fulfilment of the promise had vanished, he took to himself a concubine who was his slave, and a son was born. But this was not the child of promise, and when at last he also was given, hostility naturally arose; the child of the flesh persecuted the child of promise, and was cast out because he was not intended to inherit the special blessing of

---

* 2 Cor. iii. 13–16. † Ex. xxxiv. 29–35.
‡ Ex. xix. 5. § Gen. iii. 15.

his father. Here the Israelites, and through them the world, were shown that heavenly blessings are not tied down to the line of earthly descent, but follow rather that of the divine promise. They were taught this by a sensible and special instance, such as they could understand; but John the Baptist appreciated and expressed the underlying truth when he taught, "Think not to say within yourselves, We have Abraham to our father; for I say unto you that God is able of these stones to raise up children unto Abraham." *

It may sometimes happen that a fact of history has no prophetic teaching in itself at the time it occurred, and therefore was not originally a type, yet afterwards receives such significance by being associated with prophecies of the future. Thus it is hard to see how Jonah's three days' entombment in the sea monster could have taught his contemporaries anything of our Lord's three days in the grave; but when the Jews asked for a sign and "the sign of the prophet Jonas" was given to them, with the declaration "so shall the Son of man be three days and three nights in the heart of the earth," † then, from that time, and in consequence of that declaration, Jonah became "a foreshadowing example," a true type. Yet in some other respects, as a prophet preaching to a people lost in sin but saved in listening to him and repenting, he was always a type. As our Lord states it, "As Jonas was a sign unto the Ninevites, so shall the Son of man be to this generation." ‡

---

* Matt. iii. 9.   † *Ib.* xii. 40, cf. Jonah, ii. 1.   ‡ Luke, xi. 30.

St. Augustine has said, "The Old Testament, when rightly understood, is one great prophecy of the New."* And this is explained by Fairbairn, "Its records of the past are pregnant with the germs of a corresponding, but more exalted future. The relations sustained by its more public character, the parts they were appointed to act in their day and generation, the deliverances that were wrought for them and by them, and the chastisements they were from time to time given to experience, did not begin and terminate with themselves. They were parts of an unfinished and progressive plan, which finds its destined completion in the person and kingdom of Christ."†

(3) The third consideration mentioned is that the Old Testament itself often indicates the typical character of its narratives. Some of these instances are familiar. Moses told the people assembled in the plains of Moab, "The Lord thy God will raise up a Prophet from the midst of thee, of thy brethren, like unto me."‡ He here makes himself a type, but of what? First of a series of prophets who should make known to them God's will; but finally also of the one great Prophet who alone should make a perfect revelation. Moses therefore, was a type, first, of the human prophets in succession through the ages, and finally and chiefly of Christ. The type here, like many prophecies, has its successive antitypes, all leading on to the one final and perfect Antitype; but in all there is the same lesson—that God

---
* Contra Faust. lib. xv. 2 (also xix. 31).
† Fairbairn, *ubi sup.* p. 71.   ‡ Deut. xviii, 15.

will not leave His people without guidance, but will send to them those who shall declare His will.

So also in the case of Elijah. He is expressly declared by the last of the prophets to be a type of the forerunner of our Lord.* Malachi indeed so expresses this that the Jews, as always, clinging to the outward form, expected to see Eljiah in person ; but the angel in announcing his birth,† Zecharias in his song of thanksgiving,‡ and our Lord in two discourses with His disciples § showed that Elijah was a type fulfilled in John. He was a type because he was a messenger sent from God to turn His people from their sins and avert from them His threatened wrath. In this case the Old Testament simply sets forth the type, without expressly saying that it was only a type. That was left to be understood.

David also was a type, and his typical character becomes plain on putting different passages together. In many places the Messiah is foretold as the descendant of David who shall sit upon his throne, as " the Root and offspring of David," and under such like expressions ; on the other hand, in Jeremiah,‖ Ezekiel,¶ and Hosea,** He is simply called David. There is but one explanation of this : David, as the head of the theocracy, was a type of our Lord, and the Old Testament gives plain intimation of this by describing the Redeemer to come now as David, now as the descendant of David.

---

* Mal. iii. 1; iv. 5, 6. † Luke, i. 17. ‡ *Ib.* 76, 77.
§ Matt. xi. 14 ; xvii. 12, 13 and parallels. ‖ Jer. xxx. 9.
¶ Ezek. xxxiv. 23, 24 ; xxxvii. 24, 25. ** Hos. iii. 5.

Prophetic types form a class of themselves; but there is a point in the connection between prophesy and type which must not be passed by here, because it shows so clearly the Old Testament's recognition of its own historical types. It is a habit of the prophets to describe future events in terms of the past or the present. So common is this that some critics have erroneously laid down as the law of all prophecy, that it can only take hold of the past or the present and project it with necessary modifications into the future. As a universal rule this is thoroughly false ; as the statement of a common habit, it is eminently true. Thus when Hosea would foretell the punishment to come upon the people, he says : " They shall return to Egypt," * " Ephraim shall return to Egypt," † and again, " Egypt shall gather them up, Memphis shall bury them : " ‡ but a little further on he adds, " He shall not return into the land of Egypt, but the Assyrian shall be his king."§ That is, the bondage in Egypt was a type of the coming woe, but the actual place of suffering should be in Assyria. The passages in which the various prophets foretell the return from the Babylonian captivity or the greater Messianic deliverance under figures taken from the Exodus are too many and too familiar to require especial mention. It is not surprising therefore that the New Testament writers should have regarded these and similiar events as typical when their character in this respect had been so often intimated in the Old Testament.

---

* Hos. viii. 13. † ix. 3. ‡ ix. 6.
§ xi. 5. More elaborate instances occur in Ezek. iv. and xx.

There is one book which, from its peculiar character, may demand a word in connection with this subject. The book of Psalms is a collection of the songs of the sanctuary and even of private devotion gathered through many ages. In it the Psalmists brought their past history and the story of their present experiences before God in sacred songs of prayer and praise. It was to be expected that the typical elements of that history would come out more abundantly than elsewhere in this solemn and religious use of it. Accordingly we find the Psalms abounding in types and frequently quoted by the New Testament writers in a typical character. Especially David, the first godly monarch of Israel, the first to restore its orderly worship after long ages of abounding sin and idolatry, the first head of the theocracy who was "a man after God's own heart," yet encompassed with opposition and evil—it was natural that he should stand out in his life and in his work, as pre-eminently a type of the royal Prophet who, after the flesh, should be descended from him. So close is the type in this case that the line which separates type from prophecy is hard to be distinguished, and it is sometimes difficult to say, as in the case of Ps. xxii., whether the utterances are simply prophecies, or whether they are primarily applicable to David's own experiences, but to him as a type of his greater son. Practically, it makes little difference how this question is decided ; but in the discussion of typology it is very interesting, both as showing how typical was much of the Old Testament history, and also as showing the value of the type in this very close approximation to prophecy.

These types on the border line between the historic and the prophetic class are so numerous, and are so frequently used in the New Testament, that something further needs to be said about them. They are of two kinds:

(*a*) Those which are general in their application. These often have what Bacon calls "a springing and germinant accomplishment," and thus come to have many antitypes. Their fulfilment is not confined to a single person or event, but finds answering persons or events in many who have been in various respects made like to Christ, and in their experiences, while its highest fulfilment is in Him or in His life. Some of these germinant types are of such a nature that they must have continuous antitypes while man continues in a state of probation. Thus, when Moses chose "rather to suffer affliction with the people of God, than to enjoy the pleasures of sin for a season, esteeming the reproach of Christ greater riches than the treasures of Egypt," * he was a type of a long line of Old Testament saints as well as of the followers of Christ in all ages, but above all of Christ Himself. Other types of this kind belong so exclusively to a preparatory dispensation that when Christ came they reached their absolute fulfilment, and there could be nothing further. These two varieties need not be separated in their treatment. Several of the types already cited belong to this class, and other instances are not far to seek. At the

---

* Heb. xi. 25, 26.

time of our Lord's first purification of the temple, St. John says, "His disciples remembered that it was written, The zeal of thine house hath eaten me up." * The quotation is from the Psalms, † and was true of David and of every earnest Israelite, as Hezekiah, or Josiah, or the Maccabees, who gave up his personal ease and comfort and incurred reproach and suffering in his zeal for the house of the Lord ; it is true, again, of every faithful follower of Christ under similar circumstances. But its highest and chiefest fulfilment was in Him to whom His disciples applied its words. So also when our Lord says in reference to the traitor Judas, "that the Scripture may be fulfilled, He that eateth bread with Me hath lifted up his heel against Me." ‡ From the context, there is reason to suppose that David spoke immediately and directly of the treachery which he himself experienced. § His words have again and again been verified in the troubles of many saints. But such an experience was to be expected especially in the life of the King of Saints. The historic became a prophetic type, and thus our Lord could say of it "that the Scripture may be fulfilled"—that the words spoken of old may have their higher and greater realization. The same things are to be said of another expression of our Lord, "that the word might be fulfilled that is written in their law, They hated me without a cause." ‖ It was fulfilled in innumerable instances in the past, it continues daily to be fulfilled now ; but its greatest fulfilment was

---

* John, ii. 17.   † Ps. lxix. 9.   ‡ John, xiii. 18.
§ Ps. xli. 9.   ‖ John, xv. 25 ; Ps. lxix. 4.

in Christ. These, and many others like them, are primarily rather historical statements than prophecies; they are the record of the personal experiences of the writers. Yet they are of such a kind as to be often fulfilled in God's church and people, and preeminently in Christ when working out man's redemption. But the New Testament evidently claims for them something more than this; it points plainly to a prophetic element in them and shows that the life of our Lord, in these respects, was a fulfilment of them. The ground of such claim is this: as history these passages relate to persons who were types of Christ, and hence from being descriptive of the one, they necessarily became prophetic of the other. Not everything in the personal history of such persons is prophetic, but only what belongs to their history in their typical character. To illustrate by a more obscure example: " Jesus spoke unto the multitude in parables, and without a parable spake He not unto them; that it might be fulfilled which was spoken by the prophet, I will open my mouth in parables; I will utter things which have been kept secret from the foundation of the world."* The Psalm from which this is quoted describes the experience of the writer *as a prophet*; † the description belongs to all who bear the prophetic office, and hence must necessarily be fulfilled in Christ.

(*b*) The second subdivision of this kind of types is of the same general character, but differs from it in having only one specific application. But two instances need be given. One of these, St. Matthew's

---
* Matt. xiii. 35. † Ps. lxxviii. 2.

quotation from Hosea, "out of Egypt have I called my Son," * has already been explained in the lecture on prophecy, and unless it is to be treated as merely a use of the prophet's words by way of accommodation, must be regarded as a prophetic type having a specific application. The other instance is more doubtful. When the soldiers forebore to break the legs of our Lord upon the cross, St. John says: "These things were done that the Scripture should be fulfilled, a bone of him shall not be broken." † This may, as many think, refer to the language of the Psalm, "Many are the afflictions of the righteous; but the Lord delivereth him out of them all. He keepeth all his bones: not one of them is broken." ‡ It would then be a specific application of a general, spiritual promise, given to all who are loved of God, to a literal event in the life of the beloved Son. Another interpretation, however, brings it strictly within the class of prophetic types having a specific application. Many consider that St. John here refers to the command concerning the paschal lamb, "Neither shall ye break a bone thereof." § The Passover was certainly a prominent type of Christ in his death, and there is no other obvious reason for this command than that it might thus point more clearly to its Antitype. The difficulty in this case is that the resemblance is merely an outward one; there is no especial lesson of future truth conveyed by the command. But the answer is obvious: the type did not consist in this command, but in the truths set

---

* Hos. xi. 1; Matt. ii. 15.   † John. xix. 36
‡ Ps. xxxiv. 19, 20.   § Ex. xii. 46.

forth by the Passover, and this and other external features were merely marks of resemblance, sign-manuals as it were, to lead the mind to the deeper inward connection. The command, which had no obvious importance in regard to the paschal lamb itself, was yet made a part of its law to awaken attention and inquiry into its inward meaning, and when that meaning was fulfilled upon the cross, there was a correspondence also in the outward form that this fulfilment might be the better understood.

III.

The last general class of types are those which occur in combination with prophecy, and hence may be called Prophetic Types. No sharp line of distinction can be drawn between these and the classes already treated, since all types have a certain prophetic character; yet they have enough of common characteristics to justify their discussion as a special class.

There are three forms of combination of prophecy and type:

(1) The first form embraces those passages in which things typical in the past or the present are declared in distinct prophecy as to appear again in the future, type and prophecy being thus combined to show forth the things of the future. This is easy enough to understand in the abstract statement, for it is the ordinary action of the human mind to set forth the unknown by means of the known, and to compare the thing to be taught with something

already learned. So in prophecy the future is shadowed forth by the past or the present. Sufficient instances have already been given. It is only to be remarked that in this kind of type the connection with the antitype need not be so close, since it is here pointed out by its combination with prophecy. Thus, in the case of the crowning of the high-priest Joshua with the double crown* (a type nowhere mentioned in the New Testament), the prophet goes immediately on to speak of "the man whose name is the Branch," who " shall be a priest upon His throne," and no doubt is left as to his meaning.

(2) The second subdivision is a modification of the last. In this the type, not expressly, but in its essential principles, is embodied in prophecy foretelling things that correspond in character, but which are of higher moment. This need not be dwelt upon, but Psalm ii. and many others may be referred to as examples.

(3) The third and last kind of combination of type with prophecy is that in which the type itself is future and is foretold. In this case (a) the prophecy in foretelling the type may also look forward to the antitype; or (b) realizing the future type as if it were actually present, it may look forth from that standpoint upon the antitype. This kind of prophetic type is particularly common in the prophecies relating to the restoration from the Babylonian captivity. Taking this as a type, they either predict in connection with it the subsequent glory of Jerusalem in the Messianic restoration and the glory of the

---

* Zech. vi. 10-13.

Christian church, sometimes even passing on to the glory of the church triumphant or else they look out upon these things from the standpoint of the type as if it were already accomplished. This is very marked in the last twenty-seven chapters of Isaiah, and has been the chief reason for the controversy about the authorship of that part of the book. It is also characteristic of chapters xxxiv. and xxxv. of the same book, and in the New Testament of our Lord's prophecy of the destruction of Jerusalem and of the end of the world.*

This is the nearest approach ever made in prophecy to what is called "a double sense," of which more hereafter. Yet there is here really nothing which answers to that term as commonly understood. The prophet by no means speaks of one thing plainly, while his words are also to be understood of another and totally different thing. He simply foretells the type in connection with the antitype, the preparatory in connection with its fulfilment. The two things are not different and disconnected, but are, so to speak, on the same line of prophetic vision. Undoubtedly this sometimes leads to considerable difficulties of interpretation, but always such as may be solved by careful study and application of the principles of prophetic typology. This may be illustrated by another matter. The New Testament so continually speaks of death in immediate connection with heaven, ordinarily overlooking the intermediate state, that numberless Christians have been found to deny the existence of that state

---

* Matt. xxiv.; Mark, xiii.; Luke, xxi.

altogether. Yet it also distinctly speaks of that state, and it is a necessary consequence of the interval which it interposes between death and the resurrection. So, frequently in this kind of prophecy: the prophet gifted to foresee the type in connection with the antitype, is so absorbed in its glory that its light is reflected back upon the type, and the two are described, as it were, in one breath.

LECTURE XI.

TYPOLOGY—Concluded.

III. *Principles and Directions for the Interpretation of Particular Types.*

WHEN the general principles of typology are to be used in forming rules for the interpretation of particular types, some points may be laid down positively and definitely; and others, as in all kinds of interpretation, must be left to the good sense of the interpreter. It is impossible to give definite laws which shall apply themselves in a hard and fast way to every particular case; judgment is still required. Nevertheless, certain rules, plainly resulting from the principles which have been discussed, may be laid down with certainty, and these will go far in removing vagueness and serving as guides.

I. The first and most comprehensive of these rules is negative. Nothing in the Old Testament, in itself forbidden or sinful, can be a type of the good things of the Gospel. This rule may seem sufficiently obvious, and yet is not infrequently disregarded. Its reason lies in the nature of the connection between the type and the antitype as teaching the same essential truth; what is opposed to the Divine will cannot, except by contrast, teach what God would have to be done. To illustrate: Jacob, in the garments of Esau, receiving his father's blessing, has been often cited as a type of the Christian's being blessed in the garments of Christ! This is an utter perversion of a mere external resemblance. Recall for a moment the facts in the case, which have already been explained. Jacob, before his birth, had been promised the blessing of the first-born, which included the ancestry of the world's Redeemer. If we believe in the faithfulness of God, we know that this promise must and would have been fulfilled without a resort to any sinful devices; but it was actually obtained through a miserable fraud.

Contrast with this the Christian's being blessed in Christ. By faith and love he becomes so united with his Master that he is a member of the body of which Christ is Head. Christ dwells in him, and "his life is hid with Christ in God."* He receives blessing, not because he pretends to be, but because he is, in reality, united with the Blessed One. What connection is there between the two? What teaching of truth have they in common? There is great danger in the adducing of such things as types. The mind instinctively feels that the type and the antitype must be connected, and therefore is either led to gloss over the abominable sin of the alleged type, or else to look upon the antitype as a mere external matter, with a fearful loss of consciousness of the living inward union between Christ and the believer, or, at least, a belittling and impoverishment of its meaning.

The same vicious system of typology has been

---
* Col. iii. 3.

carried further in making the consequences of Jacob's sin prefigure Christ's life; but one example is enough to show the essential falsity of all such types in which what is unholy and wrong is made a foreshadowing example of the good.

An evil thing, however, may be typical of evil, and many examples of this are to be found. Thus, Hagar and her descendants, persecuting the child of promise and his heirs, were made by St. Paul to typify the Jews, in reliance on their carnal descent, opposing the true spiritual Church.* So also, Egypt, the land of bondage, and Edom, the persistent foe of Israel, are continually made by the old prophets to signify any and every nation which oppressed the Church of God.† And in the New Testament, Babylon is frequently used in the Book of Revelation as a type of the great worldly power opposed to the Kingdom of God;‡ and so what was spoken by David of the enmity and devices of Ahithopel, Doeg, and others, against himself as the head of the theocracy, becomes typical of the enemies of his antitype. This is but to say that, if the type cast a shadow, that shadow becomes typical of the similar shadow cast by the antitype. The truth in the antitype must expect to encounter a like opposition to that encountered by the type.

II. A second rule for the determination of types and of their meaning is, that we are to be guided, not exclusively by the ancient understanding of them, but also by the light thrown back upon them

---

* Gal. iv. 21-31.   † Zech. x. 10, 11, and frequently.
‡ Rev. xiv. 8 ; xvi. 19 ; xvii. 5 ; xviii. 2, 10, 21.

from the New Testament. This rule results from several considerations:

(*a*) *From the Preparatory Nature of Types.*—If we would understand the bud we must study it in the light thrown back upon it by the flower and the fruit, and the lungs of the embryo, or the wing-cases of the chrysalis, would be incomprehensible without a knowledge of the perfect form. It is always difficult to understand the means by which a purpose is brought to pass without a knowledge of the purpose itself. Yet, in the time when the types were given, men were unable to appreciate the more complete revelation to follow. They were the spiritual infants of the world's spring-time, learning what they might from the starting bud and the early flower; but in the harvest we must be able better to understand the meaning of the enigmas by which they were surrounded.

(*b*) *From the Analogy of Prophecy.*—The prophets themselves, in many cases, did not understand the meaning of the predictions they uttered. Daniel expressly says: "I heard, but I understood not," and the vision was not explained to him, but he was told to go his way, "for the words are closed up and sealed till the time of the end." * St. Peter says generally of the prophets of old, "of which salvation the prophets have enquired and searched diligently, ... searching what, or what manner of time the Spirit of Christ which was in them did signify...... Unto whom it was revealed, that not unto themselves, but unto us they did minister the things

---

* Dan. xii. 8-13.

which are now reported unto you." * If this were true of that clearer form of indicating the future in words, *à fortiori* must it be true of the less distinct revelation through types; and if we can only fully interpret the prophecies in the light of their fulfilment, much more must this be the case with the types. It is plain then, from the analogy of prophecy, that we must study them in the light thrown back upon them from the antitype.

(*c*) *From the History of Israel.*—This cannot indeed prove directly that use must be made of the New Testament in determining the significance of the types of the Old; but, indirectly, it has an important bearing upon the point. For the progress of teaching in the Old Testament, especially in regard to the sacrifices, leads us to expect a more perfect treatment of these, as well as of other types, in the New. The history of the older revelations shows a distinct tendency towards a better understanding of the types first given; we cannot but expect this tendency to reach its goal in the final revelation.

(*d*) *From the way in which the things of the Antitype are spoken of in the New Testament as a "Mystery" not revealed of old, but "now made known."*—Yet, those things were shadowed forth in the type, and if not then "revealed" so that men could know them, it must have been because the type could only be fully understood in connection with the antitype.

(*e*) *From the Analogy between God's works in Nature and in Revelation.*—Everywhere He gives intimations of the future; but He does not so write

---

* 1 Pet. i. 10-12.

history beforehand that men can tell more than the great and broad features of that which is to come to pass. So in nature. The knowledge gained from experience of the seasons, or from observations of the solar system, enables men to formulate laws by which they can predict future phenomena; but without that experience or observation they would be quite unable to interpret the predictions with which nature everywhere abounds. Types, as foreshadowing examples connected by deep spiritual laws with what is to follow, in the same way must be examined with the explanation of the antitype in order that their full significance may be disclosed.

Notwithstanding the importance of this principle, it is often carried too far, for it is not easy to separate in our minds between what was actually taught by the type in its time, and the instruction we are able to gather from it through the explanation of the antitype. Yet, it is very necessary to make this distinction, and while we ourselves study the type with all the advantage of our fuller knowledge, to see what it must have been, and how much instruction it actually did convey apart from that knowledge. It is only in this way that we can appreciate the true character of the Old Testament worthies. It is only by a just guaging of their religious knowledge that we can form any true estimate of their conduct. It is only by viewing the types as they stand by themselves, and generally all the revelation of old, apart from the light of the Gospel, that we can arrive at any right understanding of the Old Testament history and of the progress of its revelation. And doing this, we shall see how very much of the light that shines upon our minds from its pages is reflected back from the final revelation of the New Testament.

III. A third rule may be considered as the complement of the last, but requires a separate statement: an alleged type must be examined to see whether it is really preparatory for the antitype by teaching to the men of its time the same essential truth; otherwise it is to be rejected. This rule necessarily follows from the previous discussion of typology, and is the most important rule of all. For example, the stone which Jacob took for a pillow at Bethel has been spoken of as a type of Christ as "the corner stone" of the Church. It may be questioned whether this particular example can be admitted by common sense even to the position of an illustration; certainly its claim to be a type must be ruled out. There was here no preparatory teaching; there was nothing in the proposed type to suggest to the men of the time any truth which should fit their minds for the antitype. Certainly there was a type in connection with Jacob at that time. In his vision he saw a ladder set up from earth to heaven and the angels of God ascending and descending upon it.* Exile from home and lonely wanderer as he was, he was hereby taught that there is a connection between heaven and earth, that God will care for and watch over them that trust in Him, and that His "angels are all ministering spirits sent forth to minister for them

---

* Gen. xxviii. 12-15.

who shall be heirs of salvation;"* and our Lord taught Nathaniel that this was a type and that He was Himself the true ladder, the connection between heaven and earth, in and through whom the Father's care for man was exercised.† The difficulty is that some minds, having thus recognized the existence of a type and not content with its main truth, think it may be extended to every particular of the surrounding circumstances. It is the same disposition which seeks to give a spiritual application to every detail of a parable or illustration, forgetting the homely proverb, as true of types as of illustrations, " Parables do not run on all fours." Much of such typology may be found in a certain class of sermons and of devotional works. They are not always to be condemned if considered merely as pious meditations,—that must depend much on the character of the mind making use of them,—but in any case they are not types in the true sense of the term. In the true type, although its full meaning only appears in the antitype, yet there must have been some teaching to the men to whom it was given, designed to fit and prepare their minds for that higher truth of which it was the "foreshadowing example." This is the essential point not only of this particular rule, but of the whole of typology, and there is great danger in its neglect. There is always a more or less distinct consciousness that there should be a correspondence between the type and the antitype, and if a faulty type has been selected, there will be a tendency to

---

* Heb. i. 14. † John, i. 51

force the antitype into harmony with it. I cannot but think that much unsound teaching concerning Christ's sacrifice has resulted from dwelling in connection with it upon Abraham's sacrifice of Isaac. The one is nowhere alluded to in Scripture as a type of the other, and the points emphasized concerning it, both in the narrative and in the New Testament references to it, are always the faith and obedience of the father, while nothing is anywhere said of the voluntary action of Isaac.

IV. It is somewhat difficult to state the fourth rule in a way to avoid misunderstanding. It may be broadly put, "the type itself has but one radical idea;" yet this must be taken in connection with the qualifications that follow. The point of the rule is that the type must contain some distinct and intelligible teaching; it has no "double sense" or ambiguous and equivocal meaning, but was designed to teach consistent and comprehensible truth. Of course, that truth may be in itself many sided and separable into several truths, and so also may be the truth in the antitype, as has been already explained. The point is simply, in accordance with all that has been said, that the essence of the type consists in its teachings, and that one type cannot teach entirely different and unrelated things. It must first be determined what it teaches, and it can only be a type of that which contains essentially the same teaching.

This rule results from the educational purpose of the Old Testament transactions, laws, and institutions. If their meaning was indefinite, vague, and ambiguous, equally capable of teaching diverse things, they could have had small value for the purposes of instruction. The trumpet would have given an uncertain sound. They would have been but riddles to the men to whom they were given, and could have had no effect in preparing for that which was to follow. It may be said that while the type originally had a definite meaning and so has a definite antitype; yet it is capable of being applied to other things, and so becomes a type also of them. Certainly we may make such applications, just as we may quote any words of Scripture and apply them to circumstances which they happen to fit; but this is what is technically called "quotation by way of accommodation," and as it does not make of the words quoted a prophecy, so neither does it make of the example cited a type. It is no violation of this rule that a truth and its necessary converse should both be taught by one and the same type. Thus God's blessing on the righteous and His corresponding judgment on the wicked is taught by the same event of Lot's delivery from Sodom on its overthrow (see 2 Pet. ii. 6-9). The point is that the teaching of the type must be without ambiguity.

Sometimes the teaching of a type is a far more complex idea than a single truth and its converse, as in the institution of sacrifice. Here, an important part of the complex idea is in the relation of its several component parts to each other. Truth was taught in such complex form that it may be resolved into a whole group of correlated truths, each most closely dependent upon and connected with the others. In the case of such complex teaching the antitype must answer to the type in the relation between the ideas taught, as well as to the separate parts of the complex idea, in order that the same truth may be conveyed, because this relation itself is a fundamental part of the teaching. The separate parts of the idea may be elsewhere taught by separate types, as in the original institution of the Passover the priestly mediation was omitted; but when the complex idea with the relation of its parts to one another constitutes the main teaching of the type, the same complexity and the same relation must be expected in the antitype. Care and good judgment are necessary to discriminate between such complex teaching, and ambiguous teaching. The distinction between them is a real one, and is sufficiently obvious on careful consideration; but they may be easily confused by hasty carelessness.

While a type can have but one teaching, yet that teaching may be of such a nature as to admit of more than one antitype in another way from the "springing and germinant" types. For one event may be typical of another, and the latter still typify a third, so that there results a chain of types, each in succession rising in importance above that which went before. Thus the Exodus from Egypt was typical of the return from Babylon, and the return from Babylon is frequently used in Scripture to typify the establishment and the blessings of the Christian Church, and the Christian Church here militant on earth is an obvious type of the Church triumphant above. The same thing may be said of much of the history of the older Church, and in such cases the original type may be said to have all these successive types and their fulfilment for its antitypes; but in all this there is no double, or ambiguous, sense. There is one consistent teaching finding repeated manifestations, though sometimes in diverse ways.

V. One further rule may be given: regard must always be had to the essential difference between the type and the antitype involved in the nature of their relation to one another. The type teaches Divine truth on a lower plane, chiefly, though not entirely, in regard to the outward, present, and earthly; while the antitype rises to a higher plane, and teaches chiefly the inward, the future, and the heavenly. While this is a plain consequence of what has gone before, it is yet a vital point. An alleged type is presented; does its antitype teach the same truth in a higher form? In other words, is the teaching of the type preparatory for that of the antitype? Unless there is this advance, the alleged type must be rejected as useless and purposeless. For example, there could be no type under the old Dispensation of the unity of God; for that truth was itself already proclaimed in the fullest and most emphatic way. It was a fundamental truth of all religion, and one with which revelation must start. There could be no preparatory teaching in the nature of the case. On the other hand, the more complete doctrine of the Godhead as a unity in essence with a threefold personality, was not as yet revealed, and there might be foreshadowings, types, of this. Whether such actually existed or not is another question:

whether the minds of the people could bear even intimations of this without being led into polytheism must be decided on the evidence ; but there is no impossibility of it in the nature of a type. In the true type there is always an advance to the antitype, as from the earthly sanctuary and priesthood to the heavenly, and where this is wanting there can be no real type. For example, in Isaac's bearing the wood for the burnt offering, and Christ's bearing His own cross, there is no advance in truth ; both are external acts, and are, in themselves, on the same plane, except as they were corresponding subsidiary actions, the one in an infinitely higher and more important event than the other. In such small details as this, and in the favorite occupation of so many minds of finding the particular shape of the cross, or the color of the blood, typified in a multitude of things in the Old Testament, there may be no particular harm, although a violation of the principles of typology. But it is to be remembered that if this be harmless, it is also in great danger of being idle. It is an amusement, a spiritual amusement, if one please so to call it ; but it is not, and does not contribute to, a growth in knowledge. When, however, the same habit is applied to more important matters, and made into a means of interpreting God's purposes, it becomes most pernicious. It is one form of holding fast to the letter that killeth, to the rejection of the Spirit that giveth life.

In its broad statement, this last rule is plain enough; but there is sometimes difficulty in its application, from the fact that as the Old Testament was not merely of an earthly character, so the Gospel is not exclusively of a heavenly. Both were revelations to man in his pilgrimage through his earthly sojourn to his heavenly home. Certainly, on the one hand, "they are not to be heard which feign that the old Fathers did look only for transitory promises;"* and on the other, the very author of the Gospel was not only Himself incarnate, but had an outward and bodily obedience to fulfil. And so have His followers in the Church to the end of time. Still, there is a broad and easily recognized distinction between the two Dispensations. If heavenly truth was taught of old, it was taught chiefly through the medium of earthly transactions and duties; and if earthly duties are emphasized in the Gospel, it is in view of their spiritual source and object. The Passover was a true type of the sacrifice of Christ. The killing of the former and the crucifixion of the latter were both in themselves outward transactions, but the teaching of the one was primarily escape from temporal death and from earthly bondage; of the other, eternal salvation and deliverance alike from the punishment and from the dominion of sin. Except the Old Testament had its spiritual significance, and the Gospel had its earthly form, there could be no unity in the truths taught by them; but as the one is an advance over the other in the fulness and clearness of spiritual teaching, so there must be a corresponding advance from the type to the antitype in which that teaching is embodied.

---

* Art. 7 of the XXXIX. Articles.

TYPOLOGY—CONCLUDED.

In concluding these lectures upon typology it is well to repeat that so far as the mere word *type* is concerned, much that has been said depends upon its definition. It has here been used in the sense of " a foreshadowing example." It has been pointed out that the word is often used in other senses, and the foregoing discussion may not always apply to those other senses. Nevertheless, it is desirable to have some treatment of the subject of " foreshadowing examples," to see in what they consist, how they are to be recognized, and how dealt with ; and for this purpose there is no other word which has been sanctioned by usage.

The main points of the whole discussion may be summed up in a single sentence : A type is an institution, or a person, or an historical event in the Old Testament designed to teach, without ambiguity, truths in a form adapted to the spiritual capacity of those to whom they were given, and preparatory for the fuller revelation of the same essential truths to those who had attained a higher spiritual development through a more complete Dispensation.

LECTURE XII.

THE ALLEGED "DOUBLE SENSE" OF SCRIPTURE.

THE close of the discussion of typology seems the fitting place to speak of what is called "the double sense" of Prophecy, because, as has been noted, the nearest approach to such a sense is in some cases the combination of prophecy with type.

By "double sense" is to be understood two different senses having little or no relation to one another. The term does not include those prophecies or types which belong to the "springing or germinant" class; for in these the earlier partial fulfilments were in view from the outset, and were included in the prediction which nevertheless also looked on to a final and more complete fulfilment. Neither does it include that which was spoken of a type in its typical character, so that it must necessarily be true of the antitype. But it involves the statement that passages of Scripture which have a clear meaning in themselves, and whose meaning is apparently exhausted in their original application; yet have another sense and application in connection with some entirely distinct subject.

The notion that such a sense exists is based upon the use made of certain passages in the Old Testament by the writers of the New. It is assumed that they could not have made these quotations otherwise than in the sense in which they were intended; and since their use is entirely different from the apparent purpose of the original writer, his words, besides this apparent purpose, must also have another and a different one which is not apparent. Such a double sense, like the prophecies and the types, if it exists at all, cannot be restricted to the particular instances which happen to occur in the New Testament; if there is such a sense, then, as in the parallel cases, these can be but examples, and the whole Old Testament is thrown open to the treatment of the cabalists or the allegorists. Nevertheless, whatever be the consequences, they must be accepted, if the fundamental position is true that the New Testament writers never quote the Old Scripture in any other sense than that which was intended.

When St. Matthew* applies to the slaughter of the innocents at Bethlehem the language of Jeremiah, if he quotes according to the original sense, it is clear that there must have been a double sense in the words of the prophet of old. For he is speaking of the carrying off of the tribes into the Babylonian captivity, and is expressly charged to say, " Refrain thy voice from weeping and thine eyes from tears; for . . . . they shall come again from the land of the enemy . . . . to their own border." †
Not only is there no apparent intention of Jeremiah, or of the Spirit who spoke through him, to say anything of the infants at Bethlehem, but his full mean-

---

* Matt. ii. 17, 18. † Jer. xxxi. 15, 16.

ing seems to be exhausted in the reference to the things of old, and what he promises of the return is apparently inconsistent with any other reference. In the same way, St. Paul, speaking of the final resurrection of the body, says, "then shall be brought to pass the saying that is written, Death is swallowed up in victory. Oh, death, where is thy sting? Oh, grave, where is thy victory?" * This is a free quotation from Hosea,† and it is perfectly plain that the prophet is speaking of the captivity under the figure of death, and, as in the former case, promising a return from it. It may indeed be said in this instance that the return from the captivity was a type of the resurrection. But this is such a far-away type that it would be almost easier to accept the "double sense;" and, moreover, it is hardly possible that it could have been intended as a type. The better part of the Jews already believed in the resurrection; so far were they from needing any type to prepare them for the reception of that doctrine that here and in other places (notably in Isaiah, ‡ and less clearly in the vision of the dry bones in Ezekiel §) the literal resurrection is used as a figure to set forth that which is spiritual. When a doctrine is so well recognized as to be a basis for the teaching of other truth, it can hardly be claimed that this other truth is a type to set forth that doctrine itself. There are a few other passages in which quotations are made in an evidently different sense from that in which they were intended of old.

---

* 1 Cor. xv. 54, 55. † Hosea, xiii. 14.
‡ Isa. xxvi. 19 (cf. vs. 14). § Ezek. xxxvii.

Do these instances then establish the existence of "the double sense?" Not if we are prepared to admit that the New Testament writers may have occasionally simply cited the familiar language of the Old Testament when its words expressed what they wished to say, without regard to the original meaning of those words. This method of citation was spoken of in the lecture on Prophecy, and little more need now be said. The difficulty is felt only in cases when it is said "that it might be fulfilled which was spoken by the prophet," or some similar formula is employed. In regard to these it is first of all to be ascertained what this formula, as used by the Evangelists, was really intended to mean. If we are to understand that everything which happened "in order that the Scriptures might be fulfilled" took place for that express reason, then we shall be driven to the conclusion that our Lord's birth of a virgin,* nay even his crucifixion,† occurred because it had been so foretold; but surely the Scripture itself gives us higher and weightier reasons why these things should have been, and we recognize that these great events themselves were originally fixed in the Divine plan for the salvation of man, and then, because they were fixed, the prophecies were given to foreshadow them. When, with this understanding, we go back to our formula, it becomes equivalent to the statement, " and so, in the Divine plan, that came to pass which had been foretold." And such interpretation is but in accordance with the general softening in the sense of the illative

---
* Matt. i. 23. † Matt. xxvi. 56 ; Jno. xix. 24, 28, 36, &c.

particle (ἵνα*) which has taken place in the New Testament and still more in later Greek. It is impossible in many cases to suppose that the ground and reason of the events of the Gospel was the accomplishment of what had been predicted—that they took place, literally, *in order that* the prophecies might be fulfilled, although this formula may be used in citing them. It must be interpreted, as all other language is interpreted, according to usage and the manifest intention of the writer.

This fact being recognized, there is no longer any difficulty in understanding the use of the same formula in the citation of passages which were not prophecies, but which are merely expressed in language fitly applicable to the event narrated. In the one case as in the other, it may properly be said, "so the words uttered of old have come true, or are fulfilled." It will remain then to distinguish the true prophecy from the mere application of language, not by the form of quotation, but by the matter quoted. If follows from this that there is no necessity of supposing a "double sense" of the Scriptures on account of the quotations made from them. It is still to be determined whether—this supposed necessity being set aside—there is reason on other grounds to admit the existence of such a sense. The two opposite views taken of the matter have been involved in what has been already said: (1) The first is that many prophecies, at least, and it would seem by parity of reason, other Scriptures also, has a two-

---

* On the use of this particle in the New Testament, see Buttmann's N. Test. Grammar.

fold sense; a primary and a secondary, or, a literal and a mystical. The former is apparent, and may be called the natural meaning; the other does not seem to be conveyed at all by the words in their connection, but is supposed to inhere in the isolated words themselves applied to some different matter. (2) The opposite view is, that since the former is inadmissible, because it exposes Scripture to most arbitrary interpretation and makes it utterly unlike anything else of which we have knowledge; therefore, prophecy can have but one definite meaning and application, and when its words are applied in the New Testament in any other way, it can only be by what is called "accommodation." Neither of these views is in itself correct; yet, in considering them, the true view will come to light.

In favor of the "double sense" it is urged that "the same prophecies frequently refer to different events, the one near and the other remote—the one temporal, the other spiritual, and, perhaps, eternal; that the expressions are partly applicable to one and partly to another; and that what has not been fulfilled in the first, we must apply to the second." * That there is a certain truth in this statement has abundantly appeared both in what has been said of prophecy and in the treatment of types; but the truth is not that which establishes a double sense. A prophecy may relate to more than one thing, nay, it may relate both to temporal and spiritual things, and yet have but one sense. When it was foretold by Jeremiah, † " David shall never want a man to

---
* See Fairbairn, *ubi supra*, p. 105.   † Jer. xxxiii. 17, 18.

sit upon the throne of the house of Israel; neither shall the priests, the Levites, want a man before me to offer burnt offerings and to kindle meat offerings and to do sacrifice continually," the direct and immediate sense was plain that the Davidic throne should not cease, nor should the sacrificial system fail; and this was probably all that Jeremiah's contemporaries could understand. But when the Gospel was proclaimed, and it was made known that all these things were shadows, now absorbed in the higher substance, then it became plain that these and such-like prophecies must have their fulfilment, not in another and a different sense, but in the same sense, exalted from earthly shadows to spiritual realities. The everlasting King upon David's throne, and the everlasting Priest of the true sanctuary must be Christ, and this had been repeatedly intimated in prophecy itself, and is repeatedly insisted upon in the interpretation of those prophecies in the New Testament. This presents the message of old, not as having different senses relating to different things, but as having only one meaning—intended to have a temporal and typical application until the time should arrive for its full, spiritual and eternal fulfilment. This may be illustrated by any precept or law which is always one and the same in its meaning, but which has manifold applications. Thus, the prophet Hosea, in speaking of God's continued but ineffectual remonstrances with Israel, declares, "I desired mercy and not sacrifice," * setting forth what is required for acceptance on high. Our Lord quotes

---

* Hos. vi. 6 (cf. Micah, vi. 6-8).

this declaration twice, once in justification of His eating with "publicans and sinners,"* and once when "his disciples were an hungered" to sustain them in having plucked and eaten ears of corn on the Sabbath.† These two applications differ from each other, and both from that of the prophet; but there is no "double sense." The principle is the same throughout; it is only brought to bear on different subjects. In much the same way our Lord's enunciation of the general law, "unto every one that hath shall be given," ‡ is applied immediately and directly to spiritual things; but it is easy to see that this principle of progressive accumulation is the universal law of all created things. To whatever we turn it is true, and true in precisely the one sense in which it was uttered, though we may apply it to an endless variety of things. In this manifold application of Scripture where the same meaning is preserved (though often necessarily exalted by the subject to which it is applied), there is no foundation for attaching to its words different senses which have no connection with one another.

Nor is there any better foundation in the combination of prophecy with type. This has been sufficiently explained in the treatment of typical prophecies. What is said of the type in its typical character and relations has a further application to the antitype, but not a different sense.

On the other hand, the objections to the theory of a double sense are obvious and weighty. The first

---
* Matt. ix. 10–13. † *Ib.* xii. 1, 2, 7.
‡ Matt. xiii. 12; xxv. 29; Mark, iv. 25; Luke, viii. 18.

is, that if Scripture has thus different meanings, only one of which can be gathered from the passage itself, then we can never be certain what it really means to teach. The Holy Spirit in using human language to convey truth to the minds of men has failed to show what it meant to convey, and the inspired record, the very source and well of truth, becomes more obscure than the ordinary writings of ordinary men. In the second place, this theory destroys the value of the prophecies. For it either so complicates their meaning as to leave us in doubt and uncertainty as to their proper application ; or, if this be avoided by making them so general and comprehensive as to include the different senses proposed, then they are incapable of any close and specific fulfilment, and can no longer be used in proof of the Divine foreknowledge of the events to which they relate. They become, like the heathen oracles, ambiguous, only to be understood in their fufilment, and that fulfilment equally true, whether one event or its opposite occur. Finally, as has been seen, there are really no examples of such " double sense " which do not admit of a better explanation without resort to this theory.

The opposite view, that prophecy can have but one definite meaning and application, and therefore can relate to but one definite event, is also inconsistent with the facts in the case. It has been shown that the prophecies in the Old Testament often give intimations of a "springing and germinant" accomplishment, and certainly there are many instances in the New Testament of the application to Christian verities of passages which yet had an immediate and direct bearing upon the shadows of old. It is not necessary to add to the abundant examples already given of this; but it may be well to call attention to the fact that many of the prophecies thus interpreted under the Gospel, were generally so understood by the Jewish contemporaries of the New Testament writers. Thus, for example, the prophecy of Balaam, "There shall come a star out of Jacob, and a sceptre shall rise out of Israel, and shall smite the corners of Moab,"* etc. certainly received a marked temporal and literal fulfilment in the reign of Solomon and of some of his successors, and notably under the Maccabean dynasty, when John Hyrcanus compelled the Idumeans to accept circumcision and become incorporated with Jewish people. Yet the Hebrew students of the Old Testament saw that the meaning of this prophecy was not yet exhausted, and even the comparatively literal Targum of Onkelos translates, "when a king shall arise from the house of Jacob, and Messiah shall be anointed from the house of Israel."

The solution of the difficulty, therefore, is to be found mainly in these two things: (1) In the frequent character of prophecy as looking forward not simply to a single event or person, but to a series in the same line of progressive fulfilment, having therefore always the same sense, but with a manifold application; and (2) in the combination of type with prophecy, so that what is said of the type in

---

* Num. xxiv. 17, 18.

its typical character becomes necessarily prophetic of the antitype.

It will be observed that in this solution a certain amount of truth is allowed to the expression "double sense;" that is, there is a full admission of a manifold application of one and the same sense, and this from one point of view might be called a manifold sense. But what is denied, and emphatically denied, is an ambiguous sense; one sense apparent in the natural meaning of the utterance, and another relating to a different matter so concealed in the mere words that its existence could not be suspected.

It will still remain that there are a few quotations in the New Testament from the Old which do not thus receive an intelligible explanation. It is from these that the theory of "the double sense" has been built up. They clearly mean one thing in the Old Testament, and they are clearly used in reference to another in the New; there is no relation of type and antitype between them, and there is no common truth taught in them, and no common principle brought out by means of them. Such passages are never used in argument, never cited to establish Christian truth, or to prove the Divine foreknowledge. They are sometimes introduced without any formula of quotation at all, so that we should not know them for quotations except by the coincidence of language; they are sometimes prefaced by the simple statement "as it is written," or even by the fuller formula "that it might be fulfilled which was spoken." The extremest instance of the last is that of St. Matthew's citation from Jeremiah and application of it to the slaughter of the infants. To my mind this is simply an application. I do not understand St. Matthew to say that Jeremiah had any such meaning, that this double sense lay unsuspected in the words he used in reference to a totally different matter; but that those words, taken apart from their original meaning, aptly described what occurred, and so they again came true or were fulfilled. Why the New Testament writers alone should be entirely excluded from such a common method of using the language of Scripture, and one which was especially the habit of their contemporaries, it is hard to see. With our exact customs of citation by chapter and verse, and with careful examination of the original it is less common; but even yet one cannot hear many sermons without listening to such quotations, and one cannot read much patristic literature, or literature of any age in which scriptural language was familiar to the writers, notably that of two centuries ago, without meeting them abundantly. They are the natural expression of human thought when that thought has been trained and moulded by scriptural phraseology. The New Testament writers were certainly so trained, and if the effect of that training was the same upon them as upon all other men, there remains no foundation for the theory of "the double sense;" and this theory is encumbered by so many and such grave objections that it can only be admitted on the most convincing proof of its necessity.

LECTURE XIII.

THE NEW TESTAMENT TESTIMONY TO THE AUTHORSHIP OF THE OLD TESTAMENT BOOKS.

THIS subject is one of considerable interest and importance in connection with the relations between the Old and New Testaments; but one which has drawn out the most contradictory opinions. On the one hand, it has been alleged that every quotation from the Old Testament made by the writers of the New, fully establishes the integrity of the book from which the citation is made, and also its authorship as commonly accepted at the time; and on the other hand, it is maintained that the New Testament writers and speakers, including our Lord, merely quote the older Scriptures as the sacred books of their people, without in the least meaning to determine any critical questions in regard to them. When they mention the name of the Author, they only refer to the book, it is alleged, under its common title, without intending to pronounce upon the correctness of that designation. In favor of the latter view it is urged that this is the common custom of all times; even now, one quotes from Homer or from a disputed play of Shakespeare, when the authorship is immaterial to his purpose, although he may himself reject the imputed authorship of the passage cited. If this is done in so critical and careful an age as our own, it certainly would have been done also in the first century of the Christian era.

Before discussing these opposite opinions it will be well to have the unquestioned facts in the case distinctly before us. There are many allusions in the New Testament to events or characters of the Old, and also many phrases are used which may be found in the ancient Scriptures, which yet are not quotations in the strict sense of the word. The number of these is variously estimated by different writers, but is certainly large. They are of great value in the discussion of the canonicity and authority of those books; but may here be left out of consideration. There are also many distinct quotations made without the mention of the author, the formulas used being "the Scripture saith," or "the Spirit witnesseth," and such like. It may seem that these also should be excluded from the discussion; but before doing so, it is to be noted that this habit of quoting simply from recognized Scripture, without mention of the human author, gives a certain emphasis to that mention in instances where it does occur. When it was so customary to quote Scripture simply as Scripture, we are not at liberty to consider it a mere chance that sometimes the name of the author was mentioned. The writer need not have mentioned it. Either the name of the author was of some importance to his quotation, and then the mention of his name becomes a distinct testimony to his authorship; or else that authorship was so well known and generally accepted among his contemporaries that it made little difference whether the name was given or not. In this latter case the evidence is conclusive of the general acceptance at the time of the reputed authorship, the author being indifferently mentioned or not mentioned. The argument that the New Testament simply accommodates itself in these matters to the popular opinion of the time will be considered further on. There are also a small number of quotations in which no name is mentioned, but in which the circumstances clearly indicate that the writer or speaker accepted the commonly received authorship. Such passages will be considered in connection with those in which the author is named. With this exception we have only to consider quotations in which the name of the author is expressly mentioned.

It may be admitted at the outset that the finding of a quotation in a book now bearing the name of the author mentioned, is not sufficient proof that the writer either quoted the passage from this book or attributed it to that reputed author, unless it can be shown with reasonable probability that such book was in existence and commonly attributed to that author at the time. For example: St. Jude quotes a prophecy of Enoch,* and there is a book bearing the name of "the Book of Enoch" which contains substantially the same passage. It has been frequently assumed that St. Jude quotes this book, and this has even been made a classical example in the

---

* Jude, 14, 15.

discussion of the present subject. But the evidence is wanting that this book, in its present form, was in existence at the time when the epistle was written. The date of the book, as a whole, is variously estimated by critical scholars from the middle of the second century before Christ to the middle of the second century after. Those, however, who hold to the earlier date considers that it contains "Christian interpolations," or that " its material has apparently been used in the composition of the Apocalypse." If the former view be accepted, the latter may be set aside as altogether gratuitous. The original date of the book is of little consequence; whatever earlier germs and fragments it may contain, it must have been worked over in post-Christian times, and if so, would certainly have introduced, if it did not already contain, the prophecy authenticated by St. Jude. But admit, for the sake of argument, that the work did originally contain the prophecy in question; whence was it derived? Certainly not from revelation; for the book is undoubtedly apocryphal. It must have come either from the imagination of the writer, which is unlikely, or else it must have been derived from tradition. The latter supposition would be universally accepted, especially as the form of the language indicates long oral transmission. Why then should not St. Jude have taken it from the same source? There are many such traditions preserved in the New Testament. St. Paul mentions Jannes and Jambres as the names of the magicians who withstood Moses;* the Epistle to

---

* 2 Tim. iii. 8.

the Hebrews records that at the Mount, Moses said, "I exceedingly fear and quake;"* St. Stephen gives the age of Moses at his flight to Midian;† St. Paul states the length of the reign of Saul.‡ Whatever degree of authority may be attached by any one to these utterances, unless they were especial revelations, they must have been derived from tradition. It is plain that only a very small part of all the things said and done during the ages of Israel's history could have been recorded in the books of Scripture. Multitudes of others must have been traditionally preserved for a time, and these traditions, in the natural course of things, would either have ultimately faded away, or else have become overlaid with a mass of untrustworthy legend. Such items of these traditions as the inspired writers recognized as true and had occasion to use, they have sent forth stamped with their authority; but there is no more reason to suppose that in doing so, St. Jude quoted from the Book of Enoch, than that St. Paul quoted, in his address to the elders of Ephesus, "It is more blessed to give than to receive,"§ from some apocryphal gospel which contained the saying. It seems therefore sufficiently clear that as the author of the Book of Enoch must have quoted a traditional saying, so also St. Jude derived his quotation directly from the same source, and not indirectly, through the medium of that book. This seems the just view of the matter independently of the question of the date of the Book

---

* Heb. xii. 21. † Acts, vii. 23.
‡ *Ib.* xiii. 21. § *Ib.* xx. 35.

of Enoch; but, of course, if that book is post-Christian, wholly or partly, the question is settled out of hand. We may then meet the argument drawn from this quotation by a denial of its existence, and need not further consider the extended inferences based upon it.

There are one or two other passages appealed to on behalf of the same views which will be considered in their order. The extreme view on the other side, that every quotation from an ancient book, whether the author is mentioned or not, authenticates that book as the production of the writer under whose name it was commonly quoted at the time, scarcely needs serious refutation. There are many quotations from the Book of Proverbs, for example, and that book was commonly quoted as Solomon's, as it is still; yet the book itself expressly testifies that all beyond the twenty-fourth chapter was of later compilation. The two Books of Samuel were probably popularly quoted as the work of that prophet; but his death is recorded at the beginning of the twenty-fifth chapter of the first book. The last chapter of Deuteronomy is certainly not shown by quotations from the earlier chapters to have been written by Moses, however justly he is considered the author of the Pentateuch as a whole.

In treating of the value of the New Testament testimony to the authorship of the books cited by name, it may be well to take up first a few clear cases in which the alleged authorship is essential to the argument in support of which the passage is cited. Our Lord confounded His Jewish adversaries by the question in regard to the language of the Messianic Psalm cx., " How then doth David call him Lord?"* Here the whole difficulty consisted in the fact that the Messiah was descended after the flesh from David, and that it was David who used these words concerning Him. Here then this particular Psalm is unquestionably attributed to David by Christ, and there would otherwise be no validity in His argument. It is alleged, however, that this only shows that the Psalm was attributed to David by the Jews, and that the argument of our Lord was a mere *argumentum ad hominem*, having no force in itself, but satisfactory to them on account of their opinions in the matter. Even so, the *presumptive* evidence would be in favor of the Davidic authorship, and the burden of proof must rest upon those by whom this is denied. But it would be going very far to admit this position. It was during the last days of our Lord's life on earth. The Jews had been foiled in their utmost efforts to entrap Him in difficulty, and He now turns upon them with a question about an acknowledged prophecy of the Messiah. He claimed to be that Messiah, and they rejected Him because He did not conform to their ideas of what the Messiah should be; therefore He showed them, so clearly as to draw out a confession of their ignorance, that they did not understand this prophecy of the Messiah. It is exceedingly difficult to suppose that in doing this He would have used an unsound argument, however effective upon them; and if the argument be sound, then we have here

---

* Ps. cx. 1; Matt. xxii. 43, 45; Mark, xii. 36, 37; Luke, xx. 42, 44.

our Lord's express testimony to the Davidic authorship of Psalm cx.

In the speech of St. Peter upon the day of Pentecost he quotes from two of the Psalms,* attributing both to David, the Davidic authorship of one at least of them being necessary to the validity of His argument. His argument might indeed hold even if the Psalm just mentioned, the cx., were not by David, for when he says, " David is not yet ascended into the heavens," † the same thing would be true of any other human author. This, then, may be taken simply as a citation mentioning the name of the author, only that in this case we happen to know, from the testimony of our Lord, that the author is rightly named. His other quotation is from Psalm xvi., and it is plain that St. Peter attributed it to David, and he bases an extended argument upon the fact that it was written by him.‡

Here are two clear instances of New Testament quotations from the Old (by the mouth of our Lord and of St. Peter), giving the name of the author, and it is clear that in both the authorship, which was that commonly received, is given in the full conviction that it was right and true. Certainly the presumption must be that it is so in other cases also, unless something can be shown to the contrary. In other words, it must be assumed that the authors mentioned in the New Testament are rightly mentioned, and hence that this testimony is conclusive as to the opinion of these inspired writers, unless in-

---
* Acts, ii. 25, 34. † Acts, ii. 34 ; Ps. cx. 1.
‡ Ps. xvi. 7–10 ; Acts, ii. 25–31.

stances can be brought forward in which they have given the authorship wrongly. The *onus probandi* rests on that side.

Before going further it will be well to state the books which are actually cited with the author's name. These are Exodus, Leviticus, and Deuteronomy under the name of Moses; a number of the Psalms under the name of David,* being in every case Psalms which by their title are attributed to David, except the anonymous Psalms ii. and xcv.; Isaiah (the latter as well as the former part); Jeremiah; Daniel; Hosea; and Joel. They constitute only about forty out of many hundred citations from the Old Testament, and show that the mention of the author's name in making a quotation was, to say the least, not the ordinary custom, and is therefore somehow to be accounted for.†

---

* Ps. ii., xvi., xxxii., lxix., xcv., cix., cx.

† The following table is taken from an essay on " The New Testament witness to the Authorship of the Old Testament Books," by Prof. Francis Brown, in the *Journal of the Society of Biblical Literature and Exegesis* for Dec., 1882. The doubtful quotation from Samuel is treated of in the text.

"Genesis	is cited 28 times.	Under Moses' name	0 time.
Exodus	" " 33 "	" " "	2 times.
Leviticus	" " 12 "	" " "	1 "
Deuteronomy	" " 41 "	" " "	7 "
1 & 2 Samuel	" " 3(?) "	" Samuel's (?) "	1 "
1 Kings	" " 2 "	" Author's "	0 "
Job	" " 1 "	" " "	0 "
Psalms	" " 68 "	" David's "	10 "
Proverbs	" " 6 "	" Author's "	0 "
Ecclesiastes	" " 1 "	" " "	0 "
Isaiah	" " 61 "	" Isaiah's "	17 "

We may now take up the instances alleged to show that the New Testament writers gave the names of the authors of their quotations loosely and without intending to commit themselves to the truthfulness of the authorship. It is not to be denied that some of these present difficulties; but, I think, the difficulties are not of a kind to favor the view in support of which they are brought forward.

The stock example of St. Jude and the Book of Enoch has already been sufficiently considered, and really has no bearing upon the question.

The next instance cited is the statement of St. Peter, "all the prophets from Samuel and those that follow after, as many as have spoken, have likewise foretold of these days."* I suppose this to be a general statement that the purpose of the whole body of ancient prophecy was to point forward to the Messianic kingdom. It may be compared to the statement in the first Epistle of St. Peter, "of which salvation the prophets have inquired and searched diligently, who prophesied of the grace that should come unto you," etc.; † or to

Jeremiah	is cited	7(?)	times.	Under	Jeremiah's	name	2	times.
[Daniel	"	"	1	"	"	Daniel's	"	1	"]
Hosea	"	"	6	"	"	Hosea's	"	1	"
Joel	"	"	2	"	"	Joel's	"	1	"
Amos	"	"	2	"	"	Amos's	"	0	"
Micah	"	"	1	"	"	Micah's	"	0	"
Habbakuk	"	"	4	"	"	Habbakuk's	"	0	"
Haggai	"	"	1	"	"	Haggai's	"	0	"
Zechariah	"	"	6	"	"	Zechariah's	"	0	"
Malachi	"	"	5	"	"	Malachi's	"	0	" "

* Acts, iii. 24. † 1 Pet. i. 10.

the record of St. Luke that, while our Lord was on the way to Emmaus with the disciples, " beginning at Moses and all the prophets, He expounded unto them in all the Scriptures the things concerning Himself;"* or to the statement of St. Paul before Agrippa, that he witnessed " none other things than those which the prophets and Moses did say should come: that Christ should suffer, and that he should be the first that should rise from the dead, and should show light unto the people and to the Gentiles.†" In all these cases alike there is expressed the same view of the object of the whole body of Old Testament Scripture: that it was intended to prepare and lead forward to Christ; and in this particular instance Samuel's name is mentioned merely as the first chronologically in the long line of prophets distinctly so called. His work in the reorganization of the disordered tribes, in the restoration of the neglected worship of Jehovah, in the anointing and subsequent setting aside of the first king of Israel, and anointing in his place " a man after God's own heart," and all his teaching accompanying these acts, was in preparation for the fulfillment of the promise of the Great Deliverer and King. It was to the Messianic kingdom that all his words and works looked forward. When that kingdom had come, the disciples rightly considered that Samuel, in common with those that followed, had

---

* Luke, xxiv. 27.

† Acts, xxvi. 22, 23. The translation of the Revisers here is perhaps more accurate and certainly brings out better the point: " that He first by the resurrection of the dead should proclaim," etc.

"foretold these days" in making them the end and object of their whole life-work. That this is really what St. Peter meant to say is abundantly evident from the fact that he expressly includes "all the prophets" in the same category with Samuel, and yet of many of them, as of Elijah, Elisha, Nahum, and others, we have no distinct Messianic prophecy recorded. Why should his words be interpreted in a different way of Samuel from that in which they must be of many of the others?

But the critics will have it that St. Peter must refer to some specific prophecy in words, and as it is alleged that none was uttered, at least so far as the record goes, by Samuel himself, the reference must be to the "Book of Samuel" which contains the prophecy of Nathan spoken to David,[*] "the one great Messianic prophecy of the Book." But this prophecy was uttered many years after the death of Samuel, and could not have been recorded by him. St. Peter therefore, it is said, cites a prophecy as "Samuel's," because it is contained in a book bearing his name, although, in this part at least, not written by him. Here, then, it is claimed, is a distinct case of the citation under the name of an author of something which was not written by him, just as now when we cite a passage as "in Samuel" we do not mean "in the book which Samuel wrote," but "in the book which commonly bears his name."

This argument rests upon several assumptions, each one of which is essential to its force and none of which seem in themselves probable. In the first

---

[*] 2 Sam. vii. 12-16.

place, there is no evidence that our present Books of Samuel were called by that name in the time of St. Peter; it is not likely that they were, and, if not, the whole argument falls to the ground. It is true that, as one undivided Book, they received that name in the time of the Talmud and of our earliest Hebrew manuscripts; but these all belong to a much later date. In the Septuagint, which was the translation most used by the Apostles, they are called the first and second Books of Kings. It is not likely that the writings in question were known as the "Books" or the "Book of Samuel" in St. Peter's day. Further, if any definite prophecy must be understood, there is no necessity for supposing that of Nathan to be meant. The reference might well be to the song of Hannah at the birth of Samuel,* the close of which is generally understood as referring to the Messiah, and is so interpreted in the Chaldee Targum which embodies the current Jewish interpretation in the time of St. Peter. This song was in all probability recorded by Samuel himself. But finally, as already shown at length, there is no reason to suppose a reference to any distinct prophetic utterance. It is therefore quite impossible on any ground to consider this as a proof that a book was cited under the name of an author who was not its writer.

The next instance referred to is that of Jeremiah, twice cited by name by St. Matthew. The point for which the passages are adduced is, that while the first, in relation to Rachel's weeping for her children,

---

* 1 Sam. ii. 10.

occurs in Jeremiah substantially as it is quoted,* the other, in relation to the price of Judas' treachery and the purchase of the potter's field, with the price thereof,† does not occur at all in Jeremiah, but a somewhat similar passage is found in Zechariah. ‡ Hence it is argued that St. Matthew attributes the words of Zechariah to Jeremiah, and therefore that he was not careful about the authorship of his quotations. A great variety of explanations have been suggested to account for this discrepancy, but putting these all aside for the moment, and taking the case just as it is stated, it argues nothing for the theory which it is brought to support. There is no variation of any importance in the reading, and it is clear that the Evangelist attributes to Jeremiah a passage which is not found in the collection of his writings as we have them. Now what does this prove? No one would maintain that St. Matthew really confused in his mind the utterances of Zechariah with those of Jeremiah, since he must have been familiar with both of them. At the utmost, it was a mere slip of the pen, or of memory (so St. Augustine, Luther, Beza, Keil, Köhler, and others hold); and as an accidental mistake would only show that such mistakes were possible. We do not admit the existence of these mistakes but if allowed here, they would be far from proving that the New Testament writers were in the habit of citing authors without reference to the reality of their authorship. To sustain the theory for which it is adduced

---

* Matt. ii. 17-18 ; Jer. xxxi. 15. † Matt. xxvii. 9.
‡ Zech. xi. 12-13.

it would be necessary to show that this part of Zechariah was popularly attributed to Jeremiah, and that St. Matthew cited it accordingly.

Now it curiously happens that one of the chief efforts of modern criticism has been directed to showing that this part of Zechariah was really the writing of some earlier prophet. Mede and Archbishop Newcome led the way in this opinion, and have been followed by a host of writers both in England and on the Continent. Among these are some who assign Zechariah ix.–xi. to Jeremiah, and in this case St. Matthew would simply have stated an actual fact which modern criticism has rediscovered. But, without admitting the validity of the argument for the dismemberment of Zechariah, it may be said that whatever force it has points in the direction of a far earlier writer, a contemporary of Isaiah, and the critics who deny the authorship of Zechariah are generally agreed in this earlier date. The explanation of the difficulty by supposing Zechariah ix.–xi. to have been actually written by Jeremiah cannot therefore be accepted, nor is there the slightest evidence that any such opinion was entertained in the time of the Evangelist.

Others (notably Hengstenberg) have thought that Zechariah is expressing in other language the substance of prophecies of Jeremiah, and that St. Matthew, using the thought of Jeremiah, attributes the prophecy to him, although citing it in the form given to it by Zechariah. The subtility of the argument by which this theory is maintained is sufficient to show its inconsistency with the simplicity of the Evangelic narrative, nor even so would it meet the language, "that which was spoken by Jeremiah the prophet."

The first point to be decided is whether St. Matthew really quotes the passage of Zechariah, as alleged, and if not, from what source he derived the quotation. Certainly, if he quoted from Zechariah, he quotes the passage in a very different sense from that which it originally bore. The whole context shows that Zechariah speaks of an insufficient reward for the faithful but unavailing service of the prophet. In fact there is nothing to assimilate the two passages but the mention of the thirty pieces of silver and the casting them to the potter. The former is so slight an indication that the supposition of St. Matthew's having quoted this passage rests chiefly on the latter. It is doubtful, however, if this word occurs in the original. As the text stands the word is יוֹצֵר, a participle meaning literally *the former*. It is used frequently of a potter, also of a maker of graven images of wood, stone, or metal,* and of God as the Creator.† In the present case the meaning of *potter* is unlikely, since it can scarcely be supposed that potters would have been allowed within the temple. A change of the weak initial letter makes the word אוֹצָר = *treasury*, and either this must have been the reading of the Septuagint (*furnace*), and also the version of Symmachus, and the Chaldee (*chief officer*), as well as of the Syriac translations, or else they must have understood the word as it stands in that sense. St.

---

* Isa. xliv. 9; Heb. ii. 18.   † Jer. x. 16; xviii. 11 ; Amos, iv. 13, etc.

Matthew, according to his custom, if he quoted from Zechariah at all, would probably have quoted from the Septuagint version, and it is only necessary to put the passage from the Septuagint side by side with that from St. Matthew to show how unlikely it is that the one should have been taken from the other.

SEPTUAGINT.	ST. MATTHEW.
And the Lord said unto me, Drop them into the furnace and I will see if it is good metal, as I was tested for their sake. And I took the thirty pieces of silver and threw them into the house of the Lord, into the furnace.	And they took the thirty pieces of silver, the price of him that was valued, whom they of the children of Israel did value, and gave them for the potter's field, as the Lord appointed me.

If these same passages had been found in any two profane authors, only a bold conjecture would establish a connection between them. In the Hebrew, if the translation *potter* be retained, there is more resemblance; but still the passages are unlike. When regard is had to the dissimilarity of the context and the purport of the two passages, there certainly remains slender basis for the theory that St. Matthew here quoted Zechariah under the name of Jeremiah. Whence then was the quotation derived? In the opinion of so early and critical a scholar as Origen, and of very many commentators since his day, it was from a prophecy of Jeremiah now lost. Jeremiah prophesied in the last days of the kingdom of Judah and after its overthrow in very troubled times. His prophecies were uttered partly in Jerusalem, partly in Egypt, and some of them were sent to the captives in Chaldea. As they are collected in the book which bears his name they are in obvious chronological confusion, and there is no book of the Old Testament in which the Septuagint version varies so greatly from the Hebrew both in the translation and in the order of the latter half of the book. It also omits a number of passages. There is no improbability that other prophecies of his should have failed to be included in this collection of his writings, and some of these may well have been preserved to the time of the Christian era and have since been lost. The supposition that St. Matthew really quoted from a prophecy of Jeremiah, now lost, has much in its favor; while the supposition that he quoted from Zechariah seems to be against the evidence. But however the difficulty may be explained, there is surely here no trustworthy support for the theory that the New Testament writers, when they gave the authority for their quotations, used the names of the popularly supposed authors, without regard to accuracy. There is nothing to show that this passage of Zechariah was at the time attributed by anybody to Jeremiah.

There is one, and only one, more passage which is appealed to as evidence of the uncertainty of the authorship assigned in the New Testament to some of its quotations. It is at the opening of the Gospel of St. Mark,* and is the only quotation which that Evangelist himself makes from the Old Testament. It is made up of two passages, the first from Malachi,† the other from Isaiah.‡ In the authorized version

---
* Mark, i. 2–3. † Mal. iii. 1. ‡ Isa. xl. 3.

there is no difficulty, for the quotations are prefaced by the words, "As it is written by the prophets;" but, although this is the reading of some important manuscripts, the weight of authority is strongly for the reading, "As it is written in the prophet Isaiah," which is adopted by all the critical editors, and which called for explanation as early as the time of Origen. As the passage stands therefore, in its correct reading,* St. Mark cites Isaiah, and then proceeds to give, first a passage from another prophet, and then one from Isaiah; and hence there seems ground for the conclusion "that the citation-formula is not here an authoritative guide to the

---

* The evidence for the different readings as given by Griesbach, Lachmann, Tischendorf, and Tregelles is as follows (Westcott and Hort have not thought the reading of the *Textus Receptus* worthy of a special note, and Scrivener only refers to it as an instance of the copyist's forsaking "his proper function for that of a reviser, or critical corrector"); for ἐν τῷ (there is some variation in the omission of τῷ) ‘Ησαΐα τῷ προφήτῃ the uncials ℵ B D L Δ ; of the cursives 33, and about twenty-five others (besides 1 which gives both readings); of the versions, Itala, Vulgate, Coptic, the Peshito and Jerusalem Syriac, and the *margin* of the Harclean, the Gothic, and the Armenian in its MSS.—nearly all these being earlier than any MS. containing the other reading; of the Fathers, Irenæus in different places has both readings and notes the variation, Origen repeatedly and in an express quotation saying "that Mark has collected into one two prophecies spoken in different places by two prophets," Porphyry, as quoted by St. Jerome, and St. Jerome himself, who thinks that the name of Isaiah is an error of the scribes. Eusebius also is of the same opinion, S. Augustine, and many others. For the reading ἐν τοῖς προφήταις the remaining uncials and cursives, the most important of which are *A* and *P*; of the versions only the Æthiopic, the *text* of the Harclean Syriac (7th cent.), the Armenian in the printed edition of Zohrab, and the Arabic; of the Fathers, Photius, Theophylact, and Irenæus as above.

real authorship of the words which immediately follow." Various explanations have been suggested, from the time of Origen down. The simplest seems to be that St. Mark, like the other Synoptists,* originally wrote quoting only from Isaiah; and this is the more likely, inasmuch as his Gospel is so peculiarly restricted to what is mentioned in the other Gospels, and so especially represents what must have been the common oral teaching about our Lord's life and works. Afterwards he inserted the passage from Malachi, on account of its especial appropriateness, but neglected to put with it the name of the author. Much to the same effect is another explanation: that he originally wrote the two quotations as we have them, but that he thought chiefly of Isaiah, as the prophecy commonly used in the Christian teaching, and gave his name, and then, as a sort of after-thought, inserted the quotation from Malachi before going on to that from Isaiah. But whatever be the explanation, it is certainly a fact that this is an instance in which a New Testament writer names an Old Testament prophet and then, before giving his words, records those of another prophet without mention of his name. If we had no other sources of information, we should suppose both passages to be taken from Isaiah.

If we could accept the explanation sometimes given that Isaiah, standing first in the collection of the prophets, gave his name to the whole book, and hence that St. Mark meant to quote both prophecies under the name of Isaiah, the whole point would

---
* Matt. iii. 3; Luke, iii. 4.

be yielded, and we could also say that because Moses wrote Genesis the whole Pentateuch was called by his name, and that quotations from the four last books of it under his name prove nothing as to his authorship. But there is absolutely no evidence that the collected books of the prophets were ever so called or so quoted. The prophets (*prophetæ posteriores*) were indeed (with the exception of Daniel) anciently arranged as a separate part of the Hebrew Bible; but, as far as we know, were never called by the name of any single prophet. This explanation therefore may be dismissed.

Before the fact of these quotations can give support to the theory on behalf of which it is used, it must be shown that there was somebody who attributed the language of Malachi to Isaiah. St. Mark himself could not have done so, nor could his readers; for all alike were too familiar with the Old Testament Scriptures to confound together the utterances of the first and the last of the prophets, separated from each other by a vast interval of time. There is no evidence that anybody ever fell into such a mistake. An attempt has been made to give a parallel case by supposing a writer in English to have coupled together two quotations, one from Shakespeare and one from Milton, under the name of the latter; but the case is not parallel. The works of no English authors stand in the same relation to the English reader as the Scriptures of the Old Testament did to the early Christian. They were his sacred books, the charter of his salvation, the foundation of his faith. Such a quotation could not have passed unnoticed, and we find it did not in the earliest literature we have on the subject. And even admitting the parallel, no intelligent English writer would be supposed to have intentionally cited Shakespeare under the name of Milton; some other explanation would be sought for such a curious fact if it had ever occurred. Undoubtedly many persons have attributed the familiar words " God tempers the wind to the shorn lamb " to Scripture, without special mention of any Scripture author; but in doing so they have supposed that the words of Sterne were actually those of Scripture. There are but two ways in which it can be supposed that St. Mark intended to attribute the words of Malachi to Isaiah: (1) Either he really believed them to be Isaiah's, a supposition which no one entertains; or else (2) they were popularly so attributed, and he quotes them according to the popular opinion without thinking it worth while to correct the error. The last supposition is entirely without evidence and is contrary to all probability, and it is only by means of this that the testimony of the New Testament writers to the authorship of the Old Testament books can be impugned.

But it is still urged that here is a case of wrong citation of an author, and that, however it may be explained, it proves that no reliance can be placed on the New Testament mention of the authors of its citations. The reply is the same as in the case of St. Matthew's citation of Jeremiah; at the most it would prove simply a slip of the pen, and would invalidate the New Testament testimony just in so far as it proved errors of this kind to be possible, leaving untouched all passages in which such error could not be supposed. But it has been shown in the case of Jeremiah that there is no necessity of supposing an error, and although this is a somewhat more difficult case, there really is no such necessity here. There are instances, in regard to other matters, in the New Testament where two statements are put together in the brevity of utterance, which must be separated in order to make them accurate; and such ellipses sometimes occasion considerable difficulties of interpretation. Thus, St. Paul warns Timothy of certain false teachers " forbidding to marry, to abstain from meats,"* where our version (and also the Revision) have been obliged to insert the words *and commanding* to convey the evident meaning of the Apostle. In the question of Judas, " why was not this ointment sold for three hundred pence and given to the poor?"† familiarity with the expression almost blinds us to the ellipsis, and we fail to remember that the ointment could not have been both sold and given away, and that what was meant was, that it should be sold and the proceeds of the sale given to the poor. The elliptical form of statement concerning the use made of the price of Judas' treachery, " Now this man purchased a field with the reward of iniquity," ‡ has even been made the ground of cavil. The extremely elliptical statement in the speech of St. Stephen, " So Jacob went down into Egypt, and died, he and our fathers, and were carried over into

---
* 1 Tim. iv. 3. † John, v. 12. ‡ Acts, i. 18.

Sychem and laid in the sepulchre," * has occasioned endless exegetical difficulty, because in the brevity of the discourse the words " carried over into Sychem" grammatically apply both to Jacob and to " our fathers," while they are meant only of the latter. Similarly, St. Mark's mention of Isaiah is meant to apply and is true of only one of his quotations, while in the brevity of his writing it applies grammatically to both.

On the whole, it cannot be maintained that St. Mark meant to attribute Malachi's prophecy to Isaiah; and if not, then, whatever may be the difficulty of explaining the passage, there is no ground for arguing from it that the New Testament writers named the authors of passages of the Old without intending to commit themselves to the truth of that authorship. The same conclusion having been reached in regard to all the instances alleged, the presumption remains that when a passage of the Old Testament is cited under the name of an author, the writer or speaker intended to indicate the real authorship as much as is done in any similar quotation in any other writings at any other time. Still it may be repeated that this is not absolutely determinative of the real authorship; and that even an inspired writer might have quoted books under the name they popularly bore without committing himself to the reality of the authorship. This is possible, and, except in the few instances in which the validity of the argument depends on the authorship, no one would lose his faith in the truth of the New

---

* Acts, vii. 15, 16.

Testament if it could be proved that it sometimes quotes under the name of the currently supposed, rather than of the real author; but it is important to observe that the *presumption* that the rightful authors are given remains, and that the burden of proof rests upon the other side. Moreover, this argument presupposes that the books in question were at the time of the Christian era popularly attributed to the authors named, and this fact is of no small importance in the question of the real authorship.

Since, however, this fact has been called in question, especially as regards the Pentateuch, and it has been alleged that there is no sufficient evidence that this was popularly attributed to Moses in New Testament times, it may be well to look a moment at the effect of the opposite supposition. This is only for the sake of the argument, for it is believed that the evidence is ample that not only the Pentateuch, but the Old Testament books generally, as far as the authorship is known, were attributed to the same authors in those days as they have been since, and there is no evidence that in ancient times any other opinion was ever held. But admit the allegation, and what follows? That the New Testament writers went out of their way to mention the authors of the Old Testament books when they were not known to those whom they addressed. In this case there would be clear and express testimony to the authorship which could hardly be gainsaid without destroying altogether the reliability of the New Testament. Why should our Lord have said that Moses "wrote you this commandment," if there were no common belief that he had done so, except to assert the fact?

With the presumption therefore undiminished, that the authors mentioned in the New Testament are the real authors of the books cited, the following list may be given, in addition to those already specially discussed, of quotations from the Old Testament with the names of the authors. Some passages are included which give no express quotation, but which, nevertheless, more or less fully testify to the authorship; but simple references to facts recorded in the Old Testament are excluded.

One further remark is necessary: what is sought is testimony to the substantial authorship, not to the mere writing down of the words. For our present purpose it is of no consequence whether Moses actually wrote down the laws of the Pentateuch or whether he delivered them orally to his successors. The point is that the New Testament recognizes these laws as emanating from him.

I. The Pentateuch. (1) In the words of our Lord.

> Matt. viii. 4; Mark, i. 44; Luke, v. 14. "Offer the gift that Moses commanded." Lev. xiv. 1–31.
>
> " xix. 8. "Moses suffered you to put away your wives." Deut. xxiv. 1.
>
> Mark, vii. 10. "Moses said, Honor thy father and thy mother." Ex. xx. 12; Deut. v. 16.
>
> " x. 3, 5. "What did Moses command you? .... For your hardness of heart he wrote you this commandment." Like Matt. xix. 8.

Mark, xii. 26; Luke, xx. 37. "Have ye not read in the Book of Moses," etc. Ex. iii. 6.

Luke, xvi. 29, 31. "They have Moses and the Prophets..... If they hear not Moses and the Prophets."

" xxiv. 44. "Beginning at Moses and all the prophets, He expounded unto them in all the Scriptures," etc.

John, v. 45-47. "If ye believed Moses, ye would believe Me; for he wrote of Me. But if ye believe not his writings, how shall ye believe My words?" (In this case the argument seems to require that the leader and lawgiver " on whom ye have set your hope " should have been the author of the " writings " referred to.)

" vii. 19. " Did not Moses give you the law?"

" vii. 22, 23. " For this cause hath Moses given you circumcision..... That the law of Moses may not be broken." Lev. xii. 3. (In both these cases there is an emphasis on the fact that *Moses* gave the law.)

(2) In the words of inspired men.

A few passages may first be mentioned in which it is not expressly said that Moses wrote the words quoted, but merely, as under the previous head, that they were spoken to him or by him. They might have been recorded by some one else, but as they are contained in the writings commonly known as "the writings of Moses," the natural inference is that he was considered the author of the record.

Acts, vii. 22–26. "And Moses .... would have set them at one again, saying, Sirs, ye are brethren : why do ye wrong one to another?" Ex. ii. 13–15.

" vii. 31–34. The account of what the Lord said to Moses at the bush, taken from Ex. iii.

Rom. ix. 15. "For He saith to Moses, I will have mercy on whom I will have mercy," etc. Ex. xxxiii. 19.

Heb. viii. 5. "Moses was admonished of God. .... See, saith He, that thou make all things according to the pattern showed to thee in the Mount." Ex. xxv. 40; xxvi. 30.

" ix. 19, 20. "When every commandment had been spoken by Moses .... according to the law, he took the blood .... saying," etc.

Another class of passages refers to "the law," or to some particular law, of Moses. It is possible that these laws might have been given by Moses and orally handed down until they were recorded by some one else; but, as before, as there was at the time a written body of laws passing under the name of Moses, and in many instances expressly declaring that they were written by him, the natural inference is that this is referred to, and that its authorship is attributed to Moses.

Luke, ii. 22. "Her purification according to the law of Moses." Lev. xii. 2.

John, i. 17. "The law was given by Moses."

Acts, xiii. 39. "Could not be justified by the law of Moses."

Acts, xxi. 21. "They are all zealous of the law .... and that thou teachest .... to forsake Moses, saying that they ought not to circumcise," etc.

Heb. vii. 14. "As to which tribe Moses spake nothing concerning priests."

" x. 28. "He that despised Moses' law died."

The remaining passages all speak expressly of something which Moses wrote or said, or else of a writing under his name.

Acts, iii. 22, 23. "Moses truly said unto the fathers," quoting Deut. xviii. 15, etc.

" vii. 37. "This is that Moses which said unto the children of Israel," quoting the same passage.

" xv. 21. "Moses .... hath in every city them that preach him, being read in the synagogues every Sabbath day."

" xxviii. 23. "Persuading them concerning Jesus, both from the law of Moses," etc.

Rom. x. 5. "Moses describeth the righteousness which is of the law," quoting Lev. xviii. 5.

" x. 19. "Moses saith," quoting Deut. xxxii. 21.

1 Cor. ix. 9. "It is written in the law of Moses," quoting Deut. xxv. 4.

2 Cor. iii. 15. "Until this day remaineth the same veil untaken away in the reading of the Old Testament .... but even unto this day when Moses is read."

If one half as many passages could be found of the same period attributing the Athenian legislation to Solon, the world would consider that its authorship was settled beyond all peradventure, at least in the opinion of the writers making the quotations. It is indeed curiously argued that while these passages may establish the authenticity of the particular passages cited, they go no further, and do not show that the writers making them believed the legislation of the Pentateuch as a whole to be the work of Moses, and that the references to "the law of Moses" and "the book of Moses," etc., when there was at the time a well-known law and book passing under his name, do not prove that the writers accepted that work as his. If so, nothing could suffice short of the quotation of the whole law. But, surely, he would be thought an over-nice critic who argued that a quotation, under the name of Cicero, from the well-known work "*De Senectute*," recognized only Cicero's authorship of the particular sentence, and not of the treatise as a whole. On such principles the authorship of no ancient work could ever be established.

It remains to mention some passages in which Moses is spoken of in the New Testament by uninspired persons as the giver of the law, the receiver of revelation, or the *writer* of the law. These show the common belief of the time.

> Matt. xix. 5 ; Mark x. 4. "Why did Moses command?"—reference to Deut. xxiv. 1.
> " xxii. 24. "Moses said, If a man die," etc. Deut. xxv. 5.

Mark, xii. 19; Luke, xx. 28. "Moses wrote unto us." Reference to same passage.

John, i. 45. "Of whom Moses in the law .... did write."

" ix. 29. "We know that God hath spoken unto Moses" (in reference to the law of the Sabbath).

Acts, vi. 1. "The customs which Moses delivered unto us."

" vi. 11, 13, 14. "Blasphemous words against Moses .... against this holy place and the law .... shall change the customs which Moses delivered us."

To these may be added here the words in John, viii. 5, "In the law Moses commanded us to stone such." Lev. xx. 10.

After the Pentateuch no other books are cited under the name of the author until the Psalms are reached. These are quoted ten times as David's in the following passages:

Matt. xxii. 43, 45; Mark, xii. 36, 37; Luke, xx. 42, 44; Acts, ii. 25; ii. 34. These have already been discussed.

Acts, i. 16. "Which the Holy Ghost by the mouth of David spake .... For it is written in the Book of Psalms," followed by quotations from Ps. lxix. 25 and cix. 8.

" iv. 24–26. "Lord, ... Who by the mouth of thy servant David hast said," with quotations from Ps. ii. 1, 2.

Rom. iv. 6. "David also describeth the blessedness of the man," etc.; from Ps. xxxiv. 1, 2.
" xi. 9. "And David saith;" from Ps. lxix. 22, 23.
Heb. iv. 7. "Saying in David;" from Ps. xcv. 7, 8.

Of the prophets Isaiah is cited by name far more frequently than all the others together (17 times), and these citations are nearly equally divided between the former and the latter part of the book that bears his name.

Matt. iii. 3; Mark i. 2, 3; Luke iii. 4. "Spoken of by the prophet Esaias, saying," with quotation from Isa. xl. 3. The formulas of quotation are a little more explicit in St. Mark and St. Luke, the latter: "As it is written in the book of the words of Esaias, the prophet."
" iv. 14. "Spoken by Esaias the prophet, saying," from Isa. ix. 1, 2.
" viii. 17. The same formula, with quotation from Isa. liii. 4.
" xii. 17. The same, with quotation from Isa. xlii. 1-4.
" xiii. 14. Our Lord says "In them is fulfilled the prophecy of Esaias, which saith," quoting Isa. vi. 9, 10. In the parallel passage in Mark, iv. 12, the same passage is repeated without any indication of quotation.

Matt. xv. 7; Mark, vii. 6. Again the words of our Lord, "Well did Esaias prophesy of you," quoting Isa. xxix. 13.

Luke, iv. 17. "The book of the prophet Esaias . . . . He found the place where it is written," quoting Isa. lxi. 1, 2.

John, i. 23. "As said the prophet Esaias," with quotation from Isa. xliii. 3. This again is in the words of our Lord.

" xii. 38. "That the saying of Esaias the prophet might be fulfilled which he spake, saying," with quotation from Isa. liii. 1.

" xii. 39, 41. "Esaias said again," "These things said Esaias," with quotation from Isa. vi. 9, 10.

Acts viii. 28-33. "Read Esaias the prophet." . . . . "heard him read the prophet Esaias." . . . . "the place of the Scripture which he read was," quoting from Isa. liii. 7.

" xxviii. 25. "Well spake the Holy Ghost by Esaias the prophet unto our fathers, saying," with quotation from Isa. vi. 9, 10.

Rom. ix. 27. "Esaias also crieth concerning Israel," quoting Isa. x. 21-23.

" ix. 29. "And as Esaias said before," quoting Isa. i. 9.

" x. 16. "For Esaias saith," quoting Isa. liii. 1.

" x. 20. "First Moses saith . . . . but Esaias is very bold and saith," quoting from Isa. lxv. 1, 2.

" xv. 12. After several other quotations, it is added, "And again Esaias saith," quoting Isa. xi. 10.

It is plain that while all these prophecies are spoken of as utterances of Isaiah, in several cases they are expressly distinguished from the utterances of others. A far less amount of testimony to the authorship of any other ancient book would be considered more than enough to prove the belief of the writers in that authorship. The real question is whether it is possible that they might have been mistaken, and their private opinions be distinguished from the teaching of the Spirit who inspired them. If this is to be maintained, very clear evidence of the fact must be presented, and meantime there will be a strong presumption that the books actually proceeded from the persons to whom they are attributed.

Jeremiah is twice quoted by name. Both of these quotations have already been discussed at length: one is Matt. ii. 17, quoting Jer. xxxi. 15, and the other is Matt. xxvii. 9, in relation to the Potter's Field, and both read "that which was spoken by Jeremy the prophet."

Daniel is cited by name once by our Lord, Matt. xxiv. 15, "The abomination of desolation, spoken of by Daniel the prophet, stand in the holy place," referring to Dan. ix. 27 (cf. xi. 31; xii. 11).

Hosea has two passages, ii. 23 and i. 10, quoted together under his name in Rom. ix. 25–27.

Joel is quoted by name in Acts, ii. 16–21 in the speech of St. Peter, the passage being taken from Joel, ii. 28–32.

All the quotations from the Old Testament with the name of the writer have now been mentioned.

In regard to a very few there are some special difficulties, but it has been attempted to show that these do not bear upon the present question. About the authorship of several of them there is no question; they are simply attributed to the authors to whom they have always been and still continue to be attributed. In the case of a few others, the New Testament is absolutely committed, by the course of the argument, to the authorship assigned. The majority of them, however, are simple citations where the question of the particular authorship is not essential, but the writers of the New Testament have deviated from their custom by mentioning the author, and in several of these cases recent criticism has called that authorship in question. Do these quotations settle the question in favor of the traditional view? It seems to me that they do not do so absolutely; *i. e.*, that if it could be distinctly proved that the books in question were not written by the persons whose names they bear, it would still be possible to explain the mention of the author. But the only way of doing this is by assuming the common traditional authorship at the time, and this is in itself a strong argument for the truth of that authorship. Moreover, the citations from the Pentateuch and from Isaiah at least, even when the authorship was not essential to the argument, do in many cases imply a conviction on the part of the writers that the authors they mention were the real authors, and to suppose that they were not, would involve grave difficulties. Finally, if these citations are considered inconclusive as to the question of authorship, then almost all historic evidence of authorship of any ancient book must be set aside ; for it is far stronger here than in ordinary cases.

The question of inspiration has been purposely excluded from this discussion for obvious reasons. It is desirable to see what is the bearing of the evidence apart from this. When that is considered, a new factor of a different kind is understood. Without appeal to this, it would seem that the conclusion must be, that the New Testament testimony to the authorship of the Old Testament books in a few cases is absolute and decisive; in the others, it creates a presumption so strong that it could only be set aside by most clear and convincing proofs.

LECTURE XIV.

THE NEW TESTAMENT USE OF THE OLD.

QUOTATIONS from the Old Testament made under the name of their authors have been discussed in the last lecture. It remains to speak of the more general use of the older Scriptures in the New Testament, whether by anonymous quotations, or in a variety of other ways.

Many of the so-called quotations are without any formula of citation, and some of them, consisting only of a few words, may be mere coincidences of expression. Others are expressions of the thoughts of the New Testament writer in language familiar to him in the sacred books, but perhaps without distinct consciousness that he was using the words of others. On the other hand, there are apparent quotations from the Old Testament which do not anywhere occur in this exact form, but are rather concise summaries of the teaching of various parts of the older Scriptures. Thus St. Matthew writes, " that it might be fulfilled which was spoken by the prophets, He shall be called a Nazarene." * Our Lord declares, " He that believeth on me, as the Scripture hath said, Out of his belly shall flow rivers of living water." † St. James quotes, " The spirit

---

* Matt. ii. 23.   † John, vii. 38.

that dwelleth in us lusteth to envy."* There are several other like passages. There are also many references to characters and events in the Old Testament (as to Jonah) without express quotation. It is therefore difficult to make any precise statement of the whole number of quotations. The latest publication on the subject † enumerates nearly six hundred (592) quotations in the New Testament, many of them taken from different parts of the Old, so that by far the larger part of its books are embraced in the quotations.‡ Gough § enumerates six hundred and fourteen passages of the Old Testament quoted in the New, some of them several times, with thirteen other quotations of the more general character just mentioned. A more sober estimate would largely reduce these numbers; but the very difficulty of any precise statement shows how thoroughly the minds of the writers of the New Testament were filled both with the language and the thoughts of the Old. They used its words to express their own thoughts, and they expressed its thoughts in their own language.

On two occasions during the forty days between our Lord's resurrection and ascension He taught the disciples that the whole body of the older Scriptures pointed forward to Himself and His

---

* James. iv. 5.

† *Quotations in the New Testament.* By C: H. Toy. New York, 1884.

‡ Omitting only Judges, Ruth, Chronicles, Ezra, Nehemiah, Esther, Lamentations, Obadiah, Jonah. Express references are made to the events and persons mentioned in several of these.

§ *The New Testament Quotations.* London, 1855.

work for the redemption of mankind. On the way to Emmaus He upbraided them for their slowness of heart in not understanding this, " and beginning at Moses and all the prophets, He expounded unto them in all the Scriptures the things concerning Himself."* A few weeks later and immediately on the eve of His ascension, He explained to them " that all things must be fulfilled which were written in the law of Moses, and in the Prophets, and in the Psalms concerning Me." † Ever after they read and used the Old Testament Scriptures with this Divine guidance as the key to their meaning. It would be wholly wrong therefore to interpret the particular passages quoted as if they stood alone, and had no further meaning than the precise words, in their isolation, must convey. They are parts of a preparatory revelation, and, to be understood in their true sense, must be taken in connection with the whole teaching of that Dispensation, and also viewed in the light thrown back upon them from the Gospel. The New Testament quotations from the Old may be arranged for convenience in four general classes as they were used (1) for purposes of argument, (2) as expressions of general truth belonging alike to all ages, (3) as illustrations, and (4) simply as sacred and familiar words expressing, without regard to their original use, that which the writers wished to say. A volume would be required to treat them all in detail, and many of them have been already discussed in the previous chapters. A few instances only will here be treated under each

---

* Luke, xxiv. 26-27. † *Ib.* xxiv. 44-47.

class as examples of the method to be used, preference being given to those which have occasioned difficulties.

(1) Quotations for purposes of argument. This is in some respects the most important class, and instances of it are very abundant. Our Lord referred to the original creation of the human pair to show that monogamy had from the first been the Divine will.* Here was a citation of an old and entirely familiar fact to prove that the strictness of Christian morality, which seemed so new and of such unheard-of severity, was really God's will from the first, and the intervening laxity had been merely a Divine condescension to human weakness, suffered for the hardness of men's hearts. The argument, once put before the mind, is clear and unanswerable; but man might never have discovered it had it not been pointed out to him.

Again: He silenced the Sadducees, who denied not only the resurrection, but also said that there is "neither angel nor spirit," † by quoting the language which God addressed to Moses at the bush, "I am the God of Abraham and Isaac and Jacob." ‡ The argument is certainly a subtle one, and its force only appears to us on reflection; but it was conclusive and recognized at once as satisfactory by those to whom it was addressed.

Many passages are cited to show that the Old Dispensation looked forward to a more complete

---

* Matt. xix. 4-8 ; Mark, x. 4-7 ; Gen. i. 27 ; ii. 18-25.
† Acts, xxiii. 8.
‡ Matt. xxii. 31, 32; Mark, xii. 26-27; Luke, xx. 37-38; Ex. iii. 6-8.

revelation to follow. Several of these passages have already been considered while speaking of the teaching of the Old Testament on this subject. It remains to note how these and other passages are used in the New. The important prophecy in Jeremiah, xxxi. 31-34, is twice quoted in the Epistle to the Hebrews, the first * time to show the points just mentioned; the second, † to show that full forgiveness of sin having been the promise of the new covenant, there can no longer be a necessity for any " more offering for sin." The argument is conclusive, although it seems as difficult for Judaizing Christians of the present day to appreciate its force as it was for the Jews themselves of old.

The words of the prophet Haggai, "Yet once, it is a little while, and I will shake the heavens and the earth," ‡ as interpreted by their context and by the close of the prophecy, are used in the Epistle to the Hebrews § to show both the temporary character of the Old Dispensation and the finality of the New. The argument, as the passages appear in our version, is clear, when the reference of the prophecy to Messianic times is once admitted, as in all fairness it must be. But it is objected that the point of the Apostle's argument turns upon the expression " once more," following the Septuagint translation, and that these words do not give the sense of the Hebrew. Technically the objection is true. The exactly literal rendering of the Hebrew would be, " Yet one, it is little, and I will shake," etc.: but this has no

---

* Heb. viii. 8-12.
‡ Hag. ii. 6; cf. ver. 7-9, 22, 23.
† *Ib* x. 16-17.
§ Heb. xii. 26, 27.

meaning, and must be understood in the light of its context. The prophecy was uttered when the people were grieving over the greatly inferior glory of the second temple. God promises them that the "glory of this latter house shall be greater than that of the former," because He will bring about a great convulsion, and in this house "will give peace." He then goes on to say that He "will destroy the kingdoms of the heathen," and make Zerubbabel, as the representative of the house of David, "as a signet." The whole prophecy, in connection with the familiar prophecies that had gone before, can only be understood of the final establishment of the universal Messianic kingdom, so that the words of the Septuagint used by the Apostle are merely a summary of the whole intent and purport of the prophecy. The argument is therefore good, not because the words "once more" are actually in the original; but because their meaning is necessarily involved in what is said, and they were thus so fully justified that the Apostle had no occasion to criticise the ordinary translation.

The famous prophecy of Joel,* beginning, "It shall come to pass afterward that I will pour out my Spirit upon all flesh," was quoted by St. Peter on the day of Pentecost and applied to the outpouring of the Holy Spirit on the Christian disciples; and it was claimed that this was the meaning of the prophecy.† The last clause of it is also quoted by St. Paul as a proof of the intended universality of the Christian offer of salvation: " For there is no difference

---
* Joel, ii. 28-32.   † Acts, ii. 16-21.

between the Jew and the Greek. .... For whosoever shall call upon the name of the Lord shall be saved."* The prophecy is given after threatenings of great calamities coming upon the people. God promises, after these, to pour out His Spirit abundantly in the midst of great manifestations of His power (represented, according to ordinary poetic language, under the figure of natural wonders and convulsions), and at that time all who truly call upon Him shall be delivered. No determination of time is given when these things shall occur. From Joel's time to St. Peter's they evidently had not occurred, and then they had manifestly come to pass. It would seem that the sense in which St. Peter and St. Paul have taken this prophecy was the obvious one under the circumstances. The only point of difficulty is that Joel speaks of these things as coming " before the great and terrible day of the Lord "—an expression which we are accustomed to associate with the time of the final judgment. But that this is not the prophet's meaning is plain from the fact that he speaks of it as a time when deliverance shall still be offered to every one who "shall call on the name of the Lord." By many commentators therefore the expression is understood of the great judgment upon the unbelieving Jews in the destruction of their city and temple by the Romans. But it seems more probable that the prophet looked upon our Lord's whole work as essentially one, that being pre-eminently " the great and terrible day " when the responsibility of accepting or rejecting the offers of salva-

---
* Rom. x. 12, 13.

tion should be laid upon man. It is in the same way that the last of the prophets speaks of the coming of our Lord's forerunner.*

There are many prophecies of our Lord's coming, of His acts and offices, of His priesthood and of the blessings He should bring, which are quoted in the New Testament to show that He fulfilled the predictions concerning Him. On these there is not space here to dwell. Many of them were interpreted of the Messiah in the Jewish Targums, and undoubtedly were intended to refer to Him; others were only known to have this reference when the event came to pass exactly answering to that which had been foretold. The argument connecting prophecy and fulfillment is here something of the same nature as that which assumes that two torn pieces of paper which exactly fit together originally formed one sheet. Often, however, there are not sufficient details in the prophecy to admit of the use of this analogy, and then reliance must be placed on the scope and purpose of the prophet, on the connection with other prophecies which had gone before, on the absence of any other fulfillment, on the general interpretation of the time, and other indications which will be found in the better commentaries on the passages in question.

In all quotations which are used argumentatively, or to establish any fact or doctrine, it is obviously necessary that the passage in question should be fairly cited according to its real intent and meaning, in order that the argument drawn from it may be

---

* Mal. iv. 5, 6.

valid. There has been much rash criticism of some of these passages, and the assertion has been unthinkingly made that the Apostles, and especially St. Paul, brought up in rabbinical schools of thought, quoted the Scriptures after a rabbinical and inconsequential fashion. A patient and careful examination of the passages themselves will remove such misapprehension. Only a few of those which have occasioned most difficulty can be taken as examples. The prophet Habakkuk describes the calamities coming upon the Jews through the power and pride of the Chaldeans, and declares that in the midst of these "the just shall live by his faith."* He evidently refers to the Divine support and deliverance in the midst of these temporal calamities which shall be afforded to those who calmly trust in God and put their whole confidence in Him. St. Paul quotes the passage with the formula "as it is written" and sets it forth in the Epistle to the Romans,† and again in that to the Galatians, ‡ as embodying the fundamental principle of Christian salvation. It is used again in the Epistle to the Hebrews, § to show that this trust must still be firmly held in the midst of surrounding trials and afflictions, and there is added a clause from the Septuagint (reversing the order of the clauses), "but if any man draw back, my soul shall have no pleasure in him," which is a mistranslation of the Hebrew. In regard to this last passage there is no difficulty, for the expression "the just shall live by faith" is plainly used in the

---

* Hab. ii. 4. † Rom. i. 17.
‡ Gal. iii. 11. § Heb. x. 38.

same sense as in the prophet, and the added clause from the Septuagint is merely the converse of this, and might as well have been expressed in the Apostle's own words, if he had not found it ready to his hand in the translation in common use. But it is alleged that in Romans and Galatians the word faith is used in a different sense and with a different application from that of the prophet. Certainly the application is different, but the principle involved is the same in both cases. The word *faith* has the sense in the Old Testament of steadfastness, faithfulness in the discharge of all obligations, just as we use the term "a faithful man;" in relation to God, it means a firm belief and reliance on the Divine word, as the context shows in this passage, and as the verb is used in the expression "Abraham believed in the Lord." It is precisely this which St. Paul intends by *faith*. It is not with him a mere intellectual act; it is a principle which leads the Christian to put his whole trust in God and accept His will as the guide of life. The principle to which Habakkuk promised Divine acceptance is that to which St. Paul promises the same thing; only from the nature of the Dispensations, the one should be manifested more after an earthly, the other more after a spiritual manner.

St. Paul uses an argument in the Epistle to the Galatians which has occasioned great difficulty to the commentators, and has been often considered as altogether unsound. St. Jerome even goes so far as to say that St. Paul, in making himself all things to all men, here made himself a fool to the "foolish

Galatians!"* The passage is, "Now to Abraham and his seed were the promises made. He saith not, and to seeds, as of many; but as of one, and to thy seed, which is Christ."† The difficulty arises from the fact that the word *seed*, whether in Hebrew or in Greek, is a collective term, just as it is in English, and no inference can therefore be drawn as to the individuality of the subject of the promise from the use of the singular number. Had it been intended that the promises should be fulfilled in the whole multitude of Abraham's posterity, numerous " as the sand which is by the seashore," the same word would still have been used. The Chaldee word is also collective, though it is twice used in a different sense in the plural (Dan. i. 12, 16). ‡ It is plain, therefore, that any argument founded upon the mere number of the noun used in the promise can have no validity; nor does St. Paul intend to base his argument upon this, as is so often assumed. This is pre-eminently a case where a particular promise

---

* Apostolus qui omnibus omnia factus est, ut omnes lucrifaceret, debitor Græcis ac barbaris, sapientibus et insipientibus, Galatis quoque, quos ante stultos dixerat, factus est stultus. Hieron. in Gal. iii. 16.

† Gal. iii. 16.

‡ The Chaldee word is used in the Targums in the plural in the sense of *family* in Gen. x. 18 ; Josh. vii. 14 ; Jer. xxiii. 24 ; but in all these cases the Hebrew word is מִשְׁפָּחָה not זֶרַע and is variously rendered in the Greek. A single instance of the Greek plural is referred to in 4 Macc. xviii. 1: ὦ τῶν Ἀβραμιαίων σπερμάτων ἀπόγονοι παῖδες Ἰσραηλῖται πείθεσθε τῷ νόμῳ τούτῳ. But it may be doubted, Meyer and Lightfoot to the contrary notwithstanding, whether σπέρματα has not here rather the sense of the Chaldee plural=*families*. At most, it is a solitary and obscure example.

must be understood, as St. Paul understood it, in connection with the whole body of promises relating to the same point. When our first parents were told that the Seed of the woman should bruise the serpent's head,* the promise was from the first understood of some personal Deliverer who should rescue fallen man from the thraldom of the yoke of evil. At Cain's birth he was rashly considered the expected Restorer. † Ages after this disappointment, Noah was expected to be the one that "shall comfort us concerning our work and toil of our hands, because of the ground which the Lord hath cursed." ‡ During all the long ages when man was but falling more deeply and hopelessly under the power of evil, this promise must have been the hope and stay of every devout and God-fearing soul. It survived the terrible judgment of the flood. It passed into the expectation of the better part of every nation. Trench has well said, "No thoughtful student of the past records of mankind can refuse to acknowledge that through all its history there has run the hope of redemption from the evil which oppresses it; nor of this only, but that this hope has continually linked itself on to some single man. The help that is coming to the world, it has ever seen incorporated in a person." § This expectation surely was not wanting in the family of Shem, nor in the race of Eber; and when Abraham was called out of the world to be the father of a chosen nation, and it was promised him that "in thy seed shall all the na-

---

* Gen. iii. 15.   † *Ib.* iv. 1.   ‡ *Ib.* v. 29.
§ Hulsean Lectures, 1846. Lect. II. p. 177.

tions of the earth be blessed," he must have understood by it that the long expected Redeemer of mankind, the Seed of the woman, was to be born of his posterity.* The traditionary prophecy of Enoch, quoted in Jude 14, looks distinctly to a personal Redeemer, and so the promise was certainly understood all along through the ages as its fulfillment was determined successively to be in the tribe of Judah and in the family of David. The later prophets, one after another, bring out fresh characteristics of this Redeemer, but never waver in the idea that he is to be a *Person*, "a Priest after the order of Melchisedec," † whose birth-place at Bethlehem is foretold by Micah. ‡ Such was the general expectation of the Jews, derived from their sacred books, at the time of Christ's coming, and such was the expectation even of the Magi, from the East. § The promise having been so understood before it was confined to the seed of Abraham, having been so received by him, having been so explained by all the prophets age after age, St. Paul was certainly justified in saying that the promise was through ONE, and that one was Christ. To express this briefly in English we should say, "it was not to *seeds*, as of many; but as of one, and to thy *seed*, which is Christ," without any reference to the intrinisic etymological value of the singular and plural of that word. So St. Paul uses the plural and the singular of the Greek word, not arguing from the force of the

---

* From my article on Gal. iii. 16, in the *Bibliotheca Sacra* for Jan., 1879, p. 26.

† Ps. cx. 4.   ‡ Micah, v. 2.   § Matt. ii. 2.

number, but from the nature of the promise. He uses the singular and plural merely as a convenience to explain his meaning.

Another argument of St. Paul in this same epistle, and drawn from the same book of Genesis, has been made the ground of much unnecessary criticism. After referring to the story of Hagar and Ishmael, of Sarah and Isaac, he adds, "which things are an allegory. For these are the two covenants; the one from Mount Sinai, which gendereth to bondage, which is Agar (for this Agar is Mount Sinai in Arabia), and answereth to Jerusalem which now is, and is in bondage with her children; but Jerusalem which is above is free, which is the mother of us all. . . . . Now we, brethren, as Isaac was, are the children of promise. But as then, he that was born after the flesh persecuted him that was born after the Spirit, even so it is now," * etc. There certainly is nothing in the story of Ishmael and Isaac to show that Christians rather than Jews were the chosen people of God, and to those who suppose this to be the argument of St. Paul it must appear inconsequential. But his purpose is really very different. He has already shown in the previous part of the epistle that the true children of Abraham are those who believe: these are the children of promise and are free, while those who are merely his descendants after the flesh are under the bondage of the law. This fact having been established, he argues that the relation between the bond and the free is always the same; as it was in the days of Abraham, so it is

---
* Gal. iv. 21-31.

now. The argument is clear and satisfactory, and there was a peculiar pertinency in it for his purpose because in the illustration chosen, Ishmael was actually the child of Abraham after the flesh.*

One other instance of quotation for purposes of argument may be given. The author of the Epistle to the Hebrews, in the course of his proof that all other sacrifices are done away in Christ, writes as follows: "Wherefore when He cometh into the world, He saith, Sacrifice and offering Thou wouldest not, but a body hast Thou prepared Me: in burnt offerings and sacrifices for sin Thou hast had no pleasure. Then said I, Lo, I come (in the volume of the book it is written of Me) to do thy will, O God." † It is well known that the word *body* is taken from the Septuagint translation, and is not found in the original, ‡ which has instead, "Mine ears hast Thou opened." How the error came about it is of no importance to inquire; the Apostle quotes it as it stood in the version in common use. It is urged that in so doing he founds an important argument upon a mere error of translation, seeking to show that the old sacrifices are done away by the offering of Christ's body. But this is entirely to mistake his argument. His reasoning is really this: sacri-

---

* The minor difficulty arising from the parenthetical clause, "this Agar is Mount Sinai in Arabia," disappears from the fact that the word *Agar*, according to the weight of external evidence, should be removed from the text. It is omitted by Lachmann and Tischendorf, bracketed by Tregelles and Westcott and Hort, and its omission given as a marginal reading by the Revisers. Lightfoot (who rejects it) explains its use, if it be retained, in his Comm. *in loco*.

† Heb. x. 5–7.   ‡ Ps. xl. 6–8.

fices were only necessary because of sin ; they would cease with the perfect fulfillment of God's will ; this was predicted by the Psalmist and accomplished by Christ. The argument is concerned so entirely with Christ's obedience that in closing it the Apostle repeats the quotation without the clause containing the word *body :* his proof is complete without it. In his conclusion he does indeed use again the word *body*, but only with reference to the perfect obedience of Christ (which involved the sacrifice of himself upon the cross), not as a part of his quotation : " By the which will we are sanctified through the offering of the body of Jesus Christ once for all."

There are hardly any other argumentative quotations presenting as great apparent difficulties as those which have now been discussed. These have been purposely selected, that it may be seen that these difficulties are only apparent, and that in all cases the argument involved in the quotation is sound and was rightly used. It often happens that these arguments are too keen to have been readily perceived by us without help ; but that help being given, they become as plain as those discoveries of science which we never could have found out of ourselves, but which, once made, every one admits.

At the same time, in studying these argumentative quotations, it is very necessary to note precisely the point of the argument for which they are cited, and not to press them beyond the point intended. Thus, when our Lord made claims for Himself at Jerusalem which plainly involved His Divinity, and the Jews consequently proposed to stone Him " because that Thou, being a man, makest Thyself God,"* He foiled them by the quotation from the Psalm, "I said ye are Gods," applied to human judges.† The whole context of the passage in the Gospel forbids us to suppose that our Lord meant to disclaim a Divine character for Himself; and it is evident that the Jews understood Him still to maintain the assertion which offended them, for "they again sought to take Him." But what He did intend, and what He accomplished, was to put them in a position where, for the moment, they could have no technical right to proceed against Him. They understood perfectly that He claimed to be God; but they could lay hold on no definite expression which should give them the legal right to proceed against Him and accomplish His death before His work was finished.

It is in this connection that our Lord uses the expression which is the key to the whole use of the Old Testament in the New: "The Scripture cannot be broken."‡ He who acknowledged no other authority, who taught Divine truth as out of His own personal consciousness, who hesitated not to speak of the law and the prophets as fulfilled in Himself, and to supersede the technical requirements of the old Dispensation by the principles of the new Revelation which He brought to light, yet, from the beginning of His ministry, declared with solemn asseveration, "Verily I say unto you, Till heaven and earth pass, one jot or one tittle shall in no wise pass from the Law till all be fulfilled."§ The changes

---

* John, x. 31–36. † Ps. lxxxii. 6; cf. Ex. xxii. 28.
‡ John, x. 35. § Matt. v. 18.

He would introduce, the fresh truth He would declare, the new and higher morality He would teach, would not be a change in the Divine will, but a more full and perfect declaration of that will than man had before been able to bear. And so the older Scriptures were ever regarded by His followers—as absolutely true and reliable; whatever might be plainly proved from them rested upon a rock which nothing could by any means overthrow.

(2) But little need be said of the second class of quotations, which express truth belonging alike to all ages. Sometimes these are made with some formula of quotation, as when it is said, "Ye have forgotten the exhortation .... my son, despise not thou the chastening of the Lord,"* etc., taken from the Proverbs, and showing the purpose of afflictions, that in these, as in all else, "all things work together for good to them that love God."† This may have been less clearly understood of old, but the declaration was in God's word, nevertheless, as the universal principle of His dealings with man. Sometimes such passages are quoted without any formula. Thus, "God resisteth the proud, but giveth grace unto the humble," is quoted from the same book of Proverbs ‡ by St. James with the formula, "wherefore he saith,"§ and by St. Peter without any mark of citation. ‖ It is the expression of a universal spiritual law. In the Epistle to the Ephesians, the exhorta-

---

* Heb. xii. 5 ; Prov. iii. 11, 12. † Rom. viii. 28.
‡ Prov. iii. 34. § James, iv. 6. ‖ 1 Pet. v. 5.

tion, "Speak every man truth with his neighbor," *
is taken from Zechariah, † and the following, "Be
ye angry and sin not," ‡ from the Septuagint of
Psalms. § Similar quotations are too familiar to need
further discussion.

(3) Very frequently, passages of the Old Testament, especially historical passages, are cited as illustrations of the Apostles' teaching and examples for the Christians whom they addressed. Such quotations, also, are sometimes introduced with, " It is written," or, " the Scripture saith," but oftener there is a simple reference to the history as too familiar to require any form of citation. Thus, St. Paul, having reminded the Corinthians of the history of the Israelites at the Exodus and in the wilderness, says: " Now, these things were our examples," and then, after adding further particulars, he concludes, " Now all these things happened unto them for ensamples, and they are written for our admonition." ‖ St. James refers to Job's patience and God's mercy to him, and to the "effectual fervent prayer" of Elijah. ¶ St. Peter speaks of Sarah as an example to Christian women; ** and the example of Abraham's faith and obedience is frequently cited by various writers. †† The same custom has been followed by Christian teachers in all ages: but the frequency of such references in the New Testament shows how thoroughly the minds of its writers were filled both with its history and its language.

---

* Eph. iv. 25.   † Zech. viii. 16.   ‡ Eph. iv. 26.   § Ps. iv. 5.
‖ 1 Cor. x. 6-11.   ¶ James, v. 11, 17.   ** 1 Pet. iii. 6.
†† *E. g.* John, viii. 39, 56; Rom. iv.; Gal. iii. 6-9; Heb. xi. 8-10, 17-19; James, ii. 21-23.

(4) The fourth class of quotations, in which the writers simply use the sacred and familiar words of the older Scriptures, without reference to their original application, as a fitting means for the expression of their own thoughts, has been sufficiently discussed in the lectures on prophecy and on the alleged double sense of Scripture. Caution is needed in the consideration of such passages, lest we should imagine that some new meaning is intended to be given to the words of the older Scripture. Inspired application is very different from inspired interpretation, and the two need to be carefully distinguished. The thought, that " these present events are aptly described by what was spoken of old " is by no means the same as that " those words of old were designed to predict what is done now."

When we pass from the particular subject of quotations to other methods of the use of the Old Testament, the whole matter may be summed up in a few words. The New Testament speakers and writers, one and all, regard the older Scriptures as sacred books to which they may on all occasions appeal with confidence, whether for doctrine or for instruction in life. To them "thus saith the Scripture" is an end of controversy. It hardly matters whether in St. Paul's charge to Timothy we read with the authorized version, "All Scripture is given by inspiration of God, and is profitable,"* etc., or with the Revisers, " Every Scripture inspired of God, is also profitable," etc. In either case the

---

* 2 Tim iii. 16.

whole context shows that the reference is to the Scriptures of the Old Dispensation, and that they are regarded as an absolutely reliable basis for Christian teaching. Similarly St. Peter speaks of the " Spirit of Christ " in the prophets and of what was " revealed " to them,* and again he says that "the prophecy came not in old time by the will of man, but holy men of God spake as they were moved by the Holy Ghost."†

With such views of the Old Testament, and looking upon the Gospel as the designed completion of the Old Dispensation, the New Testament writers everywhere plant themselves upon the Old, and even in addressing the most purely Gentile converts, as in the case of the Galatians, assume, as a matter of course, that in receiving Christianity they have received the Old Testament, and will regard arguments drawn from it as conclusive of the matter in issue, and its teachings and examples as of absolute moral obligation. They but followed the example of their Master. It is impossible to read either His teachings or the writings of the Evangelists concerning Him, without seeing that they regarded the Scriptures as of Divine origin, and as revealing to man authoritatively the will of God.

Thus, just as when we examined the old Testament, we found it ever looking forward to the New as its designed fulfilment; so, when we examine the New, we find it ever turning to the Old as its Divine warrant and authority. The two are

---

* 1 Pet. i. 11-12.   † 2 Pet. i. 21.

indissolubly joined together as parts of one Divine and perfect whole. Our Lord, seeking to lead the Jews to the acknowledgment of Himself and His teaching, could say, " Search the Scriptures. . . . . They are they which testify of Me." *

"*Novum in vetere latet : vetus in novo patet.*"

---

*John, v. 39.

LECTURE XV.

CONCLUSION.

THERE are a few thoughts which belong rather to the whole subject than to any particular part of it, and which have merely been suggested in passing, to which the attention may be called at the conclusion.

The unity of the two Dispensations was the subject of the first lecture, and in those which followed it was shown how this essential unity has been modified in form and in fulness of expression to adapt it to the varying needs of men under different circumstances, and with differing degrees of spiritual enlightenment. A corresponding unity of plan is traced in nature in the adaptation of the homologous parts of very different creatures. The arm of the man, the foreleg of the horse, the wing of the bat or the bird, and the fin of the fish, are but modifications of the same part of the vertebrate structure adapted to their several environments; and comparative anatomy has carried much farther the analogies of structure between different orders of the animal kingdom, and even between the different kingdoms of nature. The "unity of nature" and the "universal reign of law" have always attracted the attention of thoughtful observers, and with advancing knowledge have become ever more and more firmly fixed as first principles of the Divine works. Not only does analogy lead us to expect the same things in Revelation; but when they are found they lead to the same conclusion of a unity of Source. Whatever may be the difficulties in nature, the unity in Revelation (extending through all the ages of the existence of our race, and under the vastly varied embodiment in human language by men of extreme divergence in character and culture and living at widely remote eras), points unmistakably to some underlying unity of Authorship, guiding and controlling all these human minds in one common course and to one common end. And this Authorship must of necessity belong to a self-conscious and personal Being. In other words, it shows that the true Source of the scriptural teaching was One Who sees the end from the beginning, and orders all things to the accomplishment of His purposes. The facts which have been reviewed concerning the ways and the extent of the preparation in the Old Testament for the New, are consistent only with the supposition that the New was distinctly foreseen and regarded throughout the whole economy of the Old. On the other hand, the New could only have planted itself upon the Old as it did, in the conviction that the same Being, " Who at sundry times and in divers manners spake in time past unto the fathers by the Prophets, hath in these last days spoken unto us by *his* Son.* The unity of the two Dispensations thus

---

* Heb. i. 1.

leads directly to the conviction of the Divine authority, and hence of the immutable truth of both.

This conviction brings us to the perception of the eternal verity of the Old Testament. This is a point which is in some danger of being overlooked. A preparatory dispensation must necessarily, in a certain sense, be temporary; and partial truth can no longer remain our highest standard when that which is more perfect has come. But it does not follow that the preparation can ever be superseded, or that this partial truth, viewed in its circumstances and relations, can ever become untrue. The present state is undoubtedly a preparation for a higher and better one, and the truths by which our souls are now nourished unto eternal life we see but as in a glass, darkly; yet that eternal life is already begun, and the higher truths of the future are taught now as far as we are able to receive them. So also in the comparison of the Old Testament with the New. It is the same Divine will which is expressed in them both, and that will is forever unchangeable. It is the same Being Who was the object of trust and hope in both, and to Whose holiness man must be conformed that he may enter into communion with Him. This it is easy to recognize; but the point we are apt to overlook is, that the New Testament teachers, familiar with the Old Testament themselves, and expecting their readers to be familiar with it, often do not repeat its instructions when really necessary to the understanding of their own teachings. When John the Baptist, himself a priest of Israel, pointed to Jesus as "the Lamb of God which taketh away the sin of the world,"* he had no need to explain the nature of vicarious sacrifice to hearers who were accustomed daily to see the lamb upon the altar in Jerusalem. When St. Paul wrote to the Ephesians that Christ "hath given Himself for us an offering and a sacrifice to God for a sweet smelling savour," † there was no occasion to enlarge upon the meaning of the familiar technical language of the Levitical law. The same thing is true in a great multitude of instances. The full sense of the New Testament teaching can only be reached by a thorough study of the Old Testament upon which it was founded. And the connection between them, it must be repeated, is not one of mere superposition, in which the Old is complete as far as it goes, and then fresh chapters of truth are added in the New; but it is a living organic connection as between the embryo and the adult, the seed and the fruit. It was the same Being, the same Divine will, the same fundamental principles of salvation, that were taught in the one as in the other; only in the former these were taught dimly and by means of types and shadows, as men were able to bear. These facts are essential to the right understanding of Scripture, and he must sorely miss the meaning of the New Testament who lets go his hold upon the conviction of the eternal truth of the Old.

There is a correspondingly important inference in regard to the New Testament. This, on the face of it, is a finality. It purports to be the last revelation of God to men while upon earth. Men have

---

* John, i. 29. † Eph. v. 2.

not always been willing to acquiesce in this. Whether in the teachings of Mohammed, in the doctrine of the Papal infallibility, in various heretical claims in various ages to the gift of prophecy, in the strange hallucinations of Swedenborgianism, or the coarser teachings of Mormonism, they have shown a craving for some further authoritative expression of the Divine will. But it results from the relations we have been considering between the Old and the New Dispensations, that no room is left for any such further revelation here upon earth. The finality which the New Testament claims for itself is fully borne out by the character of the preparation for it in the Old. It was a preparation in which a great number of lines all converged to one point; they can pass no farther without again diverging. It was a preparation for one great fact, the very heart and centre, and the explanation of all that had been done since the world began. The whole previous revelation was complete in Christ, and the very suggestion of the necessity of a further revelation is a suggestion of the insufficiency of His work. He who hath spoken to us by a Son, can speak by none higher.

It cannot be said as a qualification of these statements that after our Lord had returned "to the glory which he had with the Father before the world was," His disciples under the guidance of the Holy Spirit He had promised actually did complete and develop the revelation He had given. Their work and His own were really one. The two were continuous in point of time and in their subject-matter, the Apostles did but unfold the meaning of their master's acts and words. Undoubtedly there was an important progress in this, as has already been pointed out; undoubtedly we should have a most incomplete knowledge of the mind of Christ, if there had been given us only the narratives of the Gospels. Yet between them and the rest of the New Testament the change is not of the same kind as that which marks the passage from the Old Testament to the New. There is no new revelation, but a simple unfolding and developing by His immediate disciples of the meaning of the acts and teaching of their Master. He had Himself told them that this must be so; that while He was with them in bodily presence His work was not yet complete, and had warned them, "I have yet many things to say unto you, but ye cannot bear them now," and had added, "When He, the Spirit of truth, is come He will guide you into all truth." * When, therefore, this promised Spirit had come, and they declared His teaching, they made no new revelation, but only completed the one already begun. Well therefore could St. Paul declare this to be a finality, and in view of the possible assertion of anything further, declare with strong emotion, "Though we, or an angel from heaven, preach any other Gospel unto you than that which we have preached unto you, let him be accursed." †

It remains, therefore, that as the connection between the two Dispensations establishes the eternal verity of the Old, so does it prove the eternal

---

* John, xvi. 12, 13. † Gal. i. 8.

verity of the New as its final and complete fulfilment.

A progress has been distinctly seen in the whole course of Revelation. It is a progress made necessary by the fact that man was unable to receive the higher revelations until he had been instructed and elevated by the lower; and therefore it is a progress everywhere eloquent of the Divine love for man and tender regard for his capacities and his needs. Yet it is not a mere evolution of human thought, but is distinctly marked at every stage as having been communicated from without and from above. For the revelation has always been on the utmost verge of man's capacity to receive, far beyond his ability to invent. This was shown by the revelation in the remotest antiquity of the unity and holiness of God; it is certainly not less conspicuous in the character of Christ. One has but to read the Apocryphal Gospels, or in fact almost any literature of that period, to see how immeasurably the character of Christ as it stands forth in the Gospels, is above any merely human conception which could be formed at the time. What is true of His character is true also of His teaching: it was the confession of His enemies, " Never man spake like this man." * This fact of an external and Divine revelation, once admitted, certainly has an important bearing upon the discussion of the order of revelation; for the progress of a revelation coming from a Divine Source cannot be reduced to such definite lines as if it were entirely of human origin. In the former case fundamental

---
* John, vii. 46.

truth may be thrown out far in advance of its time, according to a human standard, simply because it is fundamental, and however imperfectly received, is yet the necessary basis for the revelation of further truth. On the other hand, when men have failed to rise to the level of a high standard given them, they may be subjected for a time to the training of a less perfect system. As the Israelites, failing to prosper under the immediate Divine government, were allowed a monarchy, and as not fulfilling the purposes of the theocracy in the promised land, they were driven into the Babylonian exile; so when they were unable to understand and live in the "Gospel preached before unto Abraham," they were, because of transgressions, subjected to the law.

The progress of revelation is therefore like the progress in nature. On the whole it is uniform, and is ever from the less to the more perfect. Yet it is marked by occasional sudden changes, " sports " as they are called in natural history, and there must sometimes be a partial and temporary retrogression, a backward swing of the pendulum to catch the next cog of the escapement, a gathering up, as it were, of force for a greater onward step. It is not a gathering up of the infinite Divine force, but of the human, upon which that must act. As in nature there must be the lightning, the earthquake, and the volcano to restore the equilibrium between opposing forces with gradually strained tension; so in revelation, eras are to be expected, followed by periods of repose. And those periods of repose must be long in proportion to the greatness of the fresh force which has been introduced, and the time required for man to assimilate this in his heart and life. As the hardness of the rock is always an element in the effect produced by the continual wearing away of the water, so the obduracy of man must be an element in the progress of revelation. Such are the phenomena which the analogies of nature would lead us to expect; and such are the phenomena which the history of the progress of revelation actually presents.

Finally, the most striking feature in all we have been considering is everywhere the Divine love and condescension in the adaptation of revelation to the wants and the capacities of men. Fallen man, in a condition of sinfulness and spiritual ignorance, was to be raised and made like to God, who is perfect in holiness. To human wisdom this might seem impossible; and in all probability, if the full light of the Gospel had shone upon the antediluvian patriarchs, or even upon such rough warriors as Gideon and Jephthah, it would but have dazzled and blinded them without useful effect. They must be raised little by little, and meantime, in so far as they honestly acted up to the light they had, there was no more difficulty in God's holding communion with them than in the Holy Spirit's dwelling in our hearts, separated as they are from His infinite holiness by all our shortcomings and sins. The difference between the best of us and the least of the saints of old is as nothing to the distance by which both are separated from the infinite perfections of God. But in the gradual elevation of man, it is plain that revelation must have been always somewhat in advance of his existing condition; and particularly it was necessary that from the outset there should be a declaration of that which man never has been able fully to learn for himself—the unity, universality and infinite holiness of God. If this was too much in advance of the ideas of the times for the mass of men to accept it for many long ages, yet it must from the first be proclaimed, because it is the necessary starting point and foundation of all true religion. It remained, the very gist and kernel of all revelation, to be apprehended, here and there, by those who were able.

Thus, little by little, in tender love and compassion, the Heavenly Father has made Himself and His will known to man. The resulting progress has been so great that men look back upon its earlier stages with the wondering question whether they could really have been revelations at all. But even now, the last great revelation has not yet been fully appreciated and embodied in our lives. When it shall be, or when even a sufficient approach to this shall have been made, we shall be transferred to that higher stage of existence where, in the open presence of the infinite Mediator, and knowing even as we are known, our present knowledge shall seem as feeble as that of the patriarchs seems now in comparison with what has been given to us. Then they and we alike shall stand in the light which none on earth can know, and God shall be "all in all."

INDEX OF SCRIPTURE TEXTS.

Reference	PAGE
Genesis, i. 27	313
ii. 18–25	313
iii. 8, 9	11
iii. 15	153, 233, 321
iv. 1	321
iv. 4, 5	111
v. 29	321
vi. 18	162
viii. 20	111
ix. 3	91
ix. 9, 12, 13, 15, 16	162
x. 18	320
xii. 1	64
xii. 3	64
xii. 12	81
xiv. 14	149
xiv. 18	138
xv. 6	25
xv. 7	64
xv. 9–21	112
xv. 18	162
xvii. 2, 9	162
xvii. 19	162
xx. 1	81
xxi. 22–32	149
xxi. 30-32	112
xxii. 13	111
xxiii. 6	149
xxv. 33	82
xxvi. 3	162
Genesis, xxviii. 12–15	253
xxxi. 54	111
xlix. 7	172
xlix. 10	68, 177
Exodus, ii. 13–15	301
ii. 24	162
iii.	301
iii. 1	138
iii. 6	300, 313
vi. 4	162
viii. 13	13
ix. 12	13
x. 20	13
xii. 46	242
xiv. 15	182
xvii. 11, 12	221
xviii. 12	138
xix. 5	139, 162, 233
xix. 6	35, 114, 151
xx. 12	299
xx. 19, 20	35
xxi. 2	105
xxi. 5, 6	105
xxii. 25	98
xxii. 28	326
xxiii. 19	97
xxiv. 7, 8	162
xxv. 40	301
xxvi. 30	301
xxviii. 38	141

344 INDEX OF SCRIPTURE TEXTS.

	PAGE		PAGE
Exodus, xxxii	35	Leviticus, xvi. 25	123
xxxiii. 19	301	xvi. 26, 28	123
xxxiii. 20	10	xvi. 27	123
xxxiv. 26	97	xviii. 5	302
xxxiv. 27	162	xix. 9, 10	98
xxxiv. 29–35	233	xix. 18	18, 230
Leviticus, i. 3, 10, 14	118	xix. 18, 24	102
iv. 3, 14	121	xix. 19	97
iv. 6, 7, 17, 18	120	xx. 10	304
iv. 20, 26, 31, 35	141	xxi. 17	141
iv. 23	121	xxii. 23	119
iv. 25, 30	120	xxiii. 10	118
iv. 28	121, 134	xxiv. 5, 6, 9	102
v. 7	121	xxv. 36, 37	98
v. 10, 13	141	xxvi. 9, 25, 42, 44, 45	162
v. 11	121	Numbers, ix. 3, 4	114
v. 11–13	101	xv. 30, 31	121
v. 14–vi. 7	122	xvi. 5	141
vii. 16, 17	119	xvi. 32, 33	23
vii. 29	119	xxi. 8, 9	211
vii. 35	141	xxii.–xxiv	138
x. 3	141	xxiii. 19	10
x. 17	141	xxiii. 21	21
xi	92	xxiv. 17	69
xi. 32–34	93	xxiv. 17, 18	271
xi. 32–35	93	xxviii. 9, 10	102
xi. 37, 38	93	Deuteronomy, v. 2	162
xii. 2	301	v. 16	299
xii. 3	300	vi. 5	102
xiv. 1–31	299	viii. 3	34
xv. 5–10	93	ix. 9	162
xv. 19–23	93	x. 12	102
xv. 26, 27	93	xi. 1, 13, 22	102
xvi. 7, 8	123	xii. 5, 11, 14, 18, 26	129
xvi. 11–14	122	xiv	92
xvi. 14, 15	120	xiv. 21	97
xvi. 15–17	122	xiv. 23–25	129
xvi. 18, 19	122	xv. 12	105
xvi. 20–22	123	xv. 13, 14	105

INDEX OF SCRIPTURE TEXTS.

	PAGE
Deuteromony, xv. 16–18....	105
xv. 20.	129
xvi. 2–8.	114
xvi. 2, 6, 7, 15, 16...	129
xvii. 8, 10.	129
xviii. 6.	129
xviii. 15......65, 235,	302
xix. 9.	102
xix. 21.	18
xxii. 6, 7.	98
xxii. 10.	97
xxiii. 19.	98
xxiv. 1.........299,	303
xxiv. 21.	98
xxv. 4.......96, 188,	302
xxv. 5.	303
xxv. 17–19.	23
xxvi. 2.	129
xxix. 1, 12, 14.	162
xxx. 6	102
xxxi. 11.	129
xxxii. 21.	302
Joshua, vii. 14.	320
ix. 27.	129
x. 24.	85
xix. 1–9.	173
Judges, i. 6, 7.	85
ii. 1.	162
iii. 18–23	84
iv. 18–21.	86
v. 24–27	86
viii. 13–17.	84
1 Samuel, ii. 10........69,	286
viii. 6, 7.	161
viii. 6, 20.	151
viii. 7.	151
xiii. 10–14.	139
xv. 2.	23
xv. 22.	123

	PAGE
1 Samuel, xv. 29	10
2 Samuel, iii. 38.	182
vii. 3, 8–12.	161
vii. 12–16 ....66, 76,	285
xii. 1–4.	195
xii. 11, 12.	88
1 Kings, viii. 63.	119
xxii. 19–23.	13
2 Kings, ii. 3, 5, 15.	160
iv. 1, 38.	160
vi. 1.	160
ix. 1.	160
1 Chronicles, iv. 36, 39–43..	174
xvi. 17.	162
xvii. 2, 4.	161
xxviii. 3.	69
2 Chronicles, xxvi. 16–21....	139
xxx. 15–19.	115
xxxv. 11.	115
xxxvi. 21.	105
Job, xi. 7, 8.	11
Psalms ii.............244,	282
ii. 1, 2 191,	304
iv. 5.	328
xvi.	282
xvi. 7–10.	281
xxii............238,	282
xxxiv. 1, 2.	305
xxxiv. 19, 20.	242
xxxv. 19.	192
xl. 6–8.... 124,	324
xli. 9.	240
li. 2–4.	222
lxix.	282
lxix. 4.........192,	240
lxix. 9.	240
lxix. 22, 23.	305
lxix. 25.	304
lxxviii. 2.	241

INDEX OF SCRIPTURE TEXTS.

	PAGE
Psalms, lxxxix. 3, 4	76
xcv	282
xcv. 7, 8	189, 305
cix	282
cx	282
cx. 1	177, 280, 281
cx. 4	180, 287
cxxxii. 11	76
Proverbs, iii. 11, 12	327
iii. 34	327
xxv. 21, 22	188
Ecclesiastes, v. 1	124
Isaiah, i. 9	306
i. 11	124
i. 25-27	154
ii. 3	76
iv. 2, 4	155
vi. 9, 10	305, 306 bis
ix. 1, 2	172, 305
x. 21-23	306
xi. 1-9	155
xi. 10	306
xxvi. 2, 3, 12, 13	155
xxvii. 9	155
xxviii. 16, 17	155
xxix. 13	126
xxix. 19-24	155
xxxii. 1, 16	155
xxxiii. 5, 14, 15, 24	155
xxxiv. xxxv	245
xl. 3	262, 291, 305
xlii. 1-4	305
xlii. 1-4, 6	155
xliii. 3	306
xliii. 25	155 bis
xliv. 9	289
xliv. 22	155 bis
xlv.-xlviii	175
xlv. 8	155
Isaiah, xlvi. 12, 13	155
lii. 11	183
lii. 13-liii. 12	70, 155
liii. 1	306 bis
liii. 4	305
liii. 7	306
lvii. 15-18	155
lviii. 6, 7	155
lix. 20	156
lx. 21	155
lxi. 1, 2	306
lxi. 8	155
lxv. 1, 2	306
lxvi. 3	125
Jeremiah, iii. 6	71
iii. 16	71
vi. 20	125
x. 16	289
xi. 1	162
xviii. 11	289
xxiii. 24	320
xxx. 9	236
xxxi. 15	183, 263, 287, 307
xxxi. 16	263
xxxi. 31	76
xxxi. 31-34	71, 162, 314
xxxi. 33, 34	71, 95
xxxi. 34	156
xxxiii. 8	156
xxxiii. 17, 18	267
xxxiv. 9, 14	105
Ezekiel, iv	237
xi. 19	156
xi. 19, 20	72
xx	237
xxi. 27	68
xxxiv. 23, 24	236
xxxvi. 25-27	73, 156
xxxvii. 24, 25	236

INDEX OF SCRIPTURE TEXTS. 347

	PAGE		PAGE
Ezekiel, xlvii. 1–12	156	Zechariah, iii. 3–5, 8, 9	74
Daniel, i. 8–16	92	vi. 10–13	244
i. 12, 16	320	vi. 11–13	74
ii. 34, 35	153	vii., viii., viii. 19	74
ii. 39–45	72	viii. 16	328
vii. 16–27	72	ix. 9	74
ix. 24	72, 156	x. 8, 10	74
ix. 27	307	x. 10, 11	249
xi. 31	307	xi. 12, 13	287
xii. 8–13	250	xiii. 1	39
xii. 11	307	xiii. 9	157
Hosea, i. 10	307	xiv. 9, 20, 21	75
ii. 23	307	Malachi, i. 6, 7	126
iii. 5	236	i. 11	75, 126
vi. 6	101, 268	ii. 12, 13	126
viii. 13	124, 237	iii. 1	236, 291
ix. 3	237	iii. 1, 2	157
ix. 6	237	iii. 2, 3	75
xi. 1	184, 242	iii. 3, 4	126
xi. 5	237	iii. 8	126
xiii. 14	183, 264	iv. 2, 5	75
xiv. 4	156	iv. 2–6	157
Amos, iv. 13	289	iv. 5	176
v. 22, 24	124	iv. 5, 6	236, 317
v. 26	205	Matthew, i.	76
vii. 14, 15	161	ii. 1–6	171
ix. 11, 12	78, 190	ii. 2	322
Jonah, ii. 1	234	ii. 15	184, 242
iii.	23	ii. 17	307
Micah, iv. 2 ss.	76	ii. 17, 18	183, 263, 287
v. 2	171, 322	ii. 23	310
vi. 6–8	125, 268	iii. 2	157
vii. 19	156	iii. 3	293, 305
Habakkuk, ii. 4	318	iii. 9	234
Haggai, i. 9–11	126	iv. 4	34, 178
ii. 6	314	iv. 14	305
ii. 6, 7	73	iv. 23	166
ii. 7–9, 22, 23	314	v. 17	3
ii. 21, 22	73	v. 18	3, 326

348 INDEX OF SCRIPTURE TEXTS.

	PAGE		PAGE
Matthew, v. 19	4	Matthew, xxii. 37-40	3
v. 21, 27, 33	8	xxii. 39	230
v. 38, 39	18	xxii. 42	76
v. 44	230	xxii. 43, 45	280, 307
viii. 4	299	xxiv.	245
viii. 17	305	xxiv. 15	307
ix. 10-13	269	xxiv. 15-22	174
ix. 13	101	xxiv. 37-39	227
ix. 27	76	xxv. 29	269
ix. 35	166	xxvi. 56	265
x. 5	77	xxvii. 9	287, 307
xi. 14	236	Mark, i. 2, 3	291, 305
xii. 1, 2, 7	269	i. 21, 39	166
xii. 3-5	4	i. 44	299
xii. 6	102	ii. 25, 26	4, 102
xii. 7	101	iv. 12	305
xii. 9-13	166	iv. 25	269
xii. 17	305	vii. 6	306
xii. 39, 40	178	vii. 10	299
xii. 40	234	x. 3, 5	299
xiii. 12	269	x. 4	303
xiii. 14	305	x. 4-7	313
xiii. 35	241	x. 6-9	4, 227
xiii. 54	166	xii. 19	304
xv. 7	306	xii. 26	300
xv. 22	76	xii. 26, 27	313
xv. 24	77	xii. 29-31	3
xvi. 4	178	xii. 36, 37	280, 304
xvii. 12, 13	236	xiii.	245
xix. 4-6	4, 227	xvi. 15	77
xix. 4-8	313	xvi. 15, 16	57
xix. 5	303	Luke, i. 17	236
xix. 8	16, 299	i. 32, 33	3
xix. 19	230	i. 41, 67	37
xx. 30, 31	76	i. 72, 73	3, 162
xxi. 9	76	i. 76, 77	236
xxii. 15-46	4	ii. 22	301
xxii. 24	303	ii. 38	70
xxii. 31, 32	313	iii. 4	293

INDEX OF SCRIPTURE TEXTS. 349

	PAGE		PAGE
Luke, iv. 15	166	John, v. 39	63, 331
iv. 16–21	4	v. 45–47	300
iv. 17	306	vi	56
iv. 33–35	166	vi. 48, 49	187
v. 14	299	vi. 59	166
vi. 3, 4	4	vii. 19	300
vii. 5	166	vii. 22, 23	300
viii. 18	269	vii. 38	310
xi. 30	234	vii. 39	37
xiv. 15	49, 67	vii. 46	338
xvi. 17	3	viii. 5	304
xvi. 29, 31	300	viii. 39, 56	328
xvii. 20, 21	158	ix. 29	304
xvii. 26, 27	227	x. 31–36	326
xviii. 1–8	229	x. 35	4, 326
xx. 28	304	xii. 38	306
xx. 37	300	xii. 39, 41	306
xx. 37, 38	313	xiii. 18	240
xx. 42, 44	280, 304	xiv.–xvi	56
xxi	245	xiv. 6	133
xxiv. 26, 27	4, 312	xv. 25	192, 240
xxiv. 27	177, 284	xvi. 4	56
xxiv. 44	300	xvi. 12, 13	54, 337
xxiv. 44–47	312	xviii. 36	159
John, i. 17	301	xix. 24, 28, 36	265
i. 23	306	xix. 36	242
i. 29	335	xx. 25	204
i. 29, 36	137	Acts, i. 6	57, 158
i. 45	304	i. 16	304
i. 51	254	i. 16, 20	5
ii. 17	240	i. 18	296
iii. 13–18	56	ii. 16–21	307
iii. 14	56	ii. 25	304
iii. 14, 15	211	ii. 25–31	281
iv. 1, 2	55	ii. 25, 34	281
iv. 10, 14, 26	56	ii. 30–36	5
iv. 22	77	ii. 34	281, 304
iv. 25	49, 65	iii. 18	5
v. 12	296	iii. 22, 23	302

	PAGE		PAGE
Acts, iii. 24	283	Acts, xxviii. 23	302
iii. 25	162	xxviii. 25	306
iv. 13-26	191	Romans, i. 17	318
iv. 24-26	304	i. 18-23	164
iv. 25, 26	5	iv.	328
vi. 1	304	iv. 3	25
vi. 11, 13, 14	304	iv. 6	305
vii. 15, 16	297	v. 12-19	227
vii. 22-26	301	v. 14	206
vii. 23	278	vi. 17	206
vii. 31-34	301	vii. 10, 12, 14	163
vii. 37	65, 302	viii. 3	38
vii. 43	205	viii. 15	165, 167
vii. 44	205	viii. 28	291
vii. 52	106	ix.-xi.	78
viii. 28-33	306	ix. 15	301
ix. 22	5	ix. 25 27	307
x.	77	ix. 27	306
xi. 19	77	ix. 29	306
xiii. 21	278	x. 5	8, 302
xiii. 39	301	x. 12, 13	316
xiii. 42, 43	166	x. 16	306
xiii. 46	77	x. 19	301
xiv. 22	159	x. 20	306
xv.	218	xi. 9	305
xv. 10	162	xi. 16-24	229
xv. 15	190	xii. 1	141
xv. 16, 17	78	xii. 5	168
xv. 21	302	xii. 20	188
xv. 28, 29	91	xiii. 9	230
xvii. 2, 3	5	xiv. 17	159
xvii. 30	16	xv. 12	306
xviii. 28	5	xv. 16	146
xx. 35	278	1 Corinthians, v. 7	115
xxi. 21	302	v. 7, 8	186
xxiii. 8	313	vi. 16	227
xxiii. 25	205	ix. 9	96, 188
xxvi. 6, 22, 23	5	x. 2	216
xxvi. 22, 23	284	x. 6, 11	205

INDEX OF SCRIPTURE TEXTS.

Reference	Page
1 Corinthians, x. 6–11	328
x. 17	168
xi. 8	227
xii. 2	6
xiii. 12	53
xv. 21, 22	227
xv. 44–46	227
xv. 50	159
xv. 54, 55	236
xv. 56	183
2 Corinthians, i. 22	167
ii. 15, 16	13
iii. 13–16	233
v. 5	167
v. 17	76
vi. 17, 18	183
Galatians, iii. 6	25
iii. 6–9	328
iii. 8	7
iii. 11	318
iii. 12	8
iii. 16	320
iii. 17	162
iii. 17, 19	25
iii. 19	7, 35
iii. 21	106
iii. 23	95
iii. 24	7, 26
iv. 6	167
iv. 9	162
iv. 21–31	181, 229, 323
iv. 24	163
v. 14	230
Ephesians, i. 14	167
ii. 11	6
ii. 15	163
ii. 19–22	169
iv. 25	328
iv. 26	328
Ephesians, v. 2	335
Philippians, iii. 17	205
Colossians i. 13	159
ii. 14, 15	26
iii. 3	248
1 Thessalonians, i. 7	205
iv. 16, 17	60
2 Thessalonians, iii. 9	205
1 Timothy, ii. 11–14	227
iv. 3	296
iv. 12	205
v. 18	96, 188
vi. 15, 16	9
2 Timothy, i. 10	37, 168
iii. 8	277
iii. 16	37, 329
Titus, ii. 7	205
Hebrews, i. 1	5, 28
i. 14	254
ii. 18	289
iii. 15–iv. 13	189
iv. 7	305
v. 1	138
v. 2	141
v. 4	140, 224
v. 6	143
v. 11, 12	202
vi. 1	232
vii. 14	302
vii. 16	143
vii. 21	143
vii. 25	143, 148, 224
vii. 27	144
vii. 28	143
viii. 1, 2	138
viii. 3	143
viii. 5	205, 301
viii. 8–12	314
ix. 5	203

	PAGE		PAGE
Hebrews, ix. 8	99	Hebrews, xiii. 10	146
ix. 12	144	James, i. 25	162
ix. 13	123	ii. 8	230
ix. 16, 17	112	ii. 21–23	328
ix. 19, 20	301	ii. 23	25
ix. 22	101, 130	ii. 25	228
ix. 24	224	iv. 5	311
ix. 26	144	iv. 6	327
x. 1–3	135	v. 11, 17	328
x. 4	24, 135	1 Peter, i. 10	63, 283
x. 5–7	324	i. 10–12	251
x. 10	144	i. 11	37
x. 12–14	135	i. 11, 12	230
x. 12	144	i. 12	192
x. 14	142, 143	iii. 6	328
x. 16, 17	314	iii. 20, 21	227, 229
x. 28	302	v. 3	205
x. 38	318	v. 5	327
xi. 7	227	2 Peter, i. 11	159
xi. 8–10	328	i. 21	37, 230
xi. 17–19	328	ii. 5	228
xi. 25, 26	239	iii. 5–7	228
xi. 31	228	1 John, iv. 11, 12	167
xii. 21	278	Jude, 14, 15	276
xii. 22–24	59	Revelation, xiv. 8	249
xii. 26, 27	314	xvi. 19	249
xii. 27	73	xvii. 5	249
xii. 28	159	xviii. 2, 10, 21	249

www.ingramcontent.com/pod-product-compliance
Lightning Source LLC
Chambersburg PA
CBHW032047220426
43664CB00008B/890